Old Frames, New Pictures

Judy Baldwin Lord
12/9/21

JUDY BALDWIN LORD

ISBN 978-1-63961-674-9 (paperback)
ISBN 978-1-63961-675-6 (digital)

Christian Faith Publishing, Inc.
832 Park Avenue
Meadville, PA 16335
www.christianfaithpublishing.com

Printed in the United States of America

To the one who gave me the words—the great I AM.

For Aunt Iva, Aunt Juanita, and Ruth,
my beautiful mom. I hope I have made you proud.
I simply adore all of you…

Acknowledgement

Grateful acknowledgement is made to the following: CFP Staff, once again, you are the best! EDNA PAK for her beautiful photographs that captured the essence of all the plots featured in OLD FRAMES, NEW PICTURES. SUE ROBINSON who took me into the 'high tech' age. She makes everything easier.

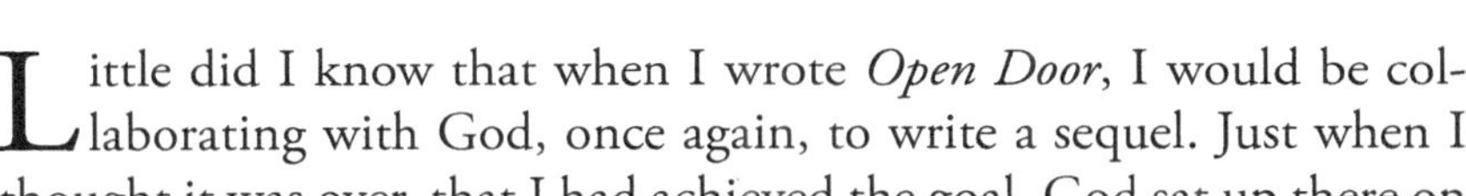

Little did I know that when I wrote *Open Door*, I would be collaborating with God, once again, to write a sequel. Just when I thought it was over, that I had achieved the goal, God sat up there on his throne, smiling.

I soon found myself sitting at my desk, remembering fondly Trudy, Kate, Jake, and all the others. It wasn't time to let them go—not quite yet. I began to write on those blank sheets of paper sitting in front of me on my desk. Where was this going?

"I'll show you," he said.

Before I knew it, Jesus and I were retracing the steps we had walked a few short years ago. There we were, climbing those mountains and resting by those streams. Some things had remained the same, yet some of the scenery was quite different.

A certain "blending" was continuing to take place in my own life, and the invitation had been delivered to me to "put it down on paper." How could I refuse? I had enjoyed the journey so much the first time around! I eagerly anticipated the paths we would walk!

I invite you once again to follow in the footsteps my Savior and I have traveled. Step into this journey where love stories are born, mysteries unfold, secrets are exposed to the light, losses happen, and miracles are just around the corner. Yes, this is a story about all of that. And there is a delightful surprise or two within these pages.

But that's just like our God, isn't it? Full of surprises. Oh, how he loves to see the wonder on our faces as he presents those unexpected gifts to us in "living color"! All we have to do is reach out. I did. In my wildest dreams, I never expected any of this. Once again, I have enjoyed the ride…

"Hope is the thing with feathers
That perches in the soul
And sings the tune without the words
And never stops at all."

(Emily Dickinson)

Prologue

Brooksport Village

It was the month of April in Brooksport Village. Another spring, another Memorial Day weekend on the horizon, coming fast. Trudy decided to close her hair salon, Trudy's Tresses and Tootsies, early. She was going to the grocery store.

"I wonder if that Seth boy is back this year," she mumbled. "He sure better remember about my Chicken in a Biskit crackers!"

Seth was there. Seth saw her coming. He ran to the back of the store, plucked the infamous crackers from a carton that had just arrived, and barely got them on the shelf before the purple-clad lady was walking down the aisle that held all her salty treats.

Before she could say a word, Seth pointed to the shelf where her favorite crackers were displayed.

"I remembered, Miss Trudy," he said proudly.

Trudy cocked her head, smiled at him, gave his shoulder a pat, put the crackers in her cart, and said, "So ya did, young man. So ya did! No more newbie trainin' needed! See ya around!"

Seth remembered the first time he had ever set eyes on that woman. She had scared him nearly to death. It had not taken him long to learn what made her happy. She needed lard, and he was going to make sure she got it. It was extremely important—staying on the good side of Miss Trudy.

Yes, another four months into a new year, and another spring had arrived. Everyone was looking forward to the warm winds blowing off the lake. No more snow. Tourists would be arriving, and Kate's bed-and-breakfast, Open Door, would be a welcome sight for all the people from the city wearing those forlorn looks. Jake had set up shop in his former room that had once been next to Kate's private quarters; he had turned it into an office. He had unpacked his clothes in, what was now, their bedroom, mingling sweaters, pants, and everything else with hers inside the drawers and closets. The only difference was a door adjoining the two rooms that had been placed in its center. There were no walls between those two anymore. And no more talks about generators, instead of important stuff. Another door had been opened. The two of them married and together at last.

Belle was still frying up those greasy doughnuts, and Stumble In was still serving those delicious burgers. Crabby's Bar didn't miss Phil at all and rejoiced with him as he continued being a dad to Charlie and a role model to all those kids he was a counselor to on missionary trips. Leon always had Phil's new drink of choice waiting for him when he did visit, what was still his favorite barstool—Coke. He never charged him. As far as Leon was concerned, he would serve Phil Coke by the case if he wanted it. Charlie finally had a father, and it was worth celebrating with free Coke for life.

Charlie and Sarah were off to college, and rumor had it that upon completion of their degrees, there would be a wedding soon. Everybody knew that small-town boys grew up to marry small-town girls, and good things were happening for those two.

Trudy still had itches. But this particular itch was the kind she could scratch. She made frequent visits to Gordy, constantly trying to "fix him up with the right girl." Gordy was having none of it. Did that stop Trudy? She was determined. And that itch would finally be scratched when Gordy was with the *right* woman.

Techy Ted made frequent visits to Brooksport Village from Detroit. He kept thinking he should move there. If Jake could set up business there, so could he. However, he wasn't so sure about Trudy. Did she want him there? She seemed to like things just the way they were. He admitted to himself that she had trust issues. Just when he thought their relationship was moving forward, she would shut him out. Boom! The door would close, and the lights would go out. She wouldn't talk to him about those issues. She wanted to keep their relationship fun. He would return to Detroit feeling lonely and depleted of energy. He loved Trudy. He wanted things to work out between them. And he loved that overgrown, spoiled cat, Buddy. They had bonded because of the cat treats he always had in his coat pocket when he arrived for a visit.

With mixed emotions, Ted realized he shouldn't judge Trudy too much about her issues when he had so many of his own, one in particular—a secret he had not dared to mention to anyone. He struggled with even talking to himself about it. He pushed it out of his mind's eye whenever he could. But it was always there. He couldn't tell Trudy. It wasn't fair to ask her to live with his demons. So maybe he was worse off than she, with his own giants that he still needed to conquer. It was better to agree with Trudy. No promises. Take life as it came, and leave his own skeleton in the closet—make their relationship no more than fun.

This little village town was finally getting a breather. So much had happened there from the storms of the past they welcomed the slow and steady heartbeat of the present. Even though change would surely come, they wanted to wait on it for a while, and they soaked up the "familiar" like a sponge. But change was in the making—and a lot of it.

A girl named Jasmine had not yet arrived. Jasmine Jones had a life of her own and a past that wouldn't let her go. She was dragging one foot in the past, trying to nudge toward the future, making her forget about the here and now. She couldn't drop the net she had been lugging around, with all her sadness packed solid inside. And when she tried, she would always look back and pick it up again. She had become numb and kept mostly to herself. Parts of her had been buried deep in the southern soil from where she came. Damaged beyond repair. She had lost her zest for life. Reality had hit her hard. Reality had splat all over the walls of her heart. She couldn't reconstruct it—it was too different now. She couldn't see the light at the end of the tunnel that she had been forced to walk. But she had not yet found that sweet small village town that had been waiting for her to step upon its streets—not yet anyway. A town by the name of Brooksport Village.

PART 1

JASMINE

Chapter 1

She held her newborn baby. A mother's smile crossed her face. Only two days ago, she was in the hospital; today, she was home. Once again, she counted every finger and every toe. All there. A little pink cap covered the tiny head of her baby daughter, Jasmine, named for the flower whose fragrance now filtered through the open window. Small fingers curled around her thumb, as those tiny white petals unfolded, one by one. It was dusk.

"Jasmine," she whispered. With secure arms, she held her daughter a little tighter. "My sweet Jasmine, born in the spring." She began to hum a mother's lullaby as she rocked her baby to sleep. The past and all its sadness was gone. Now was the time to think about tea parties with boas and floppy hats, waiting for the ice cream truck as she would clutch coins in her little hand, prom dresses with heels that weren't too high, and a sweet-sixteen birthday party. She would share it all with her mom, Ellie, whom she had just made a grandmother. She whispered a prayer, "May you always know who you are, sweet Jasmine. May you always know where you are, and most importantly, may you always know *whose* you are."

She looked out the window and could see the jasmine plant swaying in the spring breeze. She touched her daughter's tiny nose with her fingertip. She walked across the room and gently lay Jasmine in her cradle. "May your dreams be sweet, my child, my daughter." Her heart was filled to overflowing. How could one so beautiful be her very own? To hold, to love, and to cherish? Forever. "Jasmine, you are a gift from God, a beautiful gift from God." Oh, how she wished her husband could have seen this precious child, made from love.

*****

Those were the last words Jasmine ever heard from her mother, since arriving home. It would be her grandmother and this "gift from God" throughout life's ups and downs, after tragedy struck.

Ellie had rushed to the hospital with baby Jasmine in her arms; her friend Polly was driving. The ambulance had gone on ahead with lights flashing and sirens screaming.

"This can't be happening to my daughter! This can't be happening!" Ellie kept repeating over and over.

Entering the hospital ER with Ellie carrying Jasmine and Polly by her side, they were quickly ushered into a waiting area. It was there she sat with Jasmine. It was there a bottle of formula was handed to her for Jasmine. It was there Jasmine fell asleep in the comfort of her grandmother's arms. And it was there that Ellie's life changed forever. That's what happens when life strikes out at you. That's what happens when the unthinkable, the unspeakable, comes knocking on your heart's door.

The doctor entered the waiting area looking very grim. Ellie braced herself for what was to come, holding Jasmine a little tighter.

"I was hoping for the best, but from your look, it seems I better prepare for the worst," Ellie said.

"I'm so sorry, Ellie. We did everything we could—"

Ellie raised her hand in protest. "Just tell me what happened! Tell me what happened to my girl!" She lifted Jasmine to her shoulder. "Tell me what happened to this precious child's mother! And then tell me why it happened!"

The doctor sat down beside her. He tried to reach out to her, to take her hand.

"Don't take my hand," she muttered. "Can't you see my arms are full? Don't even attempt to hold my hand!"

The doctor let his arms fall to his sides and began, "Your daughter died from an amniotic-fluid embolism."

"Lay terms, please! Tell me in plain simple language what you are talking about!"

Polly continued to stare out the window, tears streaming down her face.

"It's when the amniotic fluid reenters the bloodstream after giving birth."

"Go on," Ellie whispered.

"That triggers a reaction in the body that causes cardiorespiratory arrest and hemorrhaging."

"She should have remained here in this hospital longer than two days! I told you it was wise for her to stay longer! You heard me! Do you agree now, *Doctor*?"

Yes, he did agree with her, but he had no answers that she would accept. Hell, he wouldn't have accepted them either. The insurance companies worked that way these days. He wanted to hug her. He wanted to do something—pat her shoulder? Give her a pamphlet? Say soothing, pretty words to make her feel better in this ugly situation. This was the part of his career he never could handle very eloquently. He wanted to pour them both a drink, a good stiff one. He could do none of those things. People in shock didn't hear, anyway. He was sure that if he opened his mouth to say anything at this moment, it would be the stupidest thing he had ever said in his life. So in silence, he stood to merely walk away.

Polly walked over to her friend and put her arm around her. "You left one question unanswered, Doctor," Polly murmured.

He stopped one step short of the door and turned to both women embracing each other with Jasmine between them.

"You didn't answer *why*."

*****

[They] "were with us for an hour in that exquisite room where time past and time present flowed together."

(Mary Sarton)

Chapter 2

After the funeral, Ellie went to the landscaping yard. She would not rest until she found what she was looking for. They simply had to have one to plant outside the new bedroom where Jasmine would grow up. Ellie held Jasmine closely as she walked up and down the outdoor aisles and rows of plants as she searched. Hosta, geraniums, rhododendrons, azaleas, hydrangeas—where was it?

It was dusk before she found it. She turned the corner. She smelled it. That fragrance she knew so well. The five sweet petals with a yellow circle in the middle—there it was. There was only one left. She quickly called for the aisle manager.

"I want this one," she simply said.

"May I carry it to your car for you?" he questioned.

She nodded.

*****

A man with rugged features and deep blue eyes was sitting on her porch, waiting, with a shovel propped on the wall behind him, when she arrived home. Neither said a word. They had both determined in their own minds that, at times such as these, no words were expected. He knew what to do. He took the jasmine plant from her car. He walked around to the bedroom window and dug the hole that would be its living space for years to come. The trellis had already been built for it to climb. Higher and higher it would go.

Kind of like a bridge to heaven. At least that is what he thought. Ellie had taught him about those things. Those mysterious things.

Ellie watched as she held that sweet baby in her arms while he planted. As he dug in the dirt, he could hear Ellie talking to Jasmine. "I promise you will always remember your mama. I will tell you about her. I will tell you how she loved that flower that my friend is planting."

She reached in her pocket and retrieved a tissue. Deep blue eyes looked at her, ached for her. Should he go to her? Hold her? Hold them both? She motioned for him to continue, that she was fine.

She turned and walked to the swing on the front porch and sat down. Holding little Jasmine to face her, she continued talking to her. "I will tell you how she loved kittens. I will tell you how she liked licking the bowl that held my cake batter and how she liked to iron my table napkins." Jasmine looked as if she were smiling, making little noises that only newborn babies make. "I will tell you about her walks in the woods and her love for birds that sang to her every morning outside her window."

Ellie laughed through her tears. "I will tell you how she hated rhubarb pie but loved sassafras tea. I will tell you how she laughed and sang." Remembering how creative her daughter had been, she continued. "I will tell you about her scrapbooks, and I will show them to you."

Ellie remembered her daughter's school years. "I will tell you about the teachers she liked and the ones she would have liked to forget—especially the algebra ones." Jasmine snuggled in closer to Ellie's neck as if she understood every word her grandma was telling her, as if craving to hear more.

"I will tell you about her first loves and her baton twirling. I will tell you everything you want to know, dear child. And most of all, I will tell you how very much she loved you from the time she carried you inside her tummy to the first moment she held you until her final breath."

She put her fingers on Jasmine's hand. In an instant, that tiny hand grasped her grandma's finger and held on tight. One lone tear ran down Ellie's cheek. She bent to kiss her granddaughter's forehead.

"Jasmine, sweet gift from God."

The plant had been put into the ground and watered. He stood at the corner of the house watching Ellie until she went inside. He did not want to interrupt precious moments between grandmother and granddaughter. Instinct told him Ellie would rock Jasmine to sleep as she snuggled in her arms. She would sing her a lullaby and place her in her crib. Then she would walk to the couch and cry. He would be there to hold her. He would let her tears fall upon his chest. They would say nothing to each other. They didn't need to. They both knew that some of the most intimate conversations were born in silence.

*****

Chapter 3

Ellie and Jasmine watched the seasons come and go, along with all the holidays. Ellie always made those days extraspecial, especially Christmas. They created their own Christmas decorations and strung popcorn on the tree outside to feed the birds. They addressed Christmas cards. Ellie wrote while Jasmine licked the stamps. They made cookies and decorated them. Jasmine was allowed to lick the cake batter bowl—just like her mom had done, when she had been a little girl. Oh, the memories that simple gesture invoked in Ellie. She smiled at the thought of her daughter.

Those were the toddler years where Ellie made certain that Jasmine was her priority and her main focus. She had put her own life on hold. It was a choice she had made, with one exception—the man who came to call. Jasmine secretly thought of him as their personal angel because he was always there taking care of things. One day, she would tell her grandma about her secret.

Yes, Jasmine grew up in that small southern neighborhood where nobody locked their doors and people walked next door to borrow a cup of sugar or a couple of eggs—that place where porch swings were in vogue and hummingbird feeders hung from kitchen windows, where you could see those wee birds coming for that sugar water. Red geraniums always surrounded those feeders, and the man "friend" who visited her and Ellie made doubly sure that he wore a red shirt when he came to visit. He told Jasmine that maybe one day a very special hummingbird would sit on his shoulder because red was their favorite color.

He came often to see Ellie and Jasmine, and Jasmine loved him. He was a kind soul. She always helped him water the jasmine plant outside her bedroom window. That was their special time together. Ellie always smiled a lot when he came over. He always went home at night. Jasmine always wished he would stay.

"Why do you have to go home?" she asked him one evening as he was preparing to leave.

"It's proper," he replied.

"What does *proper* mean?"

"Your grandma and I aren't married, and people would whisper."

"Whisper about what?" she continued to question.

"That I stayed overnight."

Jasmine thought about that for a while and then proclaimed, "Well, then, get married!"

He looked at Ellie. Ellie would always smile a smile that never quite reached her eyes. One could not help but see the sadness that hid beneath them.

As Ellie tucked her into bed that night, Jasmine put her arms around Ellie and held on tight.

"I love you, Grandma. You know if you and your friend got married, he could stay the night, and people wouldn't whisper. Why don't you think about it?"

Ellie smiled, hugging her back. "Oh, my sweet little one. Yes, oh yes, you are a true gift from God."

Before she tiptoed out of the room, Jasmine was asleep.

Chapter 4

The following week, while Ellie and Jasmine were working in the flower garden, Jasmine looked up at Ellie. "I think your man friend is our personal angel, Grandma."

"Do you?"

"Yes."

"Why's that, sweetness?"

"He's always here when we need him. He builds things for us. He helps me with the water hose to water the plants, and he does funerals."

"Funerals?"

"Yes."

"When did he do a funeral, sweet?"

"When you had to run to the store for toothpaste. Remember that day?"

"I do—for that special class I was teaching at church. I needed twelve sample sizes."

Jasmine nodded. "For that lesson you were teaching."

Ellie continued to pull the weeds from the flower garden. "Tell me about this funeral he performed."

"Well, I walked outside. I was going to sit on the swing, but something was sticking up from the boards in between." Ellie encouraged her to continue. "It was a hummingbird. It was dead, Grandma." Ellie continued to listen. "I started crying, and he came to vestigate."

"Investigate," Ellie corrected her.

Jasmine nodded. "Vestigate," Jasmine repeated.

Ellie smiled. "And then, what?" Ellie asked.

"He looked at the hummingbird and said that, yes, it appeared to have died."

"Did you cry harder after he told you that?"

"Yes, that's when he picked me up, looked at me, and said he thought that we should have a funeral."

"That sounds like him."

"So I ran in the house and got a tiny little box to put it in and brought it out to him."

"And then what?"

"He put the bird in the box. We covered it and took it out by the jasmine bush. He let me help him dig the hole. Then we put the box in the hole and covered it up. Then he asked me if we should sing a song."

"And what did you say?"

"I said yes. We should sing a song. I told him we should sing *Taps*."

"And did you?"

"Yes, we did."

"Did that make you feel better?"

"Yes." Jasmine got closer to her grandma, looked up at Ellie, and said, "That's why I think he is our personal angel. He made me feel better, and he knows how to do real good funerals. I think you should marry him, Grandma. Then he could be around us forever. People wouldn't whisper. We'd be 'proper.'"

Chapter 5

Unfortunately, Ellie never married him. He understood. He knew where her first commitments were, and he respected the decision Ellie had made. Her priority was her granddaughter. Turned out he had priorities too. It was only a short year later when he had to leave. Everyone cried when he left.

"His family needs him more than we do right now," Ellie had told Jasmine.

"I don't understand," Jasmine replied.

"Some things we aren't meant to understand in this life. Sometimes we don't always get what we want." Ellie stooped down and looked directly into Jasmine's eyes. "But we always get what we need."

Jasmine protested. "But he's our personal angel, Grandma—ours!"

"I know," Ellie whispered.

Jasmine turned away and left her grandma on the porch that late afternoon and walked to the side of the house. She looked at the jasmine shrub that had grown and climbed high on the trellis he had built five years ago. She sat down beside the little marker that designated the spot where they had buried the hummingbird months before. That is where her tears mingled for the loss of that tiny bird, along with the tears for the man who had gone to help someone else—someone who needed him more than her grandma, someone who needed him more than Jasmine.

Chapter 6

Soon the toddler years turned into the teens. Ellie's and Jasmine's lives continued to bloom and grow, even though a piece of them was gone forever.

Jasmine continued to lick the bowl of the remaining cake batter. She was never going to outgrow that. Raw eggs *but* mixed with sugar, milk, and flour. Good.

"I don't believe all those stories that this isn't good for you," she exclaimed to her grandma.

Ellie smiled. "I don't either."

"I think I will actually live, don't you?"

"I believe so." Ellie laughed.

Jasmine kept licking. "Remember when I ran away from home when I was six years old?"

"What made you think of that?"

"Oh, I was just thinking of your man friend of yesteryear."

Ellie looked up. Remembering his face still made her heart skip a beat. "He's the one that found you at the corner of the house in the backyard."

"And brought me back to the front door."

"I remember. You didn't run away very far."

Jasmine licked the spoon clean. "I'm sorry, Grandma."

"For what?"

"That Mama died."

"Me too."

Jasmine walked to the sink and rinsed the spoon. "And I'm sorry you had to stop living your life to raise me," Jasmine continued.

Ellie turned, untying the apron from around her waist, and walked over to Jasmine. Placing her hands on her shoulders, she turned Jasmine to face her. "Don't ever be sorry for that. I would have done anything for you. I still would. There will be plenty of time for me to meet up with my 'man friend' again—the good Lord willing."

"I hope so, Grandma. I'm old enough now to know that the two of you loved each other."

Ellie thought for a while before answering. Best to tell the truth. She walked back to the kitchen table and sat down. She looked up at Jasmine once again and said, "Yes, Jasmine, yes, we did."

*****

Later that night, Ellie found herself remembering the shadow of the man she still loved. For that's all that was left until an echo from the past kept coming back around in the form of a photo she kept tucked in a drawer for safekeeping. Her eyes would wander there every now and again. There was so much more to the story of Ellie and him. She never told Jasmine that he had been married to a woman far, far away and that woman had chosen her career over him. He had chosen a quieter life. Small-town life had not been her cup of tea. She preferred the city folk.

"Too different," he had told Ellie.

The divorce had been painful. When his ex-wife moved to the city, taking their only daughter with her was what pained him the most. He had visiting rights, and he saw his daughter every chance he got. But New York City soon claimed his daughter, just as it had his ex-wife. The visits became sporadic, and many times his daughter had canceled their visits at the last minute.

He had moved into a little town in rural New York to, at least, stay close enough to see his daughter when she called—mostly for money or when she needed something. Still, he was her father, and he had vowed to stay as close as he could—until a job offer came to him from down south—an offer that he could not refuse.

He remembered his daughter exclaiming, "You cannot possibly go down south! Are you going to be a *hillbilly* now?"

Oh yes, New York City had gotten to her, and he hated the thought that she had become so much like her mother. Nothing was good enough. They always wanted more. Money. Prestige. They cared too much about what things "looked" like. He didn't know if it was the job opportunity or his daughter's remark that he had finally said yes to the job. She was grown now and wasn't into visiting her old man anymore—not that she was ever into it. So he packed his bags, left a note to his daughter saying he would be in touch with his new phone number, and drove down south to be with the *hillbillies*.

*****

It had not taken him long to settle in. He found a nice little country home with lots of land and a horse or two. But he still wasn't too familiar with all the roads, especially the "one-way" ones. It seemed he did a lot of wrong-way turns. Nevertheless, he liked the new chapter in his life. Country music became his favorite. He was glad to be far, far away from the classical. And it wasn't long before another change would come. He met Ellie. Dear Ellie. He first saw her kneeling in her garden of flowers, with a big floppy hat on her head, singing, *"I know where I'm goin'. Don't you wanna come too?"*

"I'm lost," he had said.

She had looked up, shading her eyes from the sun. She didn't seem startled. He was glad. The last thing he would have wanted was to scare her to death. He had heard that southern women were jittery around "Yankees." And that's what he had been labeled in that small southern town—a Yankee. Until Ellie. After meeting her, he was accepted into the southern ranks. She was "somebody" down here in "hillbilly" land. And, yes, he very much wanted to go along with her, wherever she knew she was going, especially after that first cup of coffee she had invited him to share.

"Good things happen over a cup of coffee," she had said as he was leaving with his directions in hand.

Since that day, he had been there for her through all the good times. He had worked with her in the flower garden. He had grocery shopped with her, cooked for her, gone to the movies with her. He had seen her playful side with that Polly friend of hers, who was quite a character. Ellie had become his new beginning.

When tragedy struck, he was there. He had cried with her when her daughter died. He had seen her courageous spirit in the raising of her granddaughter. He had planted the jasmine shrub next to Jasmine's bedroom window. He had built the trellis, praying over each little slat he hammered together for the welfare and the protection of the woman he had grown to love, and for her granddaughter whom he had wanted to protect through the years. This was where he was meant to be. He knew it. He was going to "pop the question" soon. He would convince her that the two of them could raise Jasmine together. He was whistling, affirming his decision when the phone call had come.

*****

"I have to go," he had said to Ellie.

"I know you do," she replied.

Jasmine had walked into the room. "Will you be back for dinner?" Jasmine had asked. Being a typical five-year-old, she began dancing around the room. "Can you bring some chips? And dip?"

He had gone over to the kitchen chair and motioned for Jasmine to come sit on his lap. "No, sweetheart, I won't be back for dinner. I have to go somewhere for a long, long time."

"Why?"

"Someone needs me."

"More than Grandma and I need you?"

Her eyes were innocent—oh, so innocent.

It was Ellie who spoke. "Yes, child, someone needs him now more than us. It has to do with family, sweetheart. When it comes to family, you have to do what you have to do."

Jasmine looked up at him. "But we're your family."

He drew her close. He didn't want to leave, but his daughter had called in desperation. In one conversation that had lasted for hours, she had spilled out her heart. Yes, she had married. Yes, she was wrong to have cut him out of her life. Yes, she was glad he had discovered a new life down south. Yes, she was wrong to have married someone who was never there for her. Yes, she had a son—he was a grandfather. And now that son was sick, very sick. Her husband was gone for good, and she not only needed his help; she needed his money. She had it all figured out—he would move back to New York and live with her for a while to help take care of her son. Her mother? Well, she lived six months in Europe and six months in New York. She couldn't help in any way and had made that very clear to her daughter. She had told her she was a grown woman now and on her own. Her dad was her only hope. And he was her father. He never forgot his promise to her, *I'll always be there for you when you need me.* That was the final thing she had said to him. "I need you now. Will you come?"

He cried when he left. He knew he was leaving the only woman he had ever truly loved since the first time he had seen her in that garden of flowers. Some things you just know at first glance. Sadly, you also know that some things just couldn't be. This was one of them. His past was his past, and it would not let him go. His daughter needed him, and he would remain true to his promise that he had given her all those years ago. *"I'll be there for you."*

Chapter 7

Ellie had lived frugally. Financially secure, she had invested wisely. Her recipe books had brought in steady royalties, and her craft shop in town helped with whatever "frills" needed to be purchased, as Jasmine grew—things like prom dresses and visits to the salon for a periodic manicure. And most of all, she had saved enough for Jasmine's education.

Polly lived nearly a stone's throw away. Best friends. They knew each other's secrets. They loved sitting on the porch at dusk telling and retelling the stories of their past, present, and dreams of the future. They laughed loud and hardy, especially when Polly would let slip her only cussword she would ever speak aloud. She would drop a glass and blurt it out. She would see a good-looking man from a distance and whisper it out. She would comment on how good Ellie's cakes were, and it popped right out of her mouth again. Yes, that was Polly's trademark—her own personal cuss phrase: "S——t fire!"

"I hear Jasmine has been looking for jobs in big city hospitals," Polly said.

"Yes, she has." Ellie took a deep breath.

"Have you thought about her leaving?"

"That's all I think about lately. She's waiting on a letter, even as we sit here, from some hospital in New York."

Polly took a sip of wine. "That's why you brought out the wine instead of sweet tea this evening, eh, kiddo?"

Ellie smiled.

"Oh, of course it is. What are you going to do with yourself when she's gone?"

Ellie shrugged her shoulders.

"I'll tell you what you should do!" Polly exclaimed.

"Don't say it, Polly."

"You should call that handsome man that used to grace your premises every chance he got!"

"No, it's been too long."

"It's never too long when two people connect the way you two did! Don't give me that!"

"We did have some good times," Ellie admitted.

"S——t fire, girl! Just the mention of his name and your whole face lights up!"

"It's over, Polly. He hasn't reached out to me either. At least not lately."

"That's because you didn't answer all his phone calls. Sooner or later, you had to know he would quit trying!"

"I guess. But I couldn't intrude on what he needed to do."

"I know, I know, forever the martyr."

"I don't look at myself that way. It was just the right thing to do."

"Let him go? For good? I thought it was going to be just a temporary thing. I mean you're always saying, 'Oh, here I go again being "temporarily misplaced."' Well, my friend your 'temporarily' has lasted too long!"

"Life got in the way, Polly. He had his priorities, and I had mine."

Polly sighed. "Give me another glass, would you?" Ellie poured them both another round. "You could still call him now. Catch up. See what life has brought to the two of you between the bookends of then and now. Know what I mean?"

"No, I can't."

"Why not?"

"We've both changed, maybe too much."

"Girl, you drive me crazy!" She took another sip of her wine. "You still have remnants of the *glow*."

"Shut up."

Polly made a face.

"I saw that."

Scratching her head, Polly changed the subject and looked out to the beautiful flowers that surrounded Ellie's house. She could smell the sweet fragrance of jasmine from around the corner. The breeze was beginning to cool the hot summer day.

"Maybe I'll call him for you," Polly began.

"The subject is closed, Polly. And don't you dare! Besides, where in the world would you begin?"

Just then, Jasmine pulled up in her car. She quickly got out and ran to Ellie with the job offer in her hand. Yes, she would be leaving soon. Ellie had been preparing herself for the inevitable. All the late nights of study, all the internships, all the determination had paid off. Jasmine was now officially a member of the medical team at Morris Memorial Hospital in New York.

Polly sneaked a peek at Ellie. Of course, she was happy for Jasmine. That girl had turned out just fine.

Jasmine ran into the house for another glass to join what had now become a celebration rather than a reflection of times gone by and times yet to be.

"Even though it seems so far away, you know she will come back to visit," Polly dared to say.

"I know."

"We always return to our roots, you know?" Polly managed to say.

Jasmine returned to the porch with her glass. Polly poured her a glass from the wine bottle that was nearly empty. The three women lifted their glasses. Ellie cleared her throat.

"Here's to Jasmine, my granddaughter, flying off to another chapter, another little feisty one to make her mark in the real world. Wishing you all the best, dear one, all that a good life has to offer!"

They clinked glasses and drank. Jasmine gave her grandmother and Polly quick hugs and ran inside to call her friends about her first job in the "real world." Polly did not fail to see the tears glistening in Ellie's eyes.

"It happened too soon, didn't it, my friend?"

"Yes, it did. I thought I had a little more time with her. It seems she is a woman in demand, and a little more time is not afforded to me." Both women looked out at the flower garden that was flourishing. Ellie turned to her friend and lifted her glass. "I'm proud of that girl! So proud of her!"

"Well, s——t fire!" Polly exclaimed. "Let's open another bottle!"

*****

Jasmine had accepted the job to work at the hospital in New York. Ellie knew it was only a matter of time until Jasmine would let her know when she would be leaving. She was calming her emotions for Jasmine's imminent departure by picking up her knitting. And tonight just happened to be the night. She knew it the moment her granddaughter walked into the living room.

"I need to tell you something, Grandma."

Ellie looked up from her knitting. From the expression on Jasmine's face, she decided to take a real deep breath. "Okay," she replied, continuing to look at Jasmine.

Jasmine took a deep breath. "But, first, can you tell me again about my dad?" Jasmine asked. "I know you've told me certain details about him all my life. Now I'm all grown up, and I want to know more details."

Ellie understood. She smiled at Jasmine and put down her knitting. "Your daddy was a good man." Jasmine nodded, encouraging her grandma to tell her more. "He was a good husband, a protector, very organized, and was so happy to learn that he was going to be a daddy. Your mama told him she was expecting before he went off to the training mission. Your daddy was a marine." Ellie continued. "Oh, how your daddy loved your mama."

"So he was a man in uniform. What woman doesn't like a man in uniform? I take it he was also a lover?" Jasmine asked with a smile.

Ellie didn't even blink. "You have grown up, haven't you? Time to learn about true romance, eh? I would dare to say that, yes, your daddy was a lover."

"Somehow, I thought so." Jasmine laughed. She looked at Ellie. "Did he make people laugh, Grandma?"

"Oh yes, he was full of humor and sometimes..."

"Sometimes what?"

"Sometimes full of himself." Ellie put her knitting project on the table and pointed toward the kitchen. "Let's have tea."

*****

The two women sat at the table, facing one another.

"Everyone admired your daddy. It was almost like people stood a little straighter when he would walk into a room—like they were saluting him in their minds. He was always telling people, 'At ease, for goodness' sake, at ease.' He just had that way about him. We loved him so much." Ellie passed Jasmine the sugar bowl for her usual two scoops. "Oh yes, he was keenly respected by everyone. He stood tall in every situation. He was a fighter. He was bigger than life itself. That's why we could not accept the news when it first came to us. There are days I still can't believe it, and it's been years."

Jasmine remembered what Ellie had shared with her once before about her daddy's death. "I know it must have been hard. A man like that being brought down by a mechanical failure. A damn helicopter," Jasmine whispered.

"We were crushed. Your mama had lost the love of her life. I had lost someone I looked at as a son I never had, and you would be without a great man you would never call daddy. The whole thing was tragic."

"I never knew Mama either."

Ellie stirred sugar into her tea. "I pray I've served you well, sweetheart."

Tears were beginning to form in Jasmine's eyes. "Oh, you have, Grandma. You have!"

Ellie took a sip of her tea. "Your daddy taught us a lot, especially how to fight the good fight, *and* we came back after the shock of the news. Your mama concentrated on having a healthy, happy baby. And I did all those things grandmas-to-be do when they are expecting their first grandchild." She pointed to the living room. "You can see that I still knit!"

Jasmine smiled. "And then I was born."

"Yes, and then you were born. It was a happy day."

"But it didn't last. Mama died."

Ellie took another sip of tea. "Yes, she did."

"And you had to fight all over again."

"Yes, I did."

Jasmine looked down and back up, taking her grandma's hand. "You and I will fight together, Grandma, won't we? When we have to."

"Yes, dear child. Now tell me what is the other thing you wanted to talk to me about."

Jasmine sighed. "I'll be leaving in the fall."

Ellie took a deep breath. "I understand you have to go. I've raised you to 'set sail' one day. I always knew the day would come."

"I love you, Grandma. I'm strong because of you. I know where I'm going and what I'm supposed to do with my life."

Ellie squeezed Jasmine's hand. "I'm so proud of you, Jasmine! All those 'all-nighters' you put in with your books sure paid off! Don't you dare feel guilty about leaving. I'm going to be fine, and Polly will keep me out of trouble!"

"Sure, she will!" Jasmine laughed. "Polly's middle name is 'trouble'!"

Ellie gave her a little shove. "It's late now, child. Time to give those beautiful eyes of yours a rest. We'll talk more in the morning."

Jasmine kissed Ellie's cheek, sighed, and walked toward her bedroom. Ellie watched her go. She heard the door close and secretly wondered what she would do with her own life now that her granddaughter would be leaving.

"Time to fight again, time to swim, time to march, time to be strong," she murmured. Oh, how she hated goodbyes. She assured herself this was not a goodbye. This was a mere so long, until next time…

Chapter 8

Jasmine never forgot her roots. Just as Polly had predicted, she did return. Often. Every vacation. Every holiday. And Ellie would be waiting on the porch with open arms to welcome her home with each visit, having prepared her favorite meal of meatloaf, mashed potatoes, and green beans. Polly always joined them for dessert—chocolate pie. They were her special people, always there for her. She loved that sweet neighborhood town where she had grown up. Her town. No, she would never forget her hometown.

*****

As the years went by, Jasmine became a dedicated pretransplant coordinator at Morris Memorial Hospital. For years, she had assisted many patients until they were successfully transplanted with the organ they needed. When it was time to turn the patients over to the posttransplant coordinator, she did so with a tear, a prayer, and a red rosebud wishing them a successful and full recovery. As far back as she could remember, she had wanted to go into the medical profession. It was when her grandmother had shared with her how her mother had died that she wanted to help others to live. It became her passion, and her grandmother had seen to it that her dream came true.

Jasmine loved her job. What she didn't like was not being able to find donors quickly for patients in dire need. She had a difficult time waiting. She wanted to snap her fingers and let it be done, but reality told her to just keep calm. She was gradually learning to stay at peace in the waiting.

That was what she was doing when the phone call came from Polly.

*****

Congestive heart failure was the culprit. Polly told Jasmine she needed to hurry.

"Ellie didn't want me to tell you before. She didn't want you worrying about her. She would poo-poo me away and go to the hospital to have fluid drained out of her lungs and come home 'good as new,' she would always say. I just have to cut back on my salt intake. But this time, I told her I was calling you. She's refusing to go to the hospital."

Jasmine could tell Polly was near a tearful collapse.

"You tell her you were right to call me, and I am on my way!"

Jasmine caught the next flight out of New York LaGuardia. She prayed she wouldn't run into any delays. She prayed she would find a direct flight, but "puddle jumpers" were connectors into small towns. That was a given. But this was her grandma. This was her life. She would get there if she had to beg, borrow, or steal. She would get there. Polly had told her to hurry. She would get there.

*****

Polly was with Ellie when Jasmine arrived.

"Polly. How is she?"

"Oh, Jasmine." Polly ran to her and embraced her. "I think she's holding on for you to get back here."

Jasmine walked over to the bed. She took Ellie's hand. "I'm here, Grandma."

Ellie opened her eyes at the mere touch of her granddaughter's hand.

Polly spoke. "She wanted to be in your room. She said she wanted to smell the first fragrance of the jasmine—come April."

Jasmine understood. She remembered the times they would sit in this very room. Winter melting into spring. They would make a production of it. They popped popcorn and jazzed it up with salt and Italian spices, plus butter. They drank ginger ale that made them sneeze and laugh at the same time.

They would wait for those jasmine petals to unfold—for that fragrance to begin its spring dance that would last until October—when it was time to go back to sleep. And then Ellie would tell the story once again of how Jasmine got her name.

Grandma would tuck her in and say the four words both of them had come to cherish, "a gift from God."

Suddenly, Ellie grabbed Jasmine's other hand, and their fingers intertwined.

"Never forget, sweet, never forget how much your mama and daddy loved each other."

"I won't."

Ellie's eyes began to brim with tears. "May you find that same kind of love one day, Jasmine." Then Ellie chuckled. "You'll know him in his kiss. You don't think kissing is yucky anymore, do you, child?"

"No, Grandma, but I haven't found him yet."

"You will. Don't let him slip away when you do. Promise me."

"I promise."

Ellie coughed. "It's time, Jasmine," Ellie whispered.

"To go to sleep?" Jasmine questioned.

"Yes."

"But spring is just beginning, Grandma."

Jasmine tried desperately to protest. Polly stood helplessly nearby.

"Hold my hand tighter, Jasmine." Their hands remained interlocked. "I pray I have served you well." Ellie's breathing became more labored.

"Oh, you have!"

Ellie nodded and smiled. "I will always be with you." She held tightly to her granddaughter's hands and remembered the first time Jasmine had grasped and held tightly to her thumb. "Now it's time to walk through another door. I'll see you again, my sweet, on the other side."

Jasmine leaned close to Ellie's ear. "I love you, Grandma." She wiped away the tears streaming down her face.

"Don't cry, my sweet. Please don't cry. I'll only be a whisper away."

Jasmine leaned down again and whispered in Ellie's ear words she never wanted to say. She forced herself. "It's okay to go, Grandma. I'm going to be fine. I love you so much."

And then Ellie, her dear grandmother and friend, was gone. She breathed her last. It was dusk. Polly wept. Jasmine walked to the open window and took in the first sweet fragrance of spring. April had arrived. The jasmine was in bloom. And she, too, wept.

*****

If there ever was such a thing as a sweet funeral, Ellie's was one. It was springtime, and the flowers were in bloom. That's the way she would have wanted it.

Speaking through her tears, Jasmine gave the eulogy. She spoke of things they had shared, places they had been, and the things they had loved. And everyone listened intently. Everyone loved Ellie. She was endeared. And the entire community was there. The town cried.

The only person who went seemingly unnoticed was one of the most important; he sat in the back of the church. Tears streaking down his face. Only three people would ever know the love they had for one another. He knew. Polly knew. Ellie knew.

Silently, he left the church. Quietly, he walked to his car, got in the front seat, and looked at the bouquet he had bought only a few short hours ago. He started the engine and drove away. It was the end. It was over. The only woman he had ever really loved was gone, off to the heavenlies, she often called it.

"That woman always knew where she was going," he whispered.

He didn't want it to end like this. He took a deep breath and pushed the gas pedal to the floor. He didn't know where he was going. He didn't care. The only woman he had ever loved was now gone. But one thing he would forever be grateful for—she had died knowing how much he loved her, and he was convinced she felt the same. She had told him. And that, in the end, had been enough.

Polly had not seen him at the funeral. He was sure of that. But Jasmine—he thought she caught his eye when she was speaking to the friends who had gathered. He had looked down quickly. He didn't know what else to do. He remembered her as a little girl when he was Ellie and Jasmine's own personal angel…

Could he just walk away like this? Again? He should turn around and go to Jasmine. Ellie had been her life. He turned left into the 7-Eleven at the end of town. He was going back. He had to see Jasmine and Polly. Or would seeing them only make it worse?

*****

"Guests of my life,
You came in the early dawn, and you in the night.
Your name was uttered by the Spring flowers and
yours by the showers of rain.
You brought the harp into my house and you
brought the lamp.
After you had taken your leave I found God's footprints
on my floor."

(Rabindranath Tagore)

Jasmine drove into her hometown after the funeral. She was suspended in sorrow. She needed to touch things that were familiar. She went to Freel's Drug Store and ordered a cup of coffee. She needed to remember the days of innocent laughter, the days of meeting her high school sweetheart in this very place for hotdogs and fries. She needed to remember the days of holding hands and kisses on a blanket at Warrior's State Park. She sighed. Gone—that, too, gone.

She "cruised" up and down Broad Street, passing the State and Strand Theaters. Maybe she would go to a movie. Was that *tangible* enough? Maybe if she had popcorn. Maybe she would go into Nettie Lee and buy a new dress. Or she could ride the escalator in J. Fred Johnson's—the one that always scared her so much when she was little. Grandma would always hold out her hand. It was then she felt safe. She could go to JCPenney and buy M&M's. Life just kept going on around her. Didn't life know that she had lost someone so dear to her she didn't know what to do or where to turn?

Finally, she turned her car toward 129 Greenway Street. It was there that she would find her tangible memories. She pulled into the driveway and stared at the house. She reflected on all the memories as she sat in the car, unable to move. This house had served them well—a small house with two bedrooms, one bath, small kitchen, and a huge dining room.

She remembered every Sunday sitting around that table eating fried chicken, cooked in lard. "*Lard—that's the secret to good fried chicken!*" Ellie would exclaim. Polly had a sweet tooth for the chocolate pie. Everything was finger-lickin' good. It had always been the two of them and many times, Polly, when she was growing up. There had been a lot of laughter around that table. This place had been her shelter, her safety net.

Finally, she opened her car door and took the long walk up the sidewalk to the house she had grown up in. The house that had been filled with love every single day of her life. The house surrounded by flowers.

*****

She found herself sitting at the small kitchen table, staring at the box. Her grandmother had drawn hearts on the top with musical notes along each of the four sides. Her grandmother was always doing things like that. Drawing little music notes. Ending a sentence with little dots across the page. Drawing little stick people because that's all she knew how to draw. Jasmine smiled at the hours they would sit at this very table working on art projects, when neither one of them had the gift of artistry of any kind. Somehow, Jasmine always ended up with an A. It still confused her. How in the world did that ever happen?

She smiled at the memory. The kitchen table—where all the tea parties for two had taken place. So it seemed only fitting that she would find herself here in this particular spot, going through a memory box her grandmother had placed her name upon long before this day.

"Only you," she had said. "This is meant for only you. When I am gone, open this box. You'll understand why. Oh, there's no money in this box—only a wealth of advice and things that were important to me. I know you will take care of it and every object inside. Only you."

She had loved her grandmother. She was sure the box was packed with memories and mementos, not to mention a few teapots. Oh, how her grandmother had loved teapots. Again, she smiled at the memory.

"One day," she had said to Jasmine, "when you are as old as I am, you will remember our tea parties."

Jasmine did not have to become old to remember those parties. She remembered them now, as well as the homemade sugar cookies. Yes, they had sat there with their feathery boas and floppy hats doing "girl talk." That was when she would reveal all her sweet secrets to her grandmother.

"One day you'll tell me about your first kiss, won't you, sweet?"

"I told you I'm never kissing a boy!"

"I remember, but that will change."

They would both laugh, lick their fingers, and drink their tea. In the winter, the tea was hot. In the summer, when it was "hot as blazes" outside, it was sweet tea on ice.

Today, she sat alone—two boas on the chair next to her and two floppy hats on the window sill.

Tenderly, she placed one of the boas around her shoulders, walked to the window, and placed one floppy hat on her head. She poured herself a tall glass of sweet tea on ice because summer was coming and it would be "hot as blazes." She looked at the fan, securely fitted in the dining room window. Her grandmother did not like air conditioners. She had preferred the fan and fresh air.

She wouldn't trade one of the many memories they had made for all the riches in the world. A lone tear streaked her cheek as she walked back to the table and sat down. She took a deep breath and continued to unpack the memory box. She took off her shoes, for she felt she was on sacred ground.

*****

This was her place. Should he intrude? Would she look at him as an intrusion? Her back was to him as he watched her at the kitchen table. He watched as she put the boa around her shoulders and walk to the window sill that held the floppy hats. He watched her put on one of the hats. He saw her tears. He could not open the screen and go to her. The pain was too deep. He would not be able to help her, comfort her. He could barely stand upright, himself.

He had come back. He had planned on telling Ellie, "*Enough*!" He was going to marry her. He didn't care if they were getting older and grayer. He loved her. Too late.

He walked around to the corner where he had planted the jasmine plant all those years ago. Unnoticed, he stood there taking in the fragrance. It was dusk. Jasmine had been a newborn when that plant took its rightful corner outside her bedroom window. Ellie had stood there with Jasmine in her arms as he completed the task. Tears had rolled down her cheeks. She had lost her daughter. She had held Jasmine a little tighter. He had ached for her then. He ached for her now. He stood there as tears began to fall. He made no attempt to hide them. He had learned of Ellie's death when he had stopped at the florist to buy flowers to hand to her before he was going to say a word. Flowers had always spoken to her. He had thought they would speak for him then, showing up on her doorstep unannounced.

The florist had been busy. Flowers were being placed in delivery trucks to take to the local church. He had asked if someone was getting married. No, they had said. Sadly, someone had died. He had asked, who? His knees buckled when he heard her name. He bought the flowers, anyway. In shock, he left the florist.

Too late. He had come back too late. He turned to walk away in silence. It would be a long trip back from where he had come. He had envisioned Ellie sitting beside him, taking her back to his own hometown, laughing as they used to do. Finally, getting it right. Eternally together, looking forward to walking with their canes and leaning on each other in their garden that they would plant together. Not to be.

He turned away from Jasmine and walked the short distance to where he had parked his car, out of sight, still clutching the flowers from the florist. He had thought briefly about giving the bouquet to Jasmine. Instead, he decided to walk away. He got in his car, looked back once, and returned to the cemetery. He stopped the car in front of Ellie's grave.

"I came back, Ellie. I came back to get you. I came back for you. To talk some sense into your head. To take back what was meant to be all along."

He walked to the grave and laid the flowers beside all the others that had been placed there.

"Hello, again," he whispered. "Remember me?"

He just could not say goodbye. He had never said goodbye, and he never would. His heart was now buried with her in the grave that he stood beside. Tears of sadness fell from his eyes. Tears of regret and tears for things lost. Through the years, and now this final blow, he had come to know just how fragile life could be.

*****

Jasmine found herself roaming through the house she and her grandma had shared for so many years. It seemed so quiet now. She walked into Ellie's bedroom. The old dresser looked the same, the little stool in front of a round mirror. Two drawers on each side. Jasmine smiled as she remembered her grandma applying makeup every morning. Jasmine would sit there watching intently.

"You have to do this every morning, sweet thing."

"Why, Grandma?"

"Because you never know when you're going to meet your future intended."

"What's a 'future intended'?"

She would take the powder puff and then touch Jasmine's nose with it and say, "Your husband, sweet, your husband."

"I'm not getting married!"

Grandma's laughter would ring throughout the house.

"Oh yes, you will, sweet. You'll change your mind."

"Don't think so."

"Why not?"

"I don't want to kiss a boy."

"That, too, will change."

Jasmine shrugged. "And besides that, kissing will probably be out of style when that time comes."

Grandma laughed even louder.

Seemed she and Ellie talked a lot about kissing boys during those growing up years.

Jasmine smiled and sat down on the stool in front of the dresser. She looked into the mirror and opened one of the drawers. Sure enough, there it was. That sweet round gold and white box of Coty loose powder with the powder puff inside. Jasmine took the puff, dipped it in the powder, and touched her nose with it.

"Never leave the house with a shiny nose," her grandma had said.

A tear rolled down the cheek her grandma had kissed so many times.

Every room of her grandmother's house beckoned a memory to surface. They had experienced good times in this house. Some real good times. She walked into the kitchen and looked out the window, where she saw the old clothesline, still standing, steady and strong.

Jasmine remembered the day she was helping Ellie hang the clothes on the line.

Jasmine had asked her grandma, "If you could have anything in the world right now, what would you want?"

"Clean sheets every night," her grandmother had chirped. She turned and faced Jasmine. "Yes! That's what I would want, clean, sweet-smelling sheets from the sun after being on the clothesline outside—clean sheets every night!"

The dining room was no different. The tablecloth was the same on the oval-shaped dining room table, as if waiting for friends to arrive. And they always did. They could always smell good ole home cookin'.

Meanwhile, back in Brooksport Village

Chapter 9

Belle walked outside and stepped under the canopy to her bakery. She liked the rain. She just didn't like storms, especially storms that ripped things apart—storms that nearly destroyed her bakery a few years ago. She liked the kind of rain that promised to wash away the gloominess of a heart that had been hurt, the heaviness of a sadness that lingered around a wounded soul. She had seen so much of that.

After a rain such as this, the streets were clean, the flowers perked up. The laughter came back as tourists began to fill the streets once again. Just like hearts mended after the tears. Just like souls were revived after the sadness. Yes, this was the kind of rain Belle liked. She smiled and walked back into the bakery. Trudy would be stopping by soon for her famous deep-fried doughnuts.

"Oh, that Trudy, what in the world would we ever do without her?" she asked as she prepared the hot oil.

*****

Jasmine continued to go through her grandma's things. There were pictures. Lots of them. Mostly of Jasmine. Ellie had always told her she was special. She traced all the pictures with her fingertips. From kindergarten on into high school and through college.

She lingered upon the one that was labeled "Kindergarten." There was a teardrop stain on the corner of that picture because that was when that special man in her grandma's life had left. She remembered crying those tears. Attached to that picture was a poem about life and loss. She remembered it had been raining that day and he was holding an umbrella with Jasmine in his arms.

She looked at the photo very closely before determining that it was a picture of a younger version of the man who had been seated at the back of the church at Ellie's funeral. Yes! She held the photo closer to her eyes. Yes, indeed! It had to be him—the first man who had protected her from the rain under an umbrella. They were waiting on the bus that would take her to her first day of kindergarten.

The memory tugged at her heart. Ellie had kept the picture. Jasmine looked at that picture for a long time. There she was. Jasmine, with the innocent eyes, the pug nose, the unsure smile, and all that curly hair. Although the picture was black-and-white, she remembered the color of her dress. The dress Ellie had made for her.

She said aloud, "It was green with white buttons."

Jasmine got up and walked to the window. She poured herself another glass of sweet tea, still holding the photo in her hand. She walked back to the table and opened another box. That was when she found the jar of buttons. She laughed out loud. "I used to tease her all the time about her obsession with buttons! She would shrug her shoulders and say, 'You never know when you're going to need one.'"

Jasmine remembered always running to the jar of buttons every time she lost one and taking it to her grandma, who would merely smile and whisper, "I told you so."

She remembered especially the day her rag doll needed that special button for one of her eyes. Her grandma's eyes had gleamed when she found exactly the perfect button she was looking for to make that rag doll "whole" again.

Jasmine held the little jar of buttons up to the light, looking at them. There were square ones, round ones, red ones, green ones, and white ones—in fact, all the colors you could ever imagine. She unscrewed the lid. There on the top of all those buttons was a note, "Take care of my buttons," written in Ellie's handwriting.

Jasmine gasped. "I'll take care of your buttons, Grandma," she said. She screwed the lid back on—tight. Not one button would escape that jar under her watch. No, siree—not one button.

*****

It was beginning to rain when Jasmine had completed going through the boxes. The boa had long since fallen from her shoulders, the floppy hat was back on the windowsill, and she had switched from sweet tea to wine to coffee—strong coffee. The night had been long, and yet she knew she would not sleep, even if she tried. Morning had come. She walked outside, got in her car, and drove to the cemetery.

She walked to her grandma's grave. There beside the engraved heart on the marker was a grouping of flowers she did not recognize from the memorial. She felt a strange sensation as she looked at them. Someone had brought them after everyone had left. Someone had stood in this very spot and left them there.

Could it have been the man who looked so familiar—the one whose eyes were brimming with tears until they fell unmercifully down his face? Was he the one who had brought those flowers?

She felt it odd that they looked more like a bouquet than a funeral flower. Who, indeed, was this mystery man who had come and gone in a flash? Who was this man who came back to the cemetery while she opened and closed boxes at her grandma's home?

"Was that him, Grandma? Did our personal angel come back too late?"

She was connecting the dots. Had he been hoping to reconnect with Ellie after all the years they had spent apart? If so, it was no wonder he had cried such bittersweet tears in the church. And it was no wonder that he had vanished again so suddenly after his final goodbye.

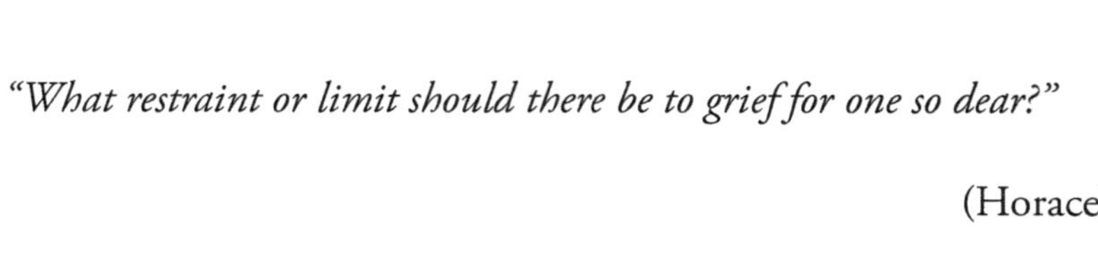

"What restraint or limit should there be to grief for one so dear?"

(Horace)

The rain became a mere drizzle as Jasmine continued to stand beside Ellie's grave. The memory box had told her much more about her grandmother than she had ever known, especially within the pages of the journals where her grandma had written through the years. She found not only fun, laughable memories captured in the words on those white pages, she also found heartfelt confidences written there for her eyes only. She found a woman with human failings—a flesh-and-blood woman who lived, breathed, pondered, made a few mistakes, learned from them, and moved on. She found a woman who had loved and lost.

Jasmine paid no attention to the drizzle of rain. She kept remembering.

"Do you believe in fairy tales, Grandma?"

"No, not really, but I do believe every girl should have at least one in her life." Ellie touched her granddaughter's nose with her fingertip. "A fairy tale to lean upon when things get dreary."

Jasmine crinkled her nose. "Did you have a fairy tale?"

Without thinking, Ellie replied, "Yes, I do believe I did."

Jasmine walked to a nearby bench and sat, staring out at all the markers of people once loved.

Jasmine was suspended in sorrow. She remembered the white bowl with the strawberry designs around the edge, sitting in the center of the table that always held a misplaced watch or ring, a dollar if you needed it, a paper clip, and sometimes an apple.

"This is our very own little lost-and-found bowl," her grandmother had said one day. "You lose something, you come look in this bowl first. It just may be there."

"Where are you now, Grandma?" Jasmine questioned. "I've lost you. I can't even find the white bowl with the strawberry designs. Is it in another box I haven't found yet?"

Unbeknownst to Jasmine, Polly had walked up behind her.

"You learn all sorts of things about life standing in the cemetery mud, don't you?" Jasmine turned to face Polly. She urged Jasmine to stand with her under the umbrella. "I went by the house to see you. I figured you'd be here." They stood in silence for a while, both grieving their own separate losses. Polly spotted the bunch of flowers held together by a ribbon. She pointed to them. "Strange, they look more like a bouquet."

Jasmine followed her gaze. "I thought so too." Polly became lost in thought. She whispered only to herself, "I wonder, was he here?" The thunder brought her back to the stark reality of where she stood.

"Come on," Polly said. "Let's get you back home. The sky is going to cut loose again any minute."

"It's not home anymore, Polly."

"I know."

As they walked the distance back to their cars, Polly put her arm around Jasmine. "We'll take my car, honey. We'll come back tomorrow and get yours. I'd like to stay with you tonight, if that's okay." She opened the passenger door for Jasmine and whispered to her as Jasmine got in, "I think I know where to look for that white bowl with the strawberry designs around it."

*****

Jasmine walked into what was once her bedroom and turned on the shower in her own private bath. It was time to shake it off. It was time to leave. She and Polly had already had the conversation of how Polly would take care of the house and especially the flower garden Ellie had loved so well—until the time came for Jasmine to sell the property. She couldn't think about that right now. She wouldn't. In time, all in time, she kept telling herself. But not right now. Weren't you supposed to wait a full year before making any major decisions? She had read that once somewhere. But then she had never lost anyone she had loved so much before.

She turned on the shower and opened the medicine cabinet. Funny how little things can cause a torrent of tears. There on the top shelf were Mercurochrome and Sal Hepatica, Ellie's natural wonder "drugs"—the "cure-alls."

It was the little basket of artificial flowers on top of the shelf just below the towel bar that caused the tears to begin. Those were the flowers that always welcomed Jasmine back to her roots. She surmised Ellie must have known she would be returning, even before the phone call from Polly summoning her home. All along, Ellie knew she was dying.

She picked the flowers up, and sure enough, on the back side was a note.

"I knew you would come. Welcome home."

She put the flowers back on the shelf. She undressed and quickly stepped into the shower, where her sobs mingled with the running water. She watched as they made a pathway down the drain.

*****

In total silence, Polly drove Jasmine to the airport. No words were said when Jasmine checked her bags. As she said goodbye, Polly grabbed her and held on tight, whispering in her ear, "Don't forget your roots, child."

Then Polly watched as Jasmine walked away.

"I can't take it," Polly whispered.

She turned and walked back to her car. She needed to get to Ellie's garden. She felt close to Ellie there. She would talk to Ellie there. She wanted to water the jasmine plant. She needed to find the white bowl with the strawberry designs. She would wrap it in paper and mail it to Jasmine. She would cut fresh flowers from Ellie's garden. Before going to bed, she would visit the cemetery one more time. She doubted very much if she would be able to sleep. But then again, perhaps she could dream of the good times they had shared. She wondered exactly when the tears of those memories would turn back to smiles of times gone by…

Meanwhile, back in Brooksport Village

Chapter 10

The sun was shining in Brooksport Village. Belle was watering the flowers outside her bakery.

"It's been dry too long," she murmured to herself.

Belle looked up.

Trudy was running from the salon to the grocery store. Kate was headed to Stumble In with Jake.

"Looks like Trudy needs her Chicken in a Biskit crackers, and those lovebirds need burgers."

Reva, Wes, and Gordy were gathering up all the riding gear at the ranch. They had canceled all the riding lessons. It was just too hot. Everybody needed an air conditioner today. Tourists were heading to Crabby's for something cold to drink.

"We need rain," Belle said to no one in particular.

She walked back into her bakery and poured a glass of lemonade. She looked over at the table in the corner and suddenly laughed. She remembered the people who had sat at that exact table and the stories that had been told, the memories that had been made.

"Jake and Trudy first met here," she said aloud. "Gordy and Trudy talked at that table. Giddy teenage girls stalked Jake at that table."

She took a sip of her drink and walked over to the infamous table, placing her hand on the flat surface.

"Lots of things have gone on at this table." She sighed. "We haven't had any excitement around this place in a long time!" She looked around and sighed again. "It's about time we had some! We need some excitement of the 'good' kind. Lord, did you hear me? Good, not bad. We've had our share of the bad. Send us some good, goose-bump-up-our-arms-and-down-our-legs kind of excitement!"

In the months to come, the Lord would do just that. But as the town had learned during the good times in its life, everything was eventually a "trade-off." Sometimes, you had to take the bad with the good. It built character. It made you stronger. The town became better when they found their way out to the other side.

Change was coming. Yes, indeed. A little lady by the name of Jasmine was coming to their fair town—in a kind of "roundabout" way…

*****

Chapter 11

The plane ride was painful. Jasmine had left a part of herself back in her small town with Polly giving her a powerful hug. *"Don't forget your roots"* kept coming back around in Jasmine's mind. She had so many memories there, and those memories were too painful to look back upon right now. She had to stay away. At least for a little while. Her mind wandered as the plane flew above the clouds.

The clouds reminded her of marshmallows. Suddenly, her mind had taken her to her grandma's kitchen. They were making cookies, sugar cookies, in that little kitchen no bigger than a matchbox. Still, somehow those cookies always ended up perfect and tasty, especially when the "princess" sprinkled red-and-green sugar all over the tops.

"You are a princess," Ellie told her granddaughter.

"But princesses don't cook, Grandma," she replied, "The queen cooks for the princess. Kind of like you and me. You're the queen, and I'm the princess."

Jasmin's expression became suddenly serious.

"What are you thinking, sweet?"

"That sometimes you cook with iron skillets. Do queens do that?"

Ellie laughed. "Maybe they do, but princesses don't. No, a princess wouldn't cook with an iron skillet. They cook with sugar. That's why they're so sweet, like you."

"But one day I will cook with iron skillets, when I become a queen!" Jasmine exclaimed.

"I have no doubt about that!" Ellie laughed.

Suddenly, Jasmine wanted an iron skillet. Whether she wanted to be or not, she was now the "queen."

The clouds broke, and Jasmine could see the city below her. She heard a little voice beside her, bringing her back to the present—a little girl talking to her mom.

"Mommy, I have the hiccups."

Jasmine looked at her and smiled. "Hiccups are funny things, aren't they?" The little girl nodded. "They sometimes just come out of the blue, don't they?"

"Like now," the little girl replied.

"If you take nine sips of water without breathing, they'll go away."

"Really?"

"Shall we try that?" the little girl's mother asked.

"Okay," her daughter answered, a little apprehensively.

Jasmine called for the airline hostess and explained the problem. A glass of water suddenly appeared. The little girl took a deep breath and began to drink the water. When she was finished drinking the water, she put the glass on the tray in front of her. She waited. No hiccups.

"It worked, Mommy. It worked!"

"So it did." Her mom smiled.

"I learned that trick when I was about your age, from my grandma," Jasmine said.

"She's smart, like my grandma!" the little girl exclaimed.

"Yes, she was. She was very smart in so many ways."

"I have a grandma. She's smart too."

"So you said!"

The interchange did not escape the young mother.

"Hiccups all gone now. Let's let the nice lady have some time to herself before we land in this crazy city."

She looked at Jasmine, as if reading her mind.

"You were very gentle with my daughter as she interrupted your own thoughts. Thank you." She smiled at Jasmine. "I hope wherever your mind was taking you that everything works out for you. You looked so sad. I noticed you said your grandmother 'was' smart."

"Yes, I did say 'was,' and I am sad, very sad," Jasmine replied. Jasmine was quiet for a moment and then turned to the woman.

"What do you think is the remedy when your heart does a hiccup and you can't get those hiccups to stop?"

"I wish it were as simple as drinking nine sips of water," the woman replied.

"Without breathing?"

"Even harder. I've been out of breath for a long time myself."

Jasmine did not ask questions. There was a silent bond between her and this young mother. People who hurt could spot another hurt person along life's highway, especially if you were sitting right next to one on a plane going to New York City. Both of them understood that. How? They were women.

*****

The plane was touching down when Jasmine realized this was not where she wanted to be. She longed to hear what the city didn't offer—the sound of crickets at night and the scent of jasmine coming through her window at dusk. She wanted something smaller. She wanted a town where everybody knew everybody. She wanted a closeness that could not be described. She wanted a town with a special burger place and a town with a drugstore, not a pharmacy. She wanted a town like the town where she grew up. She wanted a friend like Polly had been to Ellie, one who lived just around the corner. She wanted to relive that magical year when she was five and had her own personal angel. Vaguely, she remembered him and wondered where life had taken him. She knew where he wasn't—he had never come back for Ellie and her. Or had he? She had to let it go.

She vowed she would find another dream town of her own. But, first, she had to take care of the lady in room 334 at Morris Memorial Hospital. She had to see that to the end. Then, and only then, would she begin looking for a smaller town, a smaller house, preferably on a lake where she could watch the sunrise and the sunsets—a smaller everything. Maybe she'd even get a dog. Or a cat. Maybe both.

*****

Chapter 12

A day was coming when Jasmine would find another small neighborhood village town. She would leave the big city behind, just as she had vowed to do on that plane ride back to New York. It was all in the timing. That town would welcome her with open arms because of the forlorn look she would have on her face. Brooksport Village had a knack of seeing the dry tears in a person's eyes. That town knew grief when they saw it, and the people living there knew how to grieve. They didn't like it, but they knew there was no way around it. No shortcuts. Not with grief and the storms of life. You simply had to trudge through them both.

Yes, that town knew how to cry with the best of them. It also knew how to open doors to new beginnings—to healing, to smiles, just waiting to blend alongside the grief. Yes, Brooksport Village always opened its garden gate to those searching for new beginnings.

Something, unknown to Jasmine at the moment, would lure her into that town one day. But, first, there was more life to live, as Polly would say, "between the bookends" of her hometown and Brooksport Village.

New York City was still there in the distance. Her job, the hospital, now seeming like a haven to her crushed heart, was waiting for her return. She had to go back to the city that never sleeps. But far and above all the rest was something she didn't know at the time, something that would propel her into her future. Something else was about to happen. Andrew was waiting.

PART 2

CHOCOLATE EYES

"Be reverent before the dawning day. Do not think of what will be in a year, or in ten years. Think of today."

(Romain Rolland)

Andrew was a gentle giant of a man. That, in itself, was quite a surprise to him because of the turbulent life he had lived while growing up. But then again, maybe it was because of his past that he had turned into somewhat of a quiet man who just wanted to be left alone. Women found him intriguing with his mysterious demeanor, as well as his extraordinarily handsome face. They felt he was well worth the chase, and if they ended up with a few bruises along the way, so what?

He was a smart businessman, not to mention wealthy, which intrigued the ladies even more. He could have chosen any woman, and they would have followed him anywhere. A few tried, but he was not born to be "settled." There were a select few who tried to "mend" his broken spirit, but he had told them to go find a *fix-able* man—he was beyond repair. Those women would eventually get tired and disappear. He would always allow them to be the one to call it quits. Then he would sigh a sigh of relief. He didn't blame them. He could understand why a woman would want a man with "no assembly required."

He never sought to hurt anyone, and heaven knew how he hated to see women cry. He had watched his mother, Mona, cry way too often ever since he was old enough to sit up and take notice of what his father had done to her. He began to live a life of rest-lessness and discontent, trusting no one, except for his mom and his little blonde blue-eyed kindergarten friend who had grown up alongside him.

He dedicated himself to making his mother proud of him. He soon discovered he was no "honor" student. He couldn't sit still long enough to read a book. He had to keep moving. And he definitely had to be faster than his dad when that awful man would unbuckle his belt to whip him into shape. His mom had always tucked him into bed and called him her good boy. He guessed it was because she wanted to make sure that he knew someone loved him. But his father was the boss, and not a very compassionate one. His dad didn't care about the people he considered to be *below* him. And everyone was *below* the *boss*.

Andrew gradually became the good boy gone rogue. He was the neighborhood kid who planted smoke bombs on his skates and stole candy from the small grocery store located just outside of town. Once he tried cigarettes, while hiking in the woods, but never alcohol. He had seen firsthand what alcohol had done to his dad. And if there was one man he never wanted to imitate, it was his dad.

His mom was patient and prayerful. His dad was mean and strong. Plus, he was bigger than Andrew. That strength was never more evident than when that infamous belt of his dad's became the weapon of choice for Andrew's so-called rebellion. That was what he used to whip Andrew back into shape. When his mother rebelled against the actions taken against her son, his dad's hands became the weapon he used against her.

Andrew had always tried to obey his father. He was too scared not to. The corner of any room became his crouching place—until the night he saw firsthand his father's anger taking aim at his mother. No more sitting in the corner. No more being quiet. He had leapt from the chair and tackled his dad in the middle of the kitchen.

"What ya doin', boy? You think you're man enough to take me on?"

His dad had leapt at him and backhanded him clear across the kitchen. Andrew had been in the fifth grade then. Turned out he wasn't man enough at that tender age. His dad had taken his belt and literally beat Andrew into the corner to sit there and be quiet. And then he turned once again on his mom. With tears streaming down his face, he vowed right then and there that no one or nothing would ever back him into a corner again.

After the beatings, his dad would shout, "Two of a kind!" before storming out the door. Andrew and his mom didn't care where that evil man went. They were glad he left. Mona and Andrew prayed he wouldn't come back. But he always did.

*****

Now a grown man, Andrew sat at his desk looking out over the city. He remembered it all.

Mona had been forming a plan in her own mind when Andrew was a mere boy. She had to get Andrew out of the house—somewhere safe, in spite of the fact that Andrew was looking forward to the fall and beginning the sixth grade.

Andrew's attention was drawn to the reception area where his secretary placed fresh spring flowers every week.

He remembered how Mona had loved her flowers, too, and for some reason, Andrew's dad never touched her flowers. She would always have a vase of fresh flowers on the kitchen table. He supposed that those flowers brought her some kind of hope that there was something more than what life had dealt her. She found joy within those flowers. Above all else, she wanted that hope to be there for her son.

It was when she stood at her kitchen table, looking at her vase full of flowers that she made her decision. She had to save her son. For him to have any hope for his future, she had to get him out of their house. She was going to lose him if she didn't. She feared for his safety and his life. She had to guarantee that he would have a future. She touched each one of those petals on each one of those flowers as tears rolled down her cheeks. Yes, it was the right thing to do, the only thing to do. She had saved the money in secret. She had worked at the area craft store when Andrew had been at school. She had enlisted some support from friends, one in particular a fellow she had met in the support group she had joined for her own sanity. Now she had enough. It would break her heart, but it was time to let her only son go.

Andrew knew something was up. He had watched his mom that night from behind his bedroom door. He secretly vowed he would not cause any more trouble. He would not put smoke bombs on his skates. He would not steal candy. He would not cause fights at school. He would not sass his dad. He would make good grades. He would do whatever it took to make his mom happy and try to keep them both safe inside their home. He would pick her fresh flowers as long as summer stayed around. He promised God he would live up to his mom thinking he was actually a good boy. There was just something about a mom's tears.

*****

The night his mother came to him and told him her plan, a very young boy became a warrior. He wouldn't cry. His mother was doing enough of that for him. He had to be strong. He had to know that what she was doing was setting him free. But deep down in his heart, he knew that he would be leaving the only woman who had loved him unconditionally. He trusted Allie, too—his kindergarten pal he was growing up with. She kept his secrets. He had faith in his mom enough to do what she said. He loved her enough not to shed a tear. He merely nodded to her every word.

"I want you safe," she had whispered to him as she tucked the covers under his chin. She kissed him on the cheek.

"What about you?" he had asked her.

"I will take care of myself. You're not to worry about me. You just be ready tomorrow. After your dad leaves, someone will be coming here to pick you up."

He had promised. After she had left his room, he quietly got out of bed and began packing his suitcase. He waited until he heard her go to bed, and then he crept into the living room, opening the drawer of the TV stand. Gently, he lifted a photo album from the drawer and walked back to his room. He placed the album under his clothes. He would take it with him. He wanted to always remember his mother when she was a carefree spirit, laughing her way through life, dancing with the boys who made her smile *until* she met the man she married. Why? Why him? Why the man who broke her spirit when there were so many others to choose from? It was a mystery to him. Perhaps one day he would know the answer to that question. But for now, the photos would have to be enough.

*****

It took Andrew a good long while to adapt to his new life. He coped. He had to tame his restless spirit and learn a new way of "being quiet." Military school did that. He actually became an expert at it. He learned that aloneness became somewhat of a necessity for him to survive. He was most comfortable in his own room, gazing out at the world, seemingly going on without him. He wondered if there were other young boys doing things that boys do without someone hitting them. Even at his young age, he made a promise to himself that he would be the best father a son could ever have when he became a man. He wouldn't fail his son like his dad had failed him. It hadn't always been that way—before alcohol.

He missed his mom. She couldn't visit him. She couldn't risk his dad finding out where he was. For some unexplainable reason, his dad could not tolerate Andrew. His mom stayed in touch by letter, and that had to be enough for now.

He kept the photo album on his nightstand next to his bed. That helped him to remember everything good about his mom. He knew in his heart that she had saved him from the wrath of a father who suddenly forgot how to love. He prayed for her every night as he touched her picture in the frame that was placed beside the photo album. He hoped there was a God, the only one who could protect his mom from so evil a man.

*****

There were things he did like about military school. He loved the sports, even if he had to wear the school's jerseys. He liked hitting things. He liked contact sports, mostly football. Football became his way of not relinquishing total control to the school. Football allowed him to hit something and not get into trouble for doing it. He became quite the football star. To him, it was survival. Some of the money he did manage to save from the jobs assigned him during the week went directly to a small flower shop at the edge of town that could alert another flower shop in his own hometown to deliver fresh flowers to his mom at least once a month.

He continued to remember his mom touching the petals of those flowers on the kitchen table that night he crept from bed and packed his suitcase. Tears of love had dropped from her eyes. He would never forget. He understood why she could not visit him. He wanted her to know that with each month's delivery of those flowers, he was holding on to the hope that one day he would be able to give her back the spirit his father had broken.

Military school had taught Andrew a certain type of discipline, a discipline that he could not have learned anywhere else. He became a very organized person. A focused person. It also taught him to be very private. He learned not to be vulnerable. He learned to protect the people he loved. All this became a pattern with him throughout the rest of his life. He didn't share his thoughts. He became a successful man by bulldozing over whatever got in his way. If he had to be like a wrecking ball, he became a powerful one. He worked hard. He played hard. If he wanted a house overlooking the ocean, he would buy a house overlooking the ocean. If he wanted a tennis court behind that house, he would build a tennis court behind that house. A swimming pool? No problem. If he wanted a boat, he would buy a boat—"WHHSH." That was what he planned on naming his boat. He liked privacy. Whoever was fortunate enough to take a ride on that boat—well, he wanted them to have privacy too. That's why he named his prized possession WHHSH—What Happens Here Stays Here.

Yes, what he vowed in that school at such an early age that had once been a dream became a reality. He had at long last become his mom's "good boy."

The years went by, and in spite of all his successes, he was quite unsure of himself when it came to commitment, especially in a marriage. He didn't know if he could be good to a woman the way a man is supposed to be good to one. He determined he would never walk in his dad's footsteps. He would never drink alcohol. He would never hurt a woman. Women were not meant to be hurt; they were meant to be treasured. His mind kept going back to the little blonde blue-eyed friend from kindergarten who had grown up. He always smiled when he thought of her.

*****

Andrew's penthouse shouted out *roof over your head!* That was it. A roof, nothing more. No comforters. No pillows. No pictures on the wall. No dog. Merely pristine. The only thing that convinced him it was a home were fresh flowers on his kitchen table, usually wildflowers.

Perhaps his dad had been right after all. Perhaps he was a good-for-nothing-roustabout wild child who would never stay settled for long. That's why he didn't buy knickknacks you had to dust, even though his cleaning lady continued to sneak some into his living room. He saw them and would discreetly put them back into her cleaning bag before she left. She meant well. Maybe he would keep a couple the next time she made an attempt to make a house a home.

He looked in the hallway mirror, thinking of his mom.

"Well, Dad, you called me a wild child. Well, it takes one to know one, doesn't it? You were a good-for-nothing husband who didn't know squat about taking care of his woman."

He dragged his hands over his unshaven face. He resisted believing the lie that he was good for nothing. He looked around him.

"Sorry to disappoint you, *Father*, but I did amount to something."

Andrew looked at his furniture. Everything about his surroundings reeked money, and lots of it. He was set for life, but he felt empty. Maybe he would buy a knickknack, maybe two. He wanted to hit something. But now, his football days were over. Military school was over. Did that really mean he couldn't hit something anymore?

He had just talked to his mom. She was lying on a hospital bed, still pretending everything was okay, and he couldn't help her. He thought he could. He thought he could buy her what she needed, but this time, he couldn't. She had told him to "stay put." She had told him he had a business to run. She had told him she had good people surrounding her, watching over her, and she would be okay. Yes, she had told him all that.

Didn't she realize he was too fidgety to "stay put," *especially* when she needed him? She was trying to make him feel good. It was his responsibility to do the exact opposite. He could not sit in the corner anymore.

"I have to do something!" he exclaimed to no one but himself.

He walked to his bedroom and lay down on his bed, staring at the ceiling. Suddenly, he jumped up and began packing.

"Money can't buy what she needs, but I have to be there!" Instant decision. No more questions. He'd find his own answers when he got to her. He would see with his own two eyes what was going on with her health.

She had always been there for him. She had quite literally saved his life. She had squirreled money away to get him out of the house. She had dedicated and caring friends who helped her.

"I should have gone back to her after military school—been with her."

She had insisted that everything was fine, that his dad was mellowing with age, reverting to the way he was when they were first married. Yeah, right. But he had believed her; he shouldn't have.

That was why she needed a kidney now. He was at fault. He should have gone back and shown his dad how fast he could take off his own belt. But his mom had insisted he sign that pro football contract. Against his better judgement, he had done just that. Injuries happen in football. A major one that had led him into the business world. And then time got away from him.

Well, now his dad was dead, and he was glad. She didn't have to worry anymore, except for that kidney thing.

He zipped up his suitcase, made a final phone call to his second-in-command, and walked out the door. He would catch a flight out of LaGuardia and be at Morris Memorial by very early morning. He would be at her bedside. He would put a wet, cold cloth on her forehead the way she used to do for him when he had the flu. He would feed her ice chips. He would hold her hand. And although it would kill him, he promised himself that he would sit there and watch her die, if no donor could be found.

*****

The flight out of LaGuardia was rocky. His private plane was unavailable due to some mechanical problem. Andrew was worried not about the flight but what he might find at the hospital. Why couldn't they find a match, a donor? This was his mother! She deserved the best. He had the money.

"Money can't buy you everything," his mom had told him. "Please remember that," she had continued with a smile on her face.

Oh, if only it could! He would have had her a kidney long before now. His mom, the woman who had been his lifeline all those years. Why couldn't he help her now?

As he buckled himself tighter in his seat, his thoughts wandered back to those days Mona and he had suffered at the hands of, whom he now called, the devil himself. He guessed that airplane rides made people slow down enough to remember certain things when they would rather not. But there was nowhere to escape on an airplane. You had to sit there pretending to listen to the person next to you or stick a book in your face. Today he wanted neither. Today he chose to look out the window and order a drink, a good stiff one. He ordered Coke instead.

Now that he was a grown man, he had come to the realization that some questions could never be answered. But in the looking back, he realized that sometimes it can help you gaze forward with a certain determination. And he was determined to get to his mom.

He didn't know how long he could sit still on this plane. They were above the turbulence now, and, thankfully, the girl next to him had spit out her gum and was reading the newest romance novel. He wondered if young girls really believed all that *Cinderella* stuff. Gosh, he hoped not. If they did, he didn't want to be around when they finally hit that wall called "reality." He was feeling his restless spirit come back. He thought he had tamed it while in military school.

He thought he had reined it in on the football field when he played professional sports. But old habits die hard.

He took a sip from his Coke. Why had this happened to Mona when he had finally seen the "new" Mona blossom, just like those flowers on her kitchen table? She had learned to laugh again. She had become a glittery, sparkly person with a heart for humor. It was a true miracle. Once that "devil" had died, she had become a vibrant woman again. It had taken courage and strength. But he guessed there was always strength in the hope of springtime flowers. Like a boomerang, her old self was back.

"Thank God for boomerang theories," he said to himself.

He finished his Coke, sighed, and continued to look out the window. He remembered the stories Mona had told him.

"When Jesus needed to think, he would go to a quiet place, pray, and listen for the voice of God to guide him."

Andrew decided that while he was above the clouds in that plane, he was as close to heaven as he was ever going to get. It seemed a quiet enough place, regardless of the drone of the airplane's engines gliding through the clouds. Somehow, he felt those clouds knew he was a lonely heart in search of some answers. He decided this was the time he should introduce himself to God—for real. He wondered if God actually knew who he was. He wondered if he remembered him as a boy.

"Here goes," he whispered, wiping his hands on his pants.

The young girl beside him had taken off her headphones and turned slightly to look at him. She had thought he was talking to her.

Andrew continued to whisper, thinking no one could hear him. He hadn't seen that the girl had taken off her headphones.

"Hey, God, you may not know me, but I'm introducing myself to you today." The young girl continued to watch Andrew. A grown man, speaking like a little boy. "It's me, Andrew. Mona is my mother. And you know her very well. She takes good care of your flowers."

She remembered the Bible verse as she listened to Andrew. *"Truly, I tell you, unless you change and become like little children, you will never enter the kingdom of heaven."*

The young girl began to smile. She didn't want to eavesdrop on this man and his prayer, but it made her remember when she talked to God as a little girl. This adult man was finding his way as a little child.

There was a sudden dip in the plane.

Andrew wasn't afraid. He merely said, "Is that you, God? It's nice to meet you."

*****

"I liked your prayer," the young girl whispered. Startled, Andrew gazed her way. "You have nice eyes," she said.

"I thought I was whispering," Andrew replied, "and I thought you had your headphones on—and reading your book."

"You were whispering, kind of, but I have excellent hearing."

"I see you're reading one of those romance novels," Andrew said.

"I love romance," she said, showing him the book cover, "and listening to slow, dreamy music while I read."

"I could tell."

"Do you like romance?"

"I don't believe in romance."

"Maybe one day you will."

"Don't think so."

"Why not?"

"Too much disappointment in my life, I guess."

He looked at her innocent eyes and envied her. How he wished he could see life through her eyes. She merely smiled at him, opened her book, and began to read again. Headphones off.

"Just in case you want to talk," she said to him with a smile. She pointed to the headphones she had placed in her lap.

Andrew wondered if her mom had ever injured her in any way or if her dad had ever been brutal to her. He saw her hands holding the book. Soft hands. He saw her clothing. Well-groomed, high society. She had probably never been hurt in her life in any way. Not like him.

He looked out the window again thinking of the time his mom had seen the damage done to him by his father all because of a milk carton.

He was in the kitchen with the refrigerator door open. Just standing there looking at the milk carton. Should he get a glass? No. He lifted the carton to his mouth and began to drink. Seemingly, out of nowhere came the first whack across his back, followed by a gruff voice.

"What ya doin', boy?"

Andrew turned to his dad and simply said, "Drinkin' milk."

"Not out of the carton, ya don't! Nobody wants your backwash!"

And then the whacks continued. Andrew did not scream out. He took the beating, thinking all the while, I should have gotten a glass. I should have gotten a glass.

It wasn't until the next morning that his mom had seen the welts. She had been at some kind of a meeting. She went every week; he didn't know where. That morning, she had brought the folded laundry into his room. Nothing covered his back. It hurt too bad to have anything next to his skin. A sleeping Andrew awakened to the tender touch of his mom placing salve on his back.

"Did your dad do this?"

He turned to face her and nodded.

"Why?"

"I drank milk from the carton instead of getting a glass. He caught me in the act."

That was when the final decision was made by Mona. That decision, as bad as it seemed to Andrew at the time, most likely, saved his life—not only from an abusive father but from a downward spiral, due to his own actions, that would have ended in disaster. Looking back on that now, he knew how hard it was for his mother to let him go. She simply had to.

"Please fasten your seatbelts, and prepare for landing."

The announcement came over the PA system, bringing him back to the present. His dad could rot in hell for all he was concerned. Then he remembered. "Oh, he's there already. Good."

Deplaning, he saw the young girl run into the arms of a young man. He couldn't help but smile. He hoped she was right about romance, for her own sake.

It wasn't until he got into the limo that would be taking him to the hospital that he reached into his carry on that had been sitting under the vacant seat between him and the girl that he noticed something he hadn't packed. He reached in and pulled it out. The romance novel. A note had been attached.

"Someday you'll love romance like I do. Don't forget, I heard your prayer."

*****

Chapter 13

Jasmine had grown too close to the woman in room 334. The number one rule was not to get personally involved with a patient. But she had. That sweet old woman just reminded her too much of her own grandmother. She couldn't help herself. It was late; but before going home, she wanted to check on Mona, who was anxiously waiting for something to happen soon. Stage five was all Jasmine could think about. Dialysis loomed on the horizon until a match could be made.

She gathered all her research findings strewn around the table in the hospital cafeteria and began the walk toward Mona's room. She was on call tonight. Maybe tonight would be the night. Oh, how she prayed it would be. She opened the door and looked at Mona, who was sitting straight up in her bed with pillows behind her head, looking into a hand mirror and smiling.

"You're awake," Jasmine said.

"Like my sparkly earrings, love?" Mona questioned, turning her head this way and that way, as if she had not one care on her mind.

Jasmine smiled and walked to the chair beside the bed. "I actually do like those earrings. Are you going dancing in your dreams tonight?"

"I've always danced in my dreams. Reality? Well, that's another story I'd rather forget."

"So, dancing helped you escape reality?"

"Pretty much."

"Well, you'll have to teach me how you do that, Mona. I'd look forward to bedtime if I could be assured of dancing."

"Trouble sleeping?"

"Sometimes, well, a lot of times, really."

"You need a pair of these." Mona shook her head, making the dangles glitter in the lamplight.

"Maybe I do."

"Sit." Mona motioned for her to take a seat. "Tell me something good. Tell me what you've found."

"We're still looking."

Mona looked at herself again, bringing the hand mirror close to her face. "I've worn sparkly earrings a lot lately. After my drunk, abusive husband died—oh, sorry, dear—but he was… I truly don't mean to speak ill of the dead, but truth is truth. Well, after that, I would wear earrings like this to the grocery store. They just make me happy. I now believe in doing things that make me happy." Again, she touched the dangles. "I also wore them to the pharmacy and church." She circled her arms around the room. "And now the hospital."

Jasmine sighed. "We'll find something soon for you, Mona. I feel it."

"I'll keep praying you do, my dear. Until then, hand me the remote, would you?" Jasmine handed the TV remote to her. Mona switched to the online shopping network. Jasmine stood to leave. Mona looked up at Jasmine. "You must not worry so much about me. What's meant to be will be." She looked back at the TV. "Well, lookey there, would you? I've always wanted a pair like that! Talk about glitter!"

Jasmine bent down and kissed Mona on the forehead. "I'll see to it that you get them," Jasmine whispered.

"Make sure I can wear these to dance in one day, sweet girl." Mona looked at the clock on the wall. "It's so late. You should be home, getting some well-deserved rest. Go on home now. Start afresh tomorrow looking for me a kidney!"

"I will. I wanted to check in with you and say good night."

"Good night, dear child. Now you get on home, get under those covers, and I will pray for your phone to ring at some ungodly hour so you can rush back here and tell me you have found the perfect match for this tired, old body!"

*****

On the ride home, Jasmine continued to think about Mona. She had been through all the testing by all the specialists that were required for her condition. It was trauma that had caused the kidney to malfunction. Her husband had beaten her senseless when he found out what she had done all those years ago. She was willing to take it. She would have done anything for her son. She had taken his place.

And then it happened. That no-good husband of hers dropped dead of a heart attack in the corner bar down the street.

Good for her, Jasmine thought. *Good for him. Thank you, Captain Morgan.*

Jasmine could never figure out why a man would do what he did to this woman. Pure evil. That's what it was. Pure evil.

"Too close," Jasmine kept repeating to herself. "My heart is going to be broken if I don't find help for this woman."

They had been waiting for so long. They had waited over many cups of strong coffee, late-night phone calls, and praying—not necessarily in that order. Jasmine was used to waiting, but this "wait" was different. This was one of the most difficult "waits" of all. For this woman was a woman she had come to love.

*****

Jasmine finished her coffee and decided to take Mona's advice and go to bed. Coffee? What was wrong with her? She would never get to sleep now. Nevertheless, she went through the motions. Being on call this particular night, she placed her computer on the nightstand next to her bed and her phone on the pillow next to her head. She made sure she would not miss a call, if it actually came through, that a kidney was available, if they had found a match. She would then call the surgeon and set things in motion.

She prayed this would be the night for Mona and her second chance for a good, sparkly life—filled with lots of glittery earrings. A life she used to have when she was young. A life of freedom. A life of more laughter, less pain. Time to put new pictures in old frames. Time to bring hope back into a life that had not been so pleasant during those turbulent years. Time to remember and a time to move on.

"Let this be the night, Lord. Please let this be the night."

Jasmine's prayer was answered at 2:30 a.m. That ungodly hour Mona had prayed for. Jasmine leaped for the phone.

"We have a donor," the caller said, "a kidney that is a match for your patient in room 334 at Morris Memorial."

"I'm on it," Jasmine replied. She had learned to stay calm. Many things could still go wrong. Within seconds, she began the multiple phone calls to orchestrate what would happen next. Her fingers flew across the computer as the phone calls were made one by one.

She had to get back to the hospital. Within minutes, she was in her car, speeding toward Morris Memorial. She didn't park the car. It was too long of a walk, even at this early hour. This was valet time. They always knew when it was an emergency. The valet waved her in and took the car from her as she ran toward the hospital doors.

"Got one, Jasmine?"

"Sure do! I have to personally tell her!"

"Room 334?"

"Oh yes, room 334!"

The valet blew her a kiss as she disappeared through the door and into the nearest elevator.

The valet parked her car.

"That girl is special, so special," he said as he ran back to his post.

*****

The hospital was quiet. At that early hour, it was always quiet. Her phone had rung at 2:30 a.m. It took her a mere twenty minutes to make the necessary calls to the surgeons and to toss on her clothes and another fifteen minutes to get to the hospital. The nurse's station was empty, but Jasmine knew exactly where she was going. The sweet woman who reminded her so much of her grandmother was at the end of the hall, waiting. If Mona was asleep, Jasmine was going to awaken her. Shoot! She wished she had brought a brass band with her to announce her arrival with the good news.

Mona had been waiting a long time for something special to happen for her. Something that would give her new life, a kidney. And soon Jasmine would be giving her the news. There was a donor.

Jasmine ran down the hall. Although she wanted to shout out the news, she stopped short at the door, giving it a gentle knock. It was a man's voice that answered the knock, startling her.

"Yes, who is it?"

"It's Jasmine Jones. May I come in?"

The next voice was Mona's.

"Of course, dear, come in, come in!" Mona sat up in bed, her eyes brightening at the sight of Jasmine. Andrew was sitting beside the bed holding his mother's hand. "My dear, please tell me, at this ungodly hour, you have found me a kidney!"

Jasmine ran to the hospital bed, took Mona's other hand, and exclaimed, "Oh yes, Mona, we have!"

*****

Jasmine looked at Mona with questioning eyes about the man holding her hand.

"Oh, dear, where are my manners?" Mona exclaimed. She turned to her son and said, "Jasmine, please meet my son, Andrew. Andrew, I present to you, Jasmine." Without taking a breath, Mona continued. "Hand me my purse, would you please, dear?" She pointed to her purse sitting on the chair next to the window. "I must put on my lipstick."

Jasmine walked over to the chair. Andrew stood up from his chair, handing Mona her purse.

"So you are Jasmine, the lady my mom has been telling me about ever since I walked into this room and surprised her."

"That would be her," Mona interjected. Mona began rummaging through her purse, looking for her lipstick.

"You really don't need lipstick, Mona," Jasmine said with a chuckle.

"Oh yes, I do, dearie! I never go anywhere without my lipstick, especially when a handsome surgeon is waiting for me!"

"You've already met Dr. Stanley?"

"No, but I know he's handsome. Most doctors are." She began to apply a pretty pink shade to her lips, looking up from time to time to sneak a peek at Andrew. Mona looked at the two of them. Smiling, she said, "Andrew was my wild child, once upon a time—the boy with the sad chocolate eyes, the eyes that just lit up when he shook your hand."

Changing the subject, Jasmine said, "The nurses will be coming soon to take you upstairs to meet the 'handsome' doctor. So glad you put on your lipstick."

"Will you come with me, too, dear?" Mona questioned.

"I'll be right beside you." Everything became a blur after that. The preparations were beginning. Jasmine took a quick glance back at Andrew as they were leaving the room. "Don't worry. I have seen that she has the best surgeon in this place." She looked back at Mona. She bent down to her ear and whispered, "And, yes, he is handsome, Mona."

*****

Halfway down the hallway, Mona whispered to Jasmine, "I'm glad Andrew was here when you showed up."

"Why's that?"

"I think you have put a new spark in my son's eyes!" Mona looked up at the ceiling as she was being taken to the elevator. "Heaven knows, he needs a woman like you!"

Jasmine smiled. "Let's just get you your new kidney first," she replied.

"It's time someone stole his heart! And, oh, darling, I would make a wonderful mother-in-law, don't you think?"

*****

Jasmine had to admit she had felt a flutter when she saw Andrew in that dimly lit room. She thought of saxophone music. Oh yes, she did. You know the smooth kind, the kind that made you want to pour a glass of wine, look across a crowded room, and laser in on the man with the deep chocolate eyes—and those eyes of his were the most chocolate color she had ever seen.

*****

Jasmine remained in the hospital cafeteria with Andrew, drinking stale coffee, until the surgery was successfully completed. In the light of day, she had left Andrew there and gone back to her apartment. She thought that mother and son needed some "alone" time together. On the way home, she had decided she was going to marry the man with the chocolate eyes.

She whispered to herself, "And I haven't even kissed him yet, Grandma."

She had believed in love at first sight from the first time she had been read *Cinderella*. She longed to climb behind those eyes of Andrew's and take what he would give to her.

Mona was right. Her once-upon-a-time wild child shone through those sad eyes. She knew that truth from the first moment she had seen Andrew's hand clasped over his mother's hand on that hospital bed. She wanted to cozy up behind those eyes and make him smile. She had no idea why he seemed so sad, but it would become her passion to find out.

"I'm beginning to think like Polly more and more every day!" she whispered to herself. She looked in the mirror, sighed, and vowed to get hold of herself. It was ridiculous thinking the way she was thinking. They had just met, for heaven's sake!

She ran the brush through her hair. Would it be worth the pain that would certainly come into her life down the road? Was it going to be worth the journey of trying to make Andrew's smile reach his eyes? She considered herself warned. With men like him, there was always pain in the end.

She smiled when all she could think of was what Polly would tell her.

"S——t fire, yes!"

*****

Mere weeks had gone by when Mona sat up in bed as Andrew walked into her hospital room.

"Romance is about to bloom!" Mona exclaimed. She began applying her lipstick.

"It's so good to see the woman you used to be resurface, Mom." Andrew was smiling when she looked up.

"It's good to be back, son."

They both remembered the photo album that showed the perky, lively, happy girl of her past. They both knew of which they spoke. All the pain from the past seemed to be withering away. God had made wildflowers where weeds used to be. They were both grateful.

"I'm heading for my post-op appointment. Seems that handsome doctor wants to see how I'm doing."

"I figured as much—you applying your lipstick and all."

Andrew kept glancing toward the door.

"Have you asked her out yet?"

"Who?"

"Who? Really, Andrew, don't insult me!"

"Are you talking about Jasmine?"

Mona rolled her eyes. Just then Jasmine entered the room with a bouquet of flowers. "We were just talking about you," Mona nonchalantly said. Jasmine walked over to Mona and kissed her forehead. "For me?" Mona questioned.

"Yes, our star patient." Jasmine searched for a vase. Andrew stood and watched as she opened cabinet doors.

"Oh, really, you two! Jasmine, can't you see my Andrew wants a kiss too? And I don't mean on the forehead!"

Jasmine stared at both of them.

"You know she's actually right," Andrew answered his mom.

Jamie continued to look startled.

"I mean not right this minute. Maybe somewhere down the road."

Mona laughed. "When are you two going to get to the action? Snap to it. I'm leaving soon, starting my recovery. It's about time the two of you did too!"

"What exactly am I supposed to be recovering from?" Andrew questioned.

"Being alone," Mona said with a sigh.

"Well, the queen has spoken," Andrew said.

Looking at Jasmine, he asked, "Want to go have coffee?"

"Forget coffee!" Mona exclaimed. "Jasmine, go over there and open that drawer. There's a box in there I want you to have."

Jasmine walked to the nightstand and opened the drawer. She retrieved the box and opened it. She smiled and looked at Mona.

"That's right! Those are for you! I repeat, forget coffee! Do dinner! Do wine! Put on those sparkly earrings, girlie, and get to dancing!"

Meanwhile, back in Brooksport Village

Kate could not believe it. All her life she had loved and lost—until she took the exit to Brooksport Village, until she had walked into Trudy's Tresses and Tootsies. Until the cowboy had tipped his hat on that Memorial Day weekend and literally saved the annual celebration balloon launch.

She looked at Jake now, sitting at his desk, wondering when he would have to make another trip back to New York City and all the racket, as Trudy called it. Jake actually called it racket, too, now that he had discovered peace and quiet with his "hometown girl."

Oh, how she loved that man sitting there, oblivious to her stares. He was concentrating. She walked over to him, placed her hands on his shoulders, bent down, and kissed his cheek.

"Umm…what's that for?" Jake asked.

Kate smiled. "Just because." Kate turned to leave the room.

"If you're not careful, I may send you flowers," she heard Jake say as she quietly closed the door.

*****

Chapter 14

Mona had been quite the little *Miss Cupid.* The night went exactly as planned, except for the kiss. Andrew had not planned that. It just happened. Wine. Dinner. Dancing. And then somewhere in between all of that and those sparkly earrings was the kiss. Jasmine had those eyes that could look straight through a man—right to his heart. He began to tell her things, things he had never told another soul. He had to be careful with this one. It wasn't like him to reveal so much about himself. And it sure wasn't like him to kiss someone he knew would be trouble with a capital *T.* This one was different. This one was special. This one could turn his world upside down without even knowing what she had done. For that matter, neither would he. It would happen in an instant. He had a feeling it already had—with that kiss.

Now he was standing in front of his bathroom mirror, shaving.

He dared to ask himself, "Would it be worth it? He had never really trusted anyone but his mother and Allie, who had always been his confident since the third grade, before all hell had broken loose in his own house. They had kept in touch through the years. She was special—like a sister. He should tell her about Jasmine. She would tease him and accuse him of finally finding a woman he couldn't let go.

Deep down, Andrew knew this was the beginning of something he had craved all his life. All men do, he finally confessed to only himself. Men just didn't want to admit it. He seemed to be talking to himself a lot lately. His old patterns were changing. He didn't want to run away from Jasmine. He ignored old patterns that were trying to rear their ugly heads. He knew deep down that this time he was going to stay. She even had him thinking of fairy tales and happy endings. What man ever does that? Men in love, that's who.

He nicked his face. Yes, he still shaved with shaving cream and a razor. He grimaced and kept arguing with himself. Boys never read fairy tales growing up! Boys don't believe in things like that. They want adventure. They want to hunt and catch balls. Boys like to hit things. And he had hit and been hit—a lot. Quarterbacks get hit. Quarterbacks aren't protected all the time. His injury taught him that. Things changed suddenly. He had gone to sleep in one world and awakened in another.

He kept looking at himself in the mirror.

"Girls believe in fairy tales, not men."

He rubbed his hands over his shaven face.

"Fairy tales? Why in the world do I feel like I am living in one since I saw Jasmine walk through that hospital door?"

He dressed quickly. Yes, he was seeing her again—two nights in a row. He had to stop thinking about this fairy-tale crap. He would tell her tonight that if she believed in happy endings, he was so far away from that *and* she shouldn't have such high expectations of a fantasy that some people put on high pedestals in their mind. They're always disappointed when they expect too much. He would tell her tonight. Yes, he would. Maybe he would scare her away with his comments. Better to end it early before either one of them became too attached. Maybe she would think he was a crazy man, and she didn't need such craziness in her life. He just hoped she wouldn't be wearing those sparkly earrings again. They made her eyes glisten.

*****

That night, that second night, did not go as planned. Andrew was tongue-tied. And she wore those damn earrings, again. And he kissed her again. He was a goner, and he knew it.

"Might as well accept it, old chap, you are smitten. Mona will be so happy."

Andrew arrived in Mona's hospital room, ready to tell her he was giving up. As the song goes, "it's time to bring this ship into the shore and throw away the oars forever." But he didn't get the chance.

Mona looked at him and with a sternness in her voice began to speak.

"I'm moving."

Andrew stopped midstride. "What?"

"You heard me. I'm moving—to Florida."

Jasmine walked in, not far behind Andrew. "And why is that, Ms. Mona?" Jasmine asked.

"Oh, she's got a wild hair up her..."

"Andrew!" Mona exclaimed.

Andrew sighed, his eyes pleading toward Jasmine to say something that would change Mona's mind. Finally, he said, "She has the urge to surf."

Jasmine laughed. "Doesn't surprise me. But you're not quite ready to surf, Mona."

"Andrew exaggerates. I just want to get out of this godforsaken cold state. I want warmth. All year. Florida has warmth. Florida calls my name. You tell me when I'm ready."

Defiantly, Mona looked at Andrew. "When I get the 'all clear,' I'm moving!" Silence prevailed as Mona began to fiddle with her nightgown, making sure each little ruffle was in place. Looking at Jasmine with a twinkle in her eye, she asked, "You two have your coffee yet?"

Jasmine fluffed Mona's pillow, smiling at Andrew. Andrew walked over to his mother. "I was just coming to see you and tell you I've thrown away my oars."

Mona's eyes widened. "Do tell me more, my wild child!"

"We had wine, dinner, and dancing," Andrew answered while smiling at Jasmine.

"Marvelous!"

"And I'm ready for a 'mulligan,'" Andrew said.

"Stop talking in riddles, Andrew!" Mona exclaimed. "What's all this business about 'oars and mulligans'?" Mona looked from one to the other. "Well, well, no need to answer. I know love when I see it!"

*****

Mona was pleased. Pleased with her recovery. She was delighted that Andrew was smiling a lot lately, and she was especially pleased with herself in playing cupid and knowing it had not been much of an effort at all. She was pleased with the movers who had packed all her belongings, *pleased* that she would soon be in warm weather—all year round. And she was exhilarated that she was finally moving from the godforsaken cold state of New York. All clear.

"You two take care of each other," she told both Andrew and Jasmine, who were saying their goodbyes to her. "Come to visit when you can. I'm out of this frozen tundra, this polar vortex!" With a wave of her hand, she was gone.

"Mom never was one for long goodbyes." Andrew shrugged.

"I guess not," Jasmine answered.

"Want to go out tonight, plan our first trip to Florida?"

Jasmine laughed. "I'll wear my sparkly earrings."

"We'll send Mom a video. She'll be so tickled."

Nine months later…

Chapter 15

They were in love. It didn't take long. Sometimes love works that way. When you know, you just know. Why linger? Just fall and enjoy the flutter.

Andrew had been in Florida on business and visiting Mona. He called Jasmine. He couldn't wait to tell her the news. The first thing he said when she answered the phone was, "I bought a house."

"What?"

It should not have surprised her. Andrew could be quite impulsive. When he saw something he wanted, he went after it. He bought it. "A house. I bought us a house."

"Where?"

"On the ocean." It was that simple to Andrew. "We're getting married. You like being around water, so I am bringing you an ocean. We need a house. So I bought it. Did I say 'on the ocean'?" Jasmine was a little stunned, but she trusted his judgment. "When can you fly down to see it?"

"So it's somewhere 'down' there?"

"Sarasota."

"Andrew, I can't just leave my job."

"You'll like it—a lot."

"I'm sure I will, but—"

"No buts, I can run my business anywhere near an airport, and there are plenty of hospitals down here. You will find a job quickly if you want to work. You know you don't have to."

Jasmine's mind was spinning. But her face was beaming. She knew she would follow him anywhere. The wedding was a mere four months away. She had to think.

"Have your things ready. I'm sending the private plane to get you. Cannot wait to see your face!"

"Andrew, you're crazy!"

"I know."

"And a little bossy."

"I know that too."

Andrew shuffled the papers on his desk.

"Oh, one other thing," he interjected. "You may want to turn in your two-week notice. This long-distance stuff has got to end. I'm already unpacking boxes."

"You've already moved your office?"

"Yep. Just waiting for you now."

"Does Mona know we're moving closer to her?"

"Yep, she's actually dancing a jig in front of me right now."

"She's tickled?"

"She's looking forward to grandchildren."

*****

That's the way their courtship had been. Fast and furious. A love that was meant to be. Why waste time? Just do it. That is exactly what they did. They loved. Kindred spirits. And a wedding was in the making.

Jasmine turned in her notice to Morris Memorial. She called Polly and talked for hours on the phone. The next thing she knew, she was on the private plane heading for Sarasota and a house she had never seen but somehow owned. Andrew would be waiting. That was all that was important. How could life be so good? When she first looked into those eyes of his, she knew everything was about to change. She just didn't realize how quickly. It was better than better and "gooder" than good. Jasmine smiled. A fabulous new chapter was about to begin. She had to pinch herself to prove it was all real.

*****

He was standing there waiting for her as she deplaned. She ran to him.

"*Casablanca*," Andrew said.

"Except we're saying hello and not goodbye."

"Never goodbye," he replied. He took her arm and guided her to the driver of the limo that awaited them. "We're going straight to the house," Andrew announced to the driver. "You know where it is."

The driver nodded and found his way to the exit.

The house was everything Andrew had said it was. The view was breathtaking, and the sand was white as snow. Andrew took her suitcases and placed them in the hallway.

"Come on. Let's go!"

"Where?"

"To the beach… It's private. I have a surprise for you!"

They took off their shoes and ran to the edge of the white foam when Andrew pointed into the distance from where they stood. There was a table with a white linen tablecloth and a server waiting to seat them. A chilled bottle of champagne was waiting to be uncorked.

Andrew gave Jasmine his arm.

"Allow me to escort you to your welcome-home party."

Smiling, Jasmine took his arm, and they walked to the table. He pulled the chair out for her to sit. The server poured the champagne and announced that dinner would be served soon.

Jasmine was staring at Andrew.

"I wanted it to be romantic," Andrew whispered. He took her hand and bent down on one knee.

"Everyone knows we're getting married."

He cleared his throat. "I wanted it to be perfect. You don't have a ring yet." He took a small box out of his pocket, opened it, and took the ring out. Slipping the ring on her finger, he asked, "Jasmine, will you marry me?"

*****

The next three months went by in a blur. Invitations were addressed. Mona and Polly were visiting often to help with the planning. Andrew was flying back and forth with all his business dealings, and Jasmine began looking for a job to begin after their honeymoon. All was right with the world.

Had Andrew said, "Never goodbye"?

Yes, he had.

But someone once said, "Never say never."

*****

Jasmine and Andrew had just come back from a swim.

"I have to fly to New York."

"Okay, I have quite a lot to keep me busy here until you come back."

Andrew placed his arm around her shoulders. "You like it here, don't you?"

"I love it here!"

"Our little corner of the world," Andrew whispered.

She laid her head on his chest as he pulled her close. She slowly pulled away from him. "Is something wrong, Andrew?"

"I've been busy doing something all my life, from putting smoke bombs in my skates to stealing candy from the corner store." He cupped her chin in his hand. "To making business deals that no one could destroy." She kept looking at him. "What I'm trying to say is I'm slowing down. I want to be with you. I want to be the 'eye' in the hurricane swirling around me, around us. I want to protect you in that 'eye.'" Jasmine tilted her head. He took her face in his hands. "Too busy. Way too busy. Running everywhere." He put his lips close to her ear and whispered, "Then came you."

*****

Andrew decided to fly commercial. He needed people around him. The flight to New York was uneventful. Same flight magazines. Same flight instructions. He often wondered if he would ever run into the young girl from his past who gave him the romance novel. He would have liked to tell her he finally did believe. And then he would have told her about Jasmine. She would have been pleased. But he had never seen her again. He hoped she was happy with the young man who had greeted her that day. He was beginning to think that some dreams really could come true, including his own.

But this trip was not one hundred percent about business. It had to do with something much more. He couldn't tell Jasmine—not yet. He had to make sure. He made his way to his office and tried to think about pressing business matters, but there was far more on his mind.

He had some time before his visitor was to arrive. He picked up the phone and called Jasmine. He needed to hear her voice.

*****

The flowers had arrived. Jasmine was placing them in a vase when the phone rang.

"Hello?"

"Miss me?"

"Terribly."

"Get the flowers?"

"They are beautiful."

"How are we?"

"Beautiful."

"I think so too. I love you, Jasmine."

"Same here, handsome face."

Andrew was smiling when the knock came on his office door. He looked up. "Oh, Jasmine, I have to run for now. I'll call you right back. Someone's just come into my office I have to talk to. I've been waiting for them. I'll call you right back."

"Okay, until then. Here's lookin' at you, kid."

She smiled and sniffed the fresh-cut flowers, remembering their favorite movie, *Casablanca*. Perhaps she would watch it tonight.

*****

The hours went by with no call. Jasmine had errands to run, but she didn't want to miss his call. She waited. She unpacked more boxes. Still, no call.

"Must be a long meeting," she concluded.

At midnight, she gave up and went to bed. She felt unsettled. It wasn't like Andrew not to call back when he said he would. Morning would come. He would call then. He had no qualms of calling at any hour during the day or night. She tried to console herself, but sleep wouldn't come.

Morning came and went. No call. She decided to run her errands. Maybe he would call while she was away and leave a message. Maybe he would even be back in his own kitchen making coffee when she arrived back home.

She was gone longer than she had planned. She walked into Andrew's home office and looked at the message machine. No blinking lights. He still hadn't called.

"Something's wrong."

Jasmine was concerned. She called Mona.

"No, I haven't heard from him, child. But don't worry. He's just caught up in some business deal, I'm sure."

Jasmine was not so sure. Something was wrong.

*****

Andrew disappeared. He made up his mind, and nothing was going to stop him. He found it easy to revert to his earlier habits when he was a boy—the act of being reclusive. He was suddenly that lost little boy again, crouching in the corner as he watched his father unbuckle his belt. He didn't dare speak. He knew the aftermath that would follow. The blows he would have to endure stayed transfixed in his mind. One after the other. He remembered military school where he learned to be tough. Where he learned to hit things without anyone getting hurt. A wall, mostly, always in private. Yes, only walls—until football "discovered" him and it was okay to hit. In fact, the coach demanded it.

Then a calm quietness came over him. He found his success in a corporate world of "what have you done for me lately?" He would "hit" with his mind. And his darts always found their mark, like laser beams. People would fold. Obstacles were hurdled—success after success.

He never thought he would ever take a chance with love. And then came Jasmine, totally out of the blue. Lightning struck.

He shook his head in dismay. The one person he would never want to hit with a stare that would have her crumbling to the floor. He couldn't do it. He wouldn't do it. Allie—his long-ago kindergarten friend and confidant—had given him news that had stolen his future. His past was his past. Yes, he had done things that could harm him later in life, and now it seemed that his past had come back around, like a boomerang, to bite him. It was like an echo always coming around to remind you of the mistakes you made, the roads you should have traveled. It shouted out his vulnerability to a world that didn't really care.

So that's why he decided to disappear. He would rather Jasmine think of him as a son of a b——h rather than a man who could not stand in a battle he would never win. It wasn't really Allie who had signed, sealed, and delivered his fate. She only spoke the truth, the reality of it all. She had never minced words. She stood alongside the truth. And the truth had hit him between his eyes like a two-by-four.

She was the only one who ever knew he was not as strong as he portrayed himself to be. He merely put on an act, a "fake it till you make it" stance. A "walk into a place like you own it" kind of walk.

Only one thing could beat him down. And, sadly, that one thing had walked through his door with the news of a doomed man.

*****

Allie had fought the urge to rush over to him, fall to her knees in front of him, and say how sorry she was. She wanted to hold him and tell him everything was going to be all right. She was preparing to turn his world upside down with a mere word—*yes*. How could anybody do that to someone you had loved since kindergarten? She loved him. Always had. Since the very beginning. They had done so many things together. He protected those he loved; so had she. It was her that he had stolen the candy for way back when because he had no money to buy that valentine box covered in hearts.

When he had been taken to military school, even at her young age, it had killed a part of her. That's why she had studied so hard to get where she was today. She simply had to "busy" her mind. Letters going back and forth were good, but not a hand to hold when trouble beckoned.

She had not been sure what she was going to say to him now. She anticipated his reaction. He had to know. Still, she questioned how she would say it. What words could she use?

She had been standing outside his office door. He was on the phone. She could hear him talking. He loved whomever he was talking to. She knew it was a woman. Someone had finally captured his heart. She took a deep breath and knocked on his office door.

Midsentence, he looked up and saw her.

"I'll call you right back," he had said to the person on the other line. "Someone just came into my office that I have to talk to. I'll call you right back," he repeated.

He hung up. He looked at her. This tall blonde woman. Smart as a whip. Sweet, smart Allie.

"Speak to me," he had whispered.

She had looked at him, one lone tear tracking down her cheek. "Are you sure?"

He knew, even as he asked her the answer. She didn't have to speak. She could only nod.

*****

He sat at his desk for a long time after Allie left. He had known her, it seemed, all his life. He loved her in so many ways. She had been there through the years for him, especially after that football injury that had thrown him off the fifty-yard line into the corporate world. He knew she was there for him, still. He would never doubt her. He trusted her. But now? He didn't want to. He wanted something more. He wanted Jasmine. Why? Why did she have to walk into his office and just nod? She hadn't said a word. Just nodded. Her news had hit him hard. But then that's what truth does. Sometimes truth hurts. Sometimes, so does love.

He ran his hands through his hair. Time for some hard decisions. He could not, and he would not tell Jasmine. He would just disappear. Yes, that's what he would do—disappear from her life. That was best for the both of them. In the long run, that was best.

He knew he would not call Jasmine back. He knew she would be concerned. He didn't want to hurt her. He was glad he had bought the house by the ocean. She would be safe there. She had always wanted a place near the water. She had her ocean. She had her place. She had what money could buy. She just wouldn't be able to have him.

*****

Allie left his office and went into seclusion. She needed a break. She needed a respite. She cried. She went to the mountains—to her cabin. She ached. She cried again. How could this be happening? It wasn't fair. She could tell he loved the woman he had been talking to on the phone the minute she overheard his conversation. What could she do now? Nothing.

She took a deep breath. She couldn't stay here long. She had to get back. But for now, she would go to the grocery store, she would cook dinner, and she would go back to her little cabin and watch Judge Judy. Judge Judy always knew the answers. Perhaps she could answer the questions colliding in her own mind. She couldn't think of anything else to do. She would head back tomorrow and try to live life by being "busy" once again. That's what she would do. She would "busy" herself and try not to think about what was happening. She would miss him.

*****

Two months had gone by. No one could believe it. Why would they? Everything stopped, leaving skid marks a mile long. All the plans. Invitations lay on the kitchen table, never to be mailed. A wedding dress hung on the back of the bedroom door, a "no refund" tag floating between the beads.

"Those two were so in love," became whispered murmurs among guests who would never arrive on the day they had chosen to celebrate.

Jasmine walked the empty house, stopping only to make phone calls, seeking consolation from those who loved him most and trying to shed light on the knot in her gut that she felt with each passing day. She remembered the second phone call she had made to Mona.

"Mona, he's disappeared."

Mona was aghast herself. "I don't understand."

"I don't understand either." Jasmine continued, "I was talking to him. He had sent me flowers. We were talking." Jasmine knew she was repeating herself. "Someone came into his office. He was going to call me back. Right back. He didn't. It's been two months now, Mona."

Mona remained silent, thinking only to herself what in the world was Andrew doing. Had something happened to him? She couldn't believe that he would just disappear. Finally, she said, "I haven't heard a word from him."

"Something's wrong, Mona. I can feel it."

Mona was worried too. She wondered if she should call the police or send out the marine corps to look for him.

"Please call me if you hear from him."

"I promise you I will. Please do the same for me."

With that, both women broke the connection.

No sooner had Mona hung up from Jasmine that she began to dial Andrew's number, again. She and Andrew always talked at least once a week. This was not like Andrew at all. She tried every number Andrew had previously given her. No answer. Merely voice mail. She left numerous messages. All she could do was wait. She reconsidered calling the police.

*****

Andrew found himself talking to strangers in smoky out-of-the-way bars.

"What is said here stays here," Van, the bartender, told him one night. "You're becoming a regular in this bar." Andrew looked at him, running his hands over his unshaven face. "Want another ginger ale?"

"Hit me," Andrew replied.

"You amaze me," Van began. Andrew just stared at him. "Do you want to know why?" Andrew sighed. Van brought him a fresh glass of ginger ale with lots of ice. "People come in here, bearing their souls—both men and women. Drink after drink they get loose lips. You know what they say about loose lips?"

Andrew looked up from his drink.

"Loose lips sink ships."

Andrew merely nodded.

"Anyway, I could write a book about all their 'loose lip' talk. I believe most of them. They have a vacant look in their eye. Only personal deep pain can cause a look like most of them have."

Andrew wondered if he had that look. As if Van was reading his mind, he said, "You have that look, but you don't have loose lips. You only drink ginger ale."

"You respect people's privacy, don't you, Van?"

Andrew pointed to the sign hanging just above all the liquor bottles on display: *"If a phone call comes, you're not here."*

"Yep, I respect their privacy, and I try to forget most of what they tell me. Just don't want to get involved. I don't give advice. They seem to like that I just nod and listen."

"And yet you want to know my story, don't you?"

"Can't deny it."

"Why is that?"

"Maybe it's because you drink ginger ale."

"Let's just say I learned the hard way that alcohol doesn't solve anything. It only makes things worse."

"And yet you hang in here?"

"In an odd way, I find it comfortable."

"If I were a betting man, I would say this has something to do with a woman."

Andrew put his ginger ale down and looked Van straight in the eyes before answering. "It's about three women."

"Tell me about *the one*."

"The one?"

"Yeah, man, *the one*."

Andrew's face softened just thinking of Jasmine.

"Man, take my advice: get out of here, and go to that one that just made your face change from gruff and angry to silky smooth. Don't care what you've done or where you've been. She won't either. Stop running."

Van finished drying a glass and put the cloth down on the counter. He looked Andrew straight in the eye and asked, "Would you rather dance around your issues, whatever they are, or would you rather dance with your woman? Just askin'."

Before walking to the end of the bar to wait on another customer, Van turned and said over his shoulder, "You're welcome."

*****

Andrew had always been a clear thinker. He never touched booze. His drink of choice had always been ginger ale. He had seen firsthand what alcohol had done to his father. And he vowed at an early age never to touch the hard stuff. He never did.

He remembered the night he had promised his mother that he would never go near a bottle. Well, he did make one exception—champagne and wine once in a blue moon but only on celebratory occasions. And then it was only a small taste.

He was sitting on a park bench, watching toddlers play on the jungle gym when the memory came floating back. The beach. The foamy surf. The seabirds. The table. The dinner. The pop of the champagne bottle. She was there in his mind. So vividly. It was almost as if he could reach out and touch her.

He heard the murmur of Van so clearly. "Stop running." How long had it been? How many ginger ales had he consumed? How many sleepless nights had he tossed in that bed with the creaky springs?

And who in the world has springs in a mattress anymore? he thought.

Ginger ale and creaky mattresses. Is that what his life had become since Allie had come to call?

Three women on his mind. He loved them all—in different ways. But *the one*—as Van had called her—was *the one* who went with him everywhere. He slept, wept, lived, and breathed her essence every day, well into the night.

Stop running. Why would he believe that Van had such a simple answer? How could he? Did he have the strength to do exactly that?

It turned out to be the creaky mattress with springs that had him making his decision. The very next day, he found himself as a passenger on a slow train back to Florida. That slow train and transfer to a bus would give him plenty of time to think about what to do, when to do it, and what to say to two of the women he loved beyond measure. He knew where the third one was. She had retreated to the mountains where she had once said it was quiet, far away from the racket of the city. And she was probably crying her eyes out. Yes, he knew her that well.

*****

Jasmine had never slammed doors in her life. Not even when she had been a teenager. Not until now—just trying to love Andrew. It had been a full two months since she had talked to him. He was nowhere to be found. But someone once said, "People who are hard to find don't want to be found." She simply refused to believe that he had stopped loving her. She tried to rationalize why he had disappeared. She had already forgiven him. She needed closure and lots of it.

She looked at the wedding invitations. In a burst of anger, she stormed over to the table, grabbing the trash can as she ran, and slid all those invitations into the trash. Next, she marched to her bedroom that she thought one day would be theirs and grabbed the wedding dress. She had every intention of burning it. She hugged it instead. Holding the gown closely to her heart, she walked to the nightstand, picked up the framed picture of her and Andrew, touched his face with her fingertips, and turned the photo to the wall. She took a deep breath and went for a walk. She needed to see the seabirds.

After returning from her walk, she looked ambivalently at her stove. Crisis—time to boil water. Maybe chamomile tea would calm her down. She hoped so. She grabbed the phone and dialed his number, again. No answer. Had someone taken him? None of his associates knew where he was. Should she report him missing? This wasn't like him—not the Andrew she knew.

She poured her tea and sat down at the table. She scheduled out her day. But she knew she would not leave the house. She would stay until he called her. She kept rationalizing. Maybe he was planning a surprise. He was good at that. Yes, that must be it. He would walk through the door at any moment.

Waiting, with no answers, was like the corner of a puzzle piece missing. It was like a pair of sparkly shoes that you simply had to have but would never wear. You would just sit there looking at them and finally wonder why you bought them in the first place. It was like listening to someone bloviate on a barstool, making no sense at all, until finally you had to give up and do your best to walk away. The walking wounded. Still standing but disheveled.

She was tired. She had turned into a waiting machine, primed to answer the phone on the first ring. Ready to tear down any wall that had mysteriously appeared out of nowhere. She vacillated among anger, worry, and a feeling of rejection that she refused to let take root in her heart. She had never doubted him, and she had vowed she never would. But still, the nagging question kept rearing its ugly head.

Why would he have said the things he had said if he didn't mean them? Why would he have bought this house? Why would he have given her a ring, promising forever?

Her heart was full of questions those humid days of summer. Her mind tried its best to give her the answers, but she had no ears to hear. Her heart was in control. What was it someone had once said? "Emotions have no intellect." She felt she would turn into a blubbering fool if he did not contact her soon.

Tomorrow, she decided she would walk the beach and go into town for groceries. She would talk to the aisle clerk and buy chocolate brownies and a bottle of wine. She would come home, make a salad, add some chicken, and eat a brownie. Then she would open the wine. She would refuse to let the tears escape from her eyes, and she would remember the man who had told her pretty little and convincing lies. Would she cry? No, she would wail.

She had to admit that she was not made of steel when it came to Andrew. She was not one of those steel magnolias that Polly and her grandma had told her about all those years ago, while sitting on the front porch in South Carolina.

Southern women are made of steel, Polly would say. When life gets tough, we get tougher.

She felt more like her namesake at the moment. The jasmine was so fragile it was afraid to bloom in the daylight when all the racket circled around. No, the jasmine was a quiet one, a loner. It preferred to be safe and only spread its petals at dusk when the world was slowing down a bit, getting ready for a long night of silence. Only in the quietness did that precious plant sing its sweetest songs.

And that was exactly what Jasmine was doing now, preparing for the silence of another long night.

*****

Andrew thought a lot on that train and bus ride back to Sarasota. He remembered the night of the dancing with Jasmine. She had looked up at him and asked a question.

"Can you, maybe, one day, show me the part of your heart that nobody's ever seen? I'd like to be the first."

He could still hear her voice from that night when the stars seemed to dance in the heavens. That was the moment he had fallen in love. She had managed to ignite a passion for life that he had never felt before. How could he throw it away? She was the one he had let "all the way in." He decided that he couldn't leave her thinking he was a son of a b——h. That just wouldn't do.

*****

Those were his thoughts as he made his final slow journey back. But, first, he had to see the other woman, the woman he had loved from the beginning.

He powered up his phone. He saw all the messages. From Jasmine. From Mona. From Allie. He took a deep breath as it began to ring.

"Yeah." His voice sounded rough, damaged.

"Andrew, this is your mom!"

"I know that."

"Then answer me a question—what in tarnation are you doing? And where in the name of hell have you been? We have been worried sick about you! Were you kidnapped?"

Andrew couldn't help a smile forming on his lips but said nothing.

"Andrew?"

"I'm here, Mom. I'm at your front door. Let me in."

*****

"I can't hurt her, Mom."

"You have to tell her."

Andrew dragged his hands over his unshaven face. "I know."

Mona went to the linen closet and pulled out fresh towels and sheets. "Stay here tonight. Go to her tomorrow." She looked at her son. "I'm not asking you to go to her, Andrew. I am demanding you go to her. She needs to know. Come hell or high water, that girl needs to know."

Andrew sat down on the nearest chair. Mona went to him, bent down on her knees, and looked up. She took her son's face in her hands, looked directly into his eyes, and asked, "Are you sure?"

Sad eyes stared back at her. He nodded.

She stood up, took his hands, and pulled him to his feet. "Come on. I'll tuck you in."

"Just like the old days, eh, Mom?"

"Just like the old, old days but without that son-of-a-b——h father of yours hitting us."

Andrew was saddened as they walked toward the guest room of his mom's condo.

"I wish I could write a happier ending for you, Andrew."

It seemed no matter how old you get, especially in times of trouble, it felt good to have your mom tuck you in. And that is exactly what Mona did. She tucked Andrew in. She left the room, refusing to let her tears fall. She had to be strong—just like days of old. She went to her own bedroom and fell facedown beside her bed, where she prayed and cried.

"Please take care of my son. My once-upon-a-time wild child. My sweet baby. My chocolate eyes."

*****

Morning came with a whimper. Dark clouds hung low, as if hugging the earth. It was raining. Andrew looked out the window. It seemed a perfect backdrop for what he had to do. A typical heartbreak day. He walked to the kitchen where Mona was already seated with her cup of coffee. She looked up. He could tell she had been crying. He hadn't seen red eyes like that since the night she had come to him and said, *I have to get you out of here*. It saddened him to think he was the reason, once again, for her restless night.

"Are you going to go to her today?" Mona asked.

"Yes." He went to the coffeepot, poured a cup, and took a seat at the table across from his mom.

"Will you come back here afterward?"

He shrugged. "I'm not sure what I'll do, Mom. Right now, I'm not too sure of anything." He took a sip of his coffee.

Andrew took his empty coffee cup to the sink. He rinsed it out. Turning back to Mona, he said, "Promise me something."

"Anything to make this go away."

"If Jasmine calls, promise me you won't answer the phone until you hear from me, until I tell you I have talked to her."

Mona took her cup to the sink and turned to face him. "I promise." She walked across the room and took her son's face in her hands.

"I wish there were some way I could whisk you away and make this all better."

"Like when I was a mere boy going off to military school?"

"Yes, just like that."

"I think you actually saved my life, Mom."

"And you saved mine, dear boy, by becoming the person you are today. You helped me to smile again, to laugh again, to reach back into my past and discover the real me again."

"I'm glad."

A tear was rolling down Mona's cheek. Andrew wiped it away with his thumbs.

"None of that. Do you hear me? You know I can't stand to see a woman cry."

He pulled his mother to him and embraced her before walking out the door.

The rain began to envelop his car as he drove away. Mona stood on her balcony watching as he disappeared.

"It's not fair!"

She was getting soaked, but she didn't care. There was nothing she could do, nothing she could say. She stood there helplessly, asking the question, "Why?" over and over again. Why such a terrible blow in a life that held so much promise? She heard no answer. All she heard was thunder.

*****

Mona looked at the ringing phone. Jasmine. She couldn't answer. Not yet. She had to wait until Andrew contacted her that he had, indeed, seen Jasmine. Her heart ached for that sweet girl. Mona loved her like a daughter. And they were so close to becoming a family. Not to be. She wanted desperately to explain everything to her. But she would break her fingers before she answered that phone.

*****

Jasmine questioned, what was happening? Had Mona disappeared too? She didn't understand. No one was answering their phones. What was she to do? Had he merely changed his mind? Didn't she deserve an answer? She decided to walk to the ocean shore. Breathe. Look for flat rocks and sea glass. She had to do something.

*****

Andrew walked into the house. She wasn't there. He walked into the bedroom. He saw their framed picture turned to the wall.

"Why wouldn't she?" he questioned. "Why wouldn't she turn their photo to the wall? At least she hadn't replaced it with someone else. The flowers he had sent her that fateful day remained in the vase. Dead. Dried up. But still in the vase. Telephone numbers beside the phone. Numbers she had called to find him. She had been worried. She was still worried. He knew it. He had caused her pain. He was sorry for that. Now he would cause her more pain. He was sorry for that too.

He walked into the kitchen. It was so "her." He would miss her. But he absolutely had to let her go. He turned and walked out the door. He was going to find her. He knew he would find her there in the surf. He would take a deep breath. He would walk up to her. He would speak and she would know. Then he would call Mona.

*****

She knew he was near, even though her back was to him. It was a feeling. That's what he did to her. Ever since the first day they had met in Mona's hospital room. That's what happens to two people with all that "chemistry" flying around. People standing close to them were bound to get singed. It was virtuously impossible to be in a room without the other one knowing it. Jasmine took a deep breath and turned.

He was walking toward her, his hands in his pockets.

Why does he look so sad? she thought. *Why don't I run to him?*

Her feet could not move. She felt something was wrong, very wrong. Could it be that a woman from his past had come back into his life? Or someone new?

She couldn't think that. She wouldn't. He loved her. He said so. And she believed him. She would never doubt him. Could she? Should she—

What would Polly say? "S——t fire, girl! Why did you let yourself be blinded to what hides behind those sad chocolate eyes?"

He approached her slowly. Should she fight for him or flee from him? She was frozen. She could do neither, until she heard what he had to say.

He reached her. Neither said a word. He took her hands in his.

"Don't ask me any questions, not right now. Let's walk."

*****

The rain of the morning had stopped, at least for the moment, before Jasmine spoke.

"You know, I would have followed you anywhere." Jasmine broke the silence. "In fact, I did! I quit my job. I let you pick out a house without me seeing it! I trusted you! I flew to Florida with nothing but a packed suitcase! I did all that for what? To have you disappear!" She took a deep breath. "You know I made up my mind never to doubt you. I forced myself to wait for answers. I had nightly stare downs with the phone and tried calling you. You never answered. I had to force myself to face reality—the awful reality—that you didn't want to be found, by me or anyone else." She shoved her hands in her pocket when he tried to reach out to take them again.

He stared down at the sand as all her pent-up emotions bombarded him. He felt the invisible fist of her anger take powerful punches to his gut.

"I laid my heart out in words every night on blank sheets of paper. Hurt hearts sure know how to bleed. You're a complicated man, Andrew. It's hard—trying to love you." She swept the hair back from her face as the wind began to blow. "I cannot think of enough adjectives I could write about you! You're a man who would take reams and reams of paper, gallons of ink, and many midnight hours to write about, much less understand."

She secretly thought they should be having this conversation in the kitchen where she could boil some water. It was one of those "make it" or "break it" moments.

"When I didn't hear from you, I kept trying to convince myself that this trouble we had between us was a mere fragment in our lives—a little piece we would set aside, come to grips with, laugh about, somewhere down the road of our 'remember when?' and wait for our perfect ending. But there were too many questions, and I had no answers."

Andrew remained silent.

"I need answers now, Andrew, before you run away again. I'm tired of wondering how you were so tender in May and weren't anywhere in sight in June or July, with August just around the corner. How could you just disappear? What happened? Are we just a sad movie where we meet, we love, and then say goodbye? How could the life we were planning together suddenly become a shaken, blended, stirred, and poured out lie all over the floor at my feet, as I looked at wedding invitations I would never send? Tell me now! I want to know!"

Finally, Andrew broke his silence. "I love you, Jasmine."

She looked out at the horizon. "You sure have a funny way of showing it." She refused to cry. She would not allow tears to fall from her eyes. She simply would not. "You remember the picture I had of us sitting on the nightstand beside my bed?"

He nodded. He also remembered finding it turned to face the wall.

"One night after my third chocolate brownie and a Pay Day candy bar, plus half a bottle of wine, I stared at that picture. I propped myself up on my pillow, reached for it, touched your face, and turned it to the wall. Then I turned off the light and cried myself to sleep. The next morning, I put it in a box, placed it on a shelf in my closet, and vowed I'd never look at it again. That afternoon, I took it out of that closet and set it back on the nightstand. By evening, I turned it facing the wall again. That's what crazy people do while waiting for phone calls that never come, Andrew!"

He could see the tangible hurt he had caused.

"I need answers, Andrew. I don't like feeling crazy. I don't want regrets. Is that what you're feeling?"

He had resurfaced to tell her. He had come back.

Little did she know of what was to come. His truth would be stained with tears. She readied herself to listen. She had talked enough.

They sat down on the sand. She couldn't help herself. She laid her head on his shoulder. He put his arm around her and began to talk as the waves found their way to the shore. A certain reckoning was coming. Like the sandpipers, she had no clue, and she would soon be scurrying to safety, away from the onslaught of the wave. At that moment, she felt she wanted to run away from the surf with them. But she sat, deathly silent, unable to move.

She felt as if her heart would be crushed by what he was going to tell her. She took a deep breath and prepared for the storm that she sensed was coming. She could feel it. The wind would be harsh. Her eyes would sting. It was as if she already knew that, from this moment on, their lives would change drastically.

He grabbed her hands, pulling her to her feet. Again, there was a stubborn, sad silence as they walked.

Jasmine stopped suddenly, feet anchored to the sand.

"Talk to me, Andrew! Tell me what you have to say and get it over with! I'm sick to death of all this not knowing!"

Andrew reached out to take her hand. She let him. Tears were starting to roll down her cheeks. He turned to her, placing his hands on her shoulders. "Look at me, Jasmine." They were ankle deep in the surf.

Jasmine was speechless. So she said something stupid. She always said stupid things when she felt wounded. "I hear that saltwater heals all wounds."

But to Andrew, it made perfect sense. He looked at her. "It won't heal this one, Jasmine."

"Andrew, what is going on? What is happening?"

She broke away from him, taking a few steps backward. The roar of the sea was resounding in her ears. She felt as if her head was going to explode. She loved him so. She had to know. She wanted the truth.

When he only stared at her saying nothing, she began to run. She didn't know where she was going. There was really nowhere to go. The beach seemed endless, and the house was far behind her. She fell. Andrew was at her side in an instant. Reaching down to her, he fell to his knees in the sand beside her.

"Well?" she asked. "Andrew, please say something!"

They sat there in that surf for what seemed an endless time. Finally, he took her face in his hands. She looked at him, trying to read his sad chocolate eyes.

Suddenly, she was frightened. "Andrew, what is it?"

"Jasmine, there's no one else. Since I met you, there could never be anyone else—past, present, or future. You are the one. From the first moment I saw you, I knew. You are the one I want to spend the rest of my life with."

She continued to look at him, not knowing what to say, somehow knowing the gauntlet was about to fall.

He pulled her close, his face touching hers. His lips came close to her ear as he whispered, "Jasmine, my sweet, sweet Jasmine, I'm dying."

*****

Chapter 16

They held on to one another. She refused to let him go. And he wouldn't let her, even if she had tried. His lips close to her ear, he questioned, "Are you sure you want to do this? Stay with me through this?"

She pulled away from him gently. She looked at him with an intensity he had never seen in her eyes before.

"I said it in anger a short while ago. Now I say it with so much love. I cannot comprehend it myself. Andrew, I would follow you anywhere." They seemed surrounded in a cocoon of support and comfort. No regrets. She looked into his eyes. Chocolate eyes. "And that includes walking through the fire of this cancer. Yes, I want to do this."

The seabirds took flight. You could hear their cry above the clouds. They held tightly to one another. "It'll be a fierce fight," he whispered.

"I know."

"All in?"

"All in."

*****

"I have to tell you about the other woman in my life. We go way back," Andrew confessed to Jasmine after they had walked back to their house. "I met her in kindergarten."

They were sitting, curled up on the couch, fingers intertwined.

"Tell me about her," Jasmine whispered.

Their tears had been spent. They had held on to one another while walking back from the beach to the house. Now they were back in the house, still holding on to one another.

"She became a doctor. Her name is Allie."

Jasmine moved a little closer to Andrew.

"We had a special connection. She was a cute little blonde with blue eyes. For some reason, she liked my wild ways."

Jasmine smiled.

"And you liked her blonde hair and blue eyes?"

"I must confess I did. After school, we would meet and play. I may have been daring, but when I was with her, I protected her—from frogs, bugs, and bees." Andrew smiled. "One day I persuaded her to play football. I had this helmet that I placed on her head and told her she would be the opposing team but we would have to paint the helmet green because she was going to be a New York Jet."

Jasmine interrupted. "You didn't have any major falls or tackles? Please tell me you didn't!"

"No, but—"

"What!"

"We went to my mom's craft store, and I took some green paint, and while the helmet was on her head, I painted it. I didn't take the time to paint around the tiny holes in the helmet, and when I was finished, I took the helmet off her head and stood back in horror."

Jasmine was beginning to understand what had happened.

"Suddenly, she had green polka dots all over her blonde hair. She was horrified too. I'll never forget how big her eyes got when she looked in the mirror. We knew our parents, especially my dad, would be mad. So I grabbed her hand, and we ran to the small salon on the corner. As soon as we entered, the stylist looked at us, realized why we were in such a hurry with just one look at Allie, and pointed to the shampoo bowl."

Jasmine decided it was nice to have some levity in what had been such a solemn conversation on the beach. In spite of Andrew's news, they were finding a certain joy at just being together again.

"The stylist knew what to do to make it all better?" Jasmine asked.

"Yes, indeed. When we left, Allie was back to normal, but it took me a long time to pay back the salon. They put me on a payment plan."

"How did you get the money?"

"I charged boys at school to watch me fight."

"What?"

"You heard me."

"Did you always win?"

"Yes."

"But was it worth it?" Jasmine asked.

"Yes. Allie and I had a secret we never told anyone—until now. I told you."

Andrew stood and walked to the kitchen. He poured himself a glass of water.

"When I went away to military school, it killed her. It actually killed me too. I missed her."

Jasmine looked up at him.

"She loved you. And you loved her."

"Yes, we still do. But in a different kind of way than I love you."

He cocked his head, motioning for her to join him in a glass of water.

"I was her biggest cheerleader when she went to med school. I never thought she was that smart when we were little. Smart girls just didn't hang around with me. We always stayed in touch. We wrote a lot of letters back and forth and made a lot of phone calls to each other. I often kidded her that, one day, she would be my doctor and I would have to strip in front of her."

Jasmine smiled and took his hand as they walked back to the couch. Suddenly, her mind began to connect to the day of his disappearance.

"Wait, was that who came into your office that day you didn't call me back?"

"Yes."

"How long has she been your doctor?"

"A very long time."

Andrew continued, "I know it killed her to tell me the news of my test results."

"Have you seen her since that day?"

"Not yet. But I will."

"We'll fight it together, Andrew. You, me, your mom, and Allie. Please promise me you will fight this thing!"

Andrew could only smile, trying to reassure Jasmine, but deep in his heart, he knew that the looming clouds were not benign. They were huge. They were bigger than either of them could fight. The prognosis was too grave. Allie had also told him, during a phone call after she had returned to her office, that if he was lucky, he would have, perhaps, six months to live, maybe eight. There was nothing any of them could do. Treatments would not help. The tumor was too aggressive. He had not told Jasmine that part. He would tell her later. He wanted to make sure that the remaining months he had left would be good months for them. He would push the clouds away, at least for a while.

*****

Andrew and Jasmine did have their wedding. Not the one they had planned with Mona and Polly. Rather, one that had been spontaneous and, looking back, the most joyful day of Andrew's life.

They had been walking the beach that day. It was promising to be a glorious morning that would fade into the night, one that Jasmine would look back upon the rest of her life and smile.

Andrew sighed. Jasmine reached for his hand.

"What are you thinking?"

"How I don't want to leave you." They continued to walk in silence, Jasmine fighting back the tears that threatened to fall with each step they took. She looked out at the sea. "The waves are a little restless today."

Andrew followed her eyes. The waves were, indeed, cresting higher than he had ever witnessed. And yet a storm was not coming. The forecast had called for sunny weather. No humidity. A perfect beach day. Andrew sighed again. Holding tightly to Jasmine's hand, he turned her toward him.

"I've been thinking."

"About what?"

"The hereafter."

They stood there together, facing each other. It was one of those moments in time when God opens a door and you simply have to walk through it. You cannot resist it. It becomes a "pull"—like a magnet to steel.

"And how are you imagining the hereafter?"

Andrew took a deep breath and looked out at the waves that were forming, one after the other, each one a little higher than the one that had gone before it.

"I've been thinking about you and how you are so sure you are going to heaven when you die."

She nodded, continuing to look into those eyes she had come to love with her very soul.

"How are you so sure?" he asked.

"Because I let him in when he knocked."

Andrew looked perplexed.

"Everyone has a choice at some time in their life. You either let him in, or you don't."

"Let him in where?"

She placed her hand on his face. "Your heart."

The seabirds were flying all around as the waves continued to crest and fall toward the shore. They continued to walk but not along the surf's edge. It seemed the tide was going out. They found themselves walking more toward the core of the ocean.

"I've been thinking that I want to see you when you get there, but I'm wondering how I'm going to get there. I want you to see me when you turn around in heaven. I want to see the look on your face when you see me. I want to see the smile that is meant for only me. The one you smiled when you knew you first loved me. I want to see you walk across the clouds, like you walked across the room that day, and into my arms. Something is telling me I will never lose you again if I can just get to heaven."

She stopped him. Taking both his hands, she whispered, "You can, Andrew. You can see all that."

"How?"

"With a simple prayer."

"I don't pray. The last time I prayed, I introduced myself to God as Mona's son, on an airplane, seated next to a young girl that believed in romance."

Jasmine smiled. "Well, now do you feel it's time you 'come clean' as yourself?"

"Yeah, yeah, I do."

"Then pray with me, Andrew."

"Right here, right now, in the middle of this tidal wave that is bound to come if we don't start walking back to the shore?"

"Yes. Right here, right now."

With the waves continuing to rise behind them, those two prayed. With the final amen, a wave of tremendous proportions crested and came down upon them with a force that knocked them both to the sandy floor. They rose up laughing.

"Go with it, Andrew! Let's ride it to the shore!"

And that's exactly what they did. Once the shore was reached, they clung to each other, lying there on that white sandy beach. Jasmine was the first to look up to the sky. Andrew followed her gaze.

"Well, how do you like that?" Jasmine asked. "God is just full of high drama!"

Both rolled over on their backs. Their hands found each other with fingers laced together.

"Andrew, you've just become part of the family of God with the most powerful baptism I have ever witnessed! Straight from the Holy Spirit, my man! When I turn around in heaven, I will most definitely be seeing you!"

Once back in the house, they changed into dry clothes, got in the car, and headed for the small chapel that was located in a town just north of where they lived. That's where they were married. No fanfare. No long dress. No tux. Just four people. Andrew, Jasmine, the pastor, and a witness. God had planned this wedding that no human could ever duplicate. It was the most beautiful wedding both of them could have ever imagined.

"There are two tragedies in life. One is not to get your heart's desire. The other is to get it."

(Bernard Shaw)

(and not be able to keep it)

Chapter 17

They didn't fight it. Deep down, they knew they couldn't. It was too big. Pancreatic cancer always was.

Together, they went to Mona. They told her what they had decided. With a mournful heart, Mona understood. She knew her son so well.

"You were right, Mom."

"About what, son?"

"Money can't buy you everything."

They had walked out onto the balcony overlooking the ocean. Seabirds were at play. Children were splashing and building their own personal sandcastles.

"Life is never simple," Mona whispered. She took both Andrew and Jasmine's hands in hers. "I want you two to go, make yourself some precious memories—memories to fall back on, Jasmine." She squeezed their hands. "I know you don't realize it now, but you will. Memories help sustain us. They make us stronger down the road." Mona took a deep breath. "Don't think about me. Only cling to one another."

Both Andrew and Jasmine began to protest.

"No, I won't hear of it! Jasmine, you call me when the time comes. You don't need this old coot hanging around." That was Mona's excuse. Deep down in her soul, she knew she could not sit and watch her son die. She turned to Andrew. "Go make me a grandchild."

*****

They loved their beach house but decided to go to the mountains. Allie had offered them her cabin. The surroundings had a calming influence on both of them. They walked the trails and sat by a campfire at night. They made s'mores. The cabin had featured an overstuffed chair with a footstool, a TV, a bed, a small kitchenette, and a small bathroom next to a closet. That was it. They didn't need two chairs or a couch. Andrew's lap always held a personal invitation to join him. That's where they would end each day, sometimes watching *Casablanca* and sometimes just sitting in silence.

"Here's looking at you, kid," Andrew whispered every night before bed. She would smile, touch his cheek, and whisper good night. He would kiss her forehead, and they would hold each other until morning. They prayed for one more day to make one more memory. They both knew how important it would be to Jasmine as she walked the road without him.

*****

"You go on ahead without me today, Jasmine," Andrew said one morning.

"I can't do that," she replied.

"Yes, you can and you will. Those ducks we have befriended will be waiting for their breakfast. Now go get the bread and trot along. I'll be here when you get back."

"Not up to it today?"

"No, maybe tomorrow."

Andrew sighed and said, "Go on now! Mind me, or I shall spank you!"

"Promise?"

"Get out of here!"

"Okay, okay, I'm going!" She turned at the door asking one final time, "Are you sure?"

Playfully, he threw a pillow at her as she closed the door.

*****

He didn't want her to know. His legs just wouldn't cooperate. He had nearly fallen coming back into the room from outside. Her back had been turned from him while she was pouring his coffee. He was grateful for God's small favors. He knew that when she returned, he would have to tell her to take him to the hospital. She deserved one more small respite before the downhill ride on the roller coaster. He would give it to her.

She arrived back at the cabin. Running over to him, she exclaimed, "That mama duck has had her babies! Oh! Andrew, I wish you could have seen them! Tomorrow *okay*?"

Andrew was sitting in the chair. He looked up at her and whispered, "It's time, Jasmine. I need to go to the hospital." The look on her face hurt Andrew more than the pain in his legs. She went to him and crawled onto his lap. She placed her hands on his face.

"Okay."

One word was all she managed to say. They held each other in silence. It was Andrew who spoke first. "I don't think I can make it to the car. I may need some help." Jasmine stood and helped him up, wrapping her arms around his waist. Slowly, they walked to the car, his arm around her shoulder.

Jasmine called the ER on the way to the hospital and told them to have a wheelchair ready for the moment of their arrival.

*****

Andrew collapsed in the nurse's arms as soon as she pulled the curtain around them. It took all the strength he had to do that. He didn't want Jasmine to see. The rest of their days together would be spent in the hospital. Hospital rooms did not offer too much to look at. A window, a TV, and a bed. The view had no trees, the TV remained silent, and the bed had tubes hanging from stands beside the pillow the nurses kept "fluffing up."

"Stop the fluffing!" Jasmine finally shouted, "I will fluff it if it needs fluffing! Leave him alone! Leave us alone!"

They honored her wishes. Nobody came in. But someone was watching. She watched Jasmine sitting in the chair next to the bed. She watched as Jasmine sat there beside Andrew for hours. She watched until Allie appeared, put her arm around her, and guided her away. It was Mona.

Suddenly, Andrew spoke. "Jasmine, would you please rub my feet?" She was startled at the sound of his voice. He hadn't spoken for hours.

"Of course, I will rub your feet." She kissed his forehead and walked to the foot of the hospital bed. She began to rub.

"I'm upset," he said.

"About what?" she asked.

"Those damn sox on my feet. I can't feel your hands."

She smiled. "How about if I take them off?"

He nodded. "I would like that. I want to feel your touch."

Jasmine took the socks off his feet, placed them at the foot of the bed, and continued to rub his feet. "Feels good, honey."

He took a breath. "Thank you."

She smiled at him and kept rubbing. "I remember all the foot rubs you used to give me. Now it's my turn."

Andrew sighed. "Jasmine?"

She looked up.

"I need another favor. Come lay beside me."

Jasmine didn't hesitate. She went to the side of the bed, slipped off her shoes, and slid in beside Andrew, avoiding all the tubes. Her head was on his chest, and he was holding her as best he could.

"Sweetheart"—he looked at her—"I have one last favor."

Jasmine said nothing. She kept looking at him. "What is it?" she managed to whisper.

"Would you take this damned tube out of my nose?"

"Honey, it's helping you breathe."

"No, Jasmine, it's time for me to let go."

"I can't."

"Yes, you can. Please, I want to kiss you goodbye with no barriers in the way, please."

Jasmine reached up and gently removed the tube.

"Thank you. Now come here."

Sweetly, gently, their lips met.

Andrew whispered, "We had it all, kid."

Jasmine tried to hold back the tears. She knew the time had come. Andrew wiped those tears away—the ones that slid from her eyes—no matter how hard she tried to keep them hidden.

"It's okay, honey. We both know where I'm going."

"I remember your own private baptism," Jasmine whispered.

He smiled. "Quite dramatic, wasn't it? But then again, God can be very dramatic when he wants to be."

"Yes, yes, he can. I remember when that special, incomparable joy took over your life."

Andrew smiled. "It's as if God said, 'Finally, Andrew, it's about time! Let's do something out of the ordinary!'"

"And so he did," Jasmine said.

"Just you, me, and Jesus." He touched her face. "Always did like your high cheekbones," he whispered. Foreheads touching, he looked at her lying beside him. "The fight has gone out of me, dollface."

She gently kissed his lips one last time. He opened his eyes briefly and whispered, "Here's lookin' at you, kid. I'm going home."

*****

He died peacefully in her arms. Her tears fell on his chest once again. He was silent, like before, but this time, he could not feel those tears. She touched his nose with her index finger, but this time, he didn't grab her hand and pull her to him. This time, he was very still. She placed her hands on each side of his face and whispered what she could not say before. With tears streaming, she mouthed the word, "Goodbye."

Slowly, she gathered herself and put both feet on the floor. Before leaving the room, she took his left hand and then his right. Those strong hands that had held hers through the time they had been together—she now kissed them both, laying them back by his side. She stood beside the bed and kissed his forehead and then ever so gently his lips.

She turned to leave the room. Walking down the hallway, she encountered the nurse walking toward Andrew's room with the small cup of his morning pills.

"No need," Jasmine said. "He's gone."

She would have to plough through the months and years, facing an emptiness she did not know how she would handle. Andrew had been her life through the ups and downs, the tears and laughter, the goodbyes and hellos, as well as the ins and outs of the fabric of their lives. It would be a most confusing time for her.

She walked to her car and pointed it in the direction of the mountain cabin. Funny, she thought, as she began the drive, funny how both she and Andrew had loved the beach but it was the mountains that became their respite in the final days.

When she arrived, she walked to the closet and took the only familiar thing left in her world. She took the camera from the shelf. She needed to take pictures of the mama and her ducks. She needed to feel the presence of Andrew looking down on her. She needed to imagine his smile encouraging her to keep going, one step at a time. On her way out of the cabin, she gathered the bread and began her walk toward the water.

"He never saw the babies," she said to herself. "I wanted him to see the babies."

All she knew at the moment was that she had to feed those ducks.

*****

Mona had been there all along, watching the journey her son and daughter-in-law were taking with such grace. Allie had been there too. Who would have thought the little blonde, blue-eyed girl from kindergarten would grow up to be so smart and become Andrew's oncologist?

Both Andrew and Jasmine knew that those two ladies would not have had it any other way. Mona had been there wearing her sparkly earrings. Deep down inside, she knew there would be no grandchild. And she would be there for her son, always and forever.

Mona and Allie were watching, always watching, and he needed them as much as he needed Jasmine those final days. Jasmine needed them too. Everyone respected the need for privacy at moments such as these. Mona and Allie waited. They would not enter the room until Jasmine left. They had already said their goodbyes.

Mona was there in the waiting room with Allie. They watched Jasmine leave. Quietly, they walked into Andrew's room.

The nurse was preparing to call the doctor when they walked into the room. Allie walked over to the bed.

"He's gone."

Mona collapsed in the chair next to Andrew's bedside. "It's not fair, Allie! No parent should have to bury their child first! It goes against the natural order of things!"

Mona was failing at trying to hold back her tears.

Allie whispered, "He was like a brother to me."

"He loved you, too, you know?"

"He was my kindergarten beau," she whispered, bending down to kiss his cheek.

And then they wept.

"So he passed over, and all the trumpets sounded for him on the other side."

(John Bunyan)

Chapter 18

Jasmine looked in the mirror. It was over. The memorial. The final hugs of friends and family. Her family—Polly. Andrew's family—Mona and Allie. Friends—too numerous to mention. Business associates.

Andrew had been a popular guy. Everybody loved him, especially the ones who were employed by him. They had lost a friend, as well as a "boss." He had been their "chief." They would miss him. He had trained them well. The business would continue to prosper, and people would move on.

Jasmine, on the other hand, felt that she did not know herself anymore. Who was this stranger in the mirror looking back at her? Her identity had left with Andrew. The best part of her was gone. It left her the moment Andrew had whispered his last words. She kept looking at her reflection. She touched her face.

"I don't know you. You're a widow."

She wondered why women who lost their husbands were called "widows." She shook her head, as if to clear the cobwebs from the corner of her mind. She looked up at the ceiling, searching for spiders.

"I think of black widow spiders when I think of myself as a *widow*."

She looked back at her reflection once again.

"I don't like spiders. I don't like the word *widow*. Can't someone come up with a better name than that?"

She turned away from the dark shadows under her eyes and walked to the window, wishing it were dusk. Then she could smell the jasmine as its fragile petals unfolded. Then she could remember the good times, the loving times.

"We can land a man on the moon and can't come up with a better word than *widow*. I wonder why that is?"

She walked back to the mirror.

She pictured a big *W* on her forehead. People would know she was alone now. Stripped of couple-hood—stripped of her identity. Stripped from the love of her life. It was more than an amputation—this loss. She felt as if her very heart had been ripped from her chest.

She took a deep breath.

This path she was to walk would be like walking in a different country, learning a new language, new customs. She would have to learn how to survive. She vowed that she would. She would learn how to mow the grass and fix the sprinkler system. She would learn how to take care of "salt blocks" in the water purifier. She would learn how to be alone.

She knew she was thinking of things that didn't really mean much. She was trying to think of things that would not sting so badly. Things that would set her heart free, encouraging it to keep beating. She was trying to distract her heart from one final explosion.

Without Andrew? There would be a hole in the pillow next to her. There would be empty shoes that could never be filled. The laughter was gone. The smiles? A mere shadow. The nights would be darker and the days not so bright. She didn't want to be in this new land. She hated this new land. She wanted to go back to what she knew. She wanted to walk the shore with her Andrew. She wanted to see the tiny seabirds running from the surf. She wanted the waves to crash around them. She wanted to watch *Casablanca* while curled in Andrew's lap, his arms around her. She didn't want this to be happening! She couldn't comprehend this type of loss. She wasn't going to try. She wanted to throw things. She wanted to run screaming through the streets. She wanted people to think she was crazy and put her in a rubber room or a straight jacket—anything to numb the pain.

Through all of her rantings, she could see the grievous mountain before her. It seemed too steep, too rocky. She wondered if the mountain before her would shake before she took the first step on the path leading to the promised summit she so desperately needed to reach. It was only then that she would be able to look out upon how far she would have come—when she was able to stand tiptoe on that summit. It would be only then that she could rest and be lifted up on eagles' wings. She had to believe that she would be protected on her *widow's* journey. She had to trust. With only a brief moment of hesitation, she walked to her front door, opened it, and walked out. She breathed in the air deeply and took her first step.

"I'm leaning on you, God. Hold me up. Guard my steps. Catch me when I stumble, stoop down, and wipe the tears from my eyes. I am forever yours. Walk me through this barren land of which I feel like an alien with no familiar ground. Let me stand upon the foundation of your love. And please let the mountain shake. Let me know you are there waiting for me. Reach out, my God, and take my hand."

And with that prayer, she fell to her knees and wept.

He heard every word. He was there. He honored her request and did so much more. He began to wipe her tears, picked her up from the ground, and carried her—as the mountain began to shake.

"Should her heart break and the grief pour out, it would flow over the whole earth, it seems, and yet, no one sees it."

(Anton Chekhov)

Jasmine drove back to the beach house and sat watching the waves crash against the shore. The ocean was angry today. Well, that was just fine because she was angry too. She was full of questions. How could it be? Life going on through her river of tears? Life constantly moving as if nothing had ever happened? People continued to laugh. Cars continued to be driven up the street. The tide of the ocean continued to roll. Seabirds continued to fly. Didn't they know her world had stopped turning? She wanted to shout at them. She wanted to get on her soapbox and tell them how much she hurt. Instead, she shouted at God. Maybe he would acknowledge her grief. Surely, he wouldn't pass her by like the other adults having their "happy hours" on the beach. Not like the children running to flag down the ice cream truck.

She needed company. She didn't need people passing her by, along with the world. She was off-balance. The earth had tilted. At any given moment, she would be falling off the edge, sliding down into the unknown with no arms to catch her as she fell.

Her grandmother had always been there at the bottom of the sliding board, arms outstretched. Where was she now? With Andrew? Both gone. She had to claim her own little box of space to grieve.

She jumped up from the beach chair and walked to her kitchen. She wanted to clean out things, throw out things, slam some more doors.

She had always thrown food out on their expiration date. That's what she was doing now. "Shelf life" was something she had always paid careful attention to since that bout with food poisoning. No, she would never forget that. Nothing would ever get past her mouth with an expired shelf life.

Wilted lettuce. Gone. Soup cans? Expired a month ago. Gone. Bread and cheese. Molded. Gone. Was she having fun yet?

People have shelf lives, too, she decided. She vowed then and there cleaning out those cabinets and that refrigerator that she would never let someone ever get that close to her again. And besides, no one could ever fill Andrew's shoes. His feet had been far too big.

She slumped to the floor, sitting there in the middle of all that expired food in all those trash cans thinking of Andrew's feet. This is what it had all come to. She didn't dare move. In a single moment, her life had changed. Shattered. Upside down. Exploded. She wasn't one bit sure that she would find all the pieces to put herself back together. No, she was not sure of that at all. She had unraveled.

How could a man so big, so full of life be gone so quickly? Here, a moment ago, gone now. How could a man with such big feet be gone? A man who walked into a room and filled it with laughter and charm? A man with such charisma? How could he be gone? It wasn't fair that God would take such a man away from a world that needed the special light that Andrew sent forth. It wasn't fair at all!

By the time Jasmine had taken all the cans of expired and moldy food to the end of the street for pick up the next morning, darkness was not far behind. She kept visualizing the face she had seen in that hospital bed. That wasn't Andrew! She jumped up from the couch and, with a frenzy, began opening drawers and closets collecting every frame she could find. She opened boxes of photos and began placing them in the frames, and then she placed them one by one throughout her house. She would see his eyes following her. She would feel his presence in every room. She stared at each framed photo. She walked to the TV and opened the drawer that harbored all the old movies. She pulled one from the drawer, inserted it into the DVD player, walked to the couch, and sat back down. *Casablanca.*

*****

Sleep evaded her. She had forced herself to the bed after crying over the movie. With covers a shamble, she put both feet on the floor and found her way through the now-clean kitchen to the back door. She sought the softness of the cool summer night. It was there she could look up and see the stars.

Jasmine sat on the porch steps and remembered a particular night she had sat with her grandmother on that special back porch of the home where she had grown up. They had been sitting together wrapped in her grandma's favorite quilt.

"This is where I come to sit when I need to feel close to your mother," Ellie had said.

Tonight, Jasmine needed both her mother and her grandmother. She wanted to feel their embrace. She needed so desperately to hear their soft, soothing words. She stood up from the steps and walked back into her bedroom. She gently took the quilt her grandma had given her, walked back to the porch, wrapped herself in it, and sat down. She could almost hear her grandma's words from that long-ago night.

"When things seem lost, Jasmine," her grandma had said, *"you must breathe in faith and breathe out trust. Faith and trust are the bottom line. It's where the rubber meets the road."*

Jasmine once again gazed at the stars.

"I have to be still in the silence, don't I, God?"

The memory faded as the night grew darker. Jasmine was alone on those steps now. She could hear the ocean waves in the distance.

In a word, she felt "gutted." Like a fish out of water. No kind hand had caught her and flung her back into the deep so she could breathe again. She felt as if she were on a desert, a very dry terrain with no escape.

"Breathe in through your nose, sweet girl, and out through your mouth."

Faith and trust.

She did exactly that.

*****

Polly had decided it was time to go back to the beach. Jasmine needed her. And it was on that porch she found Jasmine early in the morning upon her arrival. Sitting wrapped up in Ellie's favorite blanket. She had promised Ellie years ago that she would always take care of her special garden. She would water it, pull up the weeds, and plant new seeds. And when she would start to sweat, she would say, "S——t fire!" She would do the same for Jasmine. She would give her water, put salve on her wounded heart, and give her a hope for the future. Yes, she would help the most beautiful flower in Ellie's garden, Jasmine, herself.

Polly went to Jasmine softly. She sat down beside her, not wanting to startle her. Jasmine had finally fallen asleep, propped up, alongside the guardrail. She slowly put her arm around Jasmine. Jasmine awakened.

"Polly!" she exclaimed.

"I'm here. I'm here."

"I didn't know you were coming."

"Neither did I." Polly took her in her arms. "I'm here to help you cry, as long as you want me to stay."

*****

Chapter 19

Jasmine and Polly walked arm in arm into the kitchen.

"All my senses ache, Polly. How can I move forward? How can I possibly unlove Andrew?"

Polly began to make coffee and listened to Jasmine.

"Who am I now?"

"A woman whose heart has been shattered, sweet girl. A woman who loved so intensely that the pain is almost unbearable," Polly replied.

"Have you ever loved that way, Polly?"

"I wish I could say that I have, but, no, I haven't."

"The hurt that follows isn't worth it, Polly."

"Oh, my child, I beg to differ. Loving like that is so very rare. You were blessed to have found it and lived it. It's special."

*****

So many different griefs accumulate into one solid core when someone close to you dies. Lover's grief. Mother's grief. Friend's grief...

And so it was with Allie. She went into seclusion. She needed a break. She needed a respite. She cried. She went to the mountains. She ached. She cried again. How could this have happened? It wasn't fair. They had it all. She took a deep breath. She knew she would have to return to the hospital soon, but for now, she would rest.

She was sitting on her front porch cabin swing one early morning, listening to the birds. It was a habit of hers to retreat to the woods when the pressure became too strong—away from hospitals and family awaiting bad news in emergency rooms. She sat there looking out at the woods. She heard the creek nearby, gurgling over the rocks, making its way to the waterfall not far from her cabin. Ducks always returned to the same little pond beyond that waterfall. She had read somewhere that ducks mated for life. Jasmine had told her she had come back to feed the babies after Andrew died.

Again, she thought of the unfairness of Andrew's death. He had found love. Jasmine and he were so happy together. Everything was perfect. Why? Why, indeed? She had a right to question, just like Jasmine and Mona. Not everyone knew all the memories that he and Allie had shared. They had proven that members of the opposite sex could, indeed, be friends—best friends.

He was her protector. She was his princess. He had told her he would always protect a princess. She remembered the growing up years before he had to go to military school. But Mona had done the right thing. Allie thought she would surely die then. But now she understood that some decisions a mother has to make breaks a lot of hearts.

She held her coffee cup in her hands. She sat back and let the memories explode in her mind. She remembered the night Andrew had come to her house and crawled through the bedroom window. His dad had been in one of his drunken moods, and Mona had scurried him out of the house telling him to go to Allie's.

He had looked around her room and said, "I'll sleep on the couch."

"You can sleep here," she had replied. "I'll go to the couch and tell Mom you're here."

Her mom had always understood what was going on and had told Mona that Andrew could come any time, day or night. That night had been one of those nights.

"I can't sleep in here!" he had exclaimed.

"Why not?"

"A pink room with a canopy bed?" He pointed to the corner right next to the bed. "And a Barbie dressing table?"

She had laughed at the expression on his face and had thought that he had just escaped hell itself—and his main worry was about sleeping in a canopy bed with a Barbie dressing table close beside it?

"Oh, simmer down, I'm not going to take pictures," she had answered him.

She didn't know if he was merely exhausted or if he just didn't think that fighting was a good idea with his best friend, before he actually fell into the canopy bed. He was asleep in seconds.

Tears rolled down her cheeks as she remembered. She got up from the rocking chair and walked into the cabin. She pulled her sweater around her a little tighter and slowly walked to the bookcase and pulled down a photo album from the shelf. She opened the album and found the photo she was looking for. She released it from the plastic backing, placed it in her pocket, and walked back to the porch. Evening was approaching. Soon it would be pitch-black dark. She didn't care. That's just how the woods reacted when the sun left the sky. No one ever came to this part of the woods. And darkness didn't scare her anymore. The cabin was "out of the way" with no disturbances. That's why she had offered it to Andrew and Jasmine when they both made the decision not to fight his illness. The prognosis had not been good, even with treatment. She had agreed with them, and they needed their privacy. They had accepted her offer.

She smiled. She was glad they had captured their moment in time here. It was the least she could do for Andrew. And Jasmine.

She thought, once again, of Andrew's protection of her, especially in his letters, when they corresponded as teens from his military school. He was always giving her advice about everything, especially when she had begun to date. At least, she had tried to date. But Andrew's words of wisdom about boys always kept whispering in her ear, "Not good enough." So she had become quite serious in her studies and became a doctor. She didn't know then that she would be the one who would have to tell him that he was dying. She didn't understand how such a man, such a hero that he was to her, could die. How could a man so strong and vibrant one year die the next? Men like him didn't just up and die!

She only hoped that one day she could get it right like Andrew and Jasmine. They were meant for each other. She continued to question, why God would take him away now. Of all times.

She sighed and decided to "bench" coffee and have wine "suit up." She would open the bottle of wine she had purchased on the way up to the cabin. Again, she went into the cabin and opened the wine, not bothering to retrieve a glass. She resolved to drink it straight from the bottle.

She returned to the porch, thinking that she had been doing a lot of walking these past few days, especially in the woods. But that's what grieving people did. They walked around not knowing why they went into a particular room or down a particular path. They made wrong turns while driving their cars. And they got lost in the woods, as she had done only yesterday. She had followed the running water back to the cabin.

I learned to do that in Girl Scouts, she thought now. She was very glad to be back on her porch. Now that her protector was gone, she had to fend for herself.

She took her first gulp of wine and reached inside her sweater pocket, dragging out the photo she had plucked from the album. She smiled as she looked down at the picture.

"I lied, Andrew."

She touched that youthful face with her fingertip and took another gulp of wine.

He had been sleeping so soundly. She had gone over to the bed and pulled the pink coverlet close to his chin before snapping the picture. Andrew—in a canopy bed right next to the Barbie dressing table. He had never known. Tonight, this photo was more precious than ever. Tonight, she would sleep with that photo pressed inside the palm of her hand. She took another gulp of wine.

No one else would ever see the picture. There would be no frame for it. It was her treasure and her treasure alone. It was meant to be precious. It was meant only for her eyes. It was a part of her childhood, her life, forever to be cherished. Those innocent years that all too soon blended into adulthood where everything changed.

"Rest in sweet peace, my protector and dear friend. Rest in sweet peace."

She looked up at the darkening sky and asked God once again, "Why?"

*****

Mona sat on her balcony overlooking the ocean. Her face was expressionless. She was beyond questions. She had done everything a mother could do to protect her son, from birth and beyond. But she couldn't protect him from death.

Now she sat on her Adirondack chair not knowing what to do with her hands. Her Andrew. The one who fought so many battles and won had lost this one. The war inside her heart would rage on; of this, she was sure.

Losing a child. How does one even begin to cope with it? To survive it? She felt numb. The warmth of the sun didn't help. She thought about walking to the shore. The water would be somewhat cool. Maybe she would lie down in the surf and let people think she, too, was dead. That's how she felt.

She began talking to herself, "Anybody who loses a child should be able to do whatever crazy thing they want to do."

Still, she sat. She didn't think she could move, anyway.

She wanted to be alone.

"But Andrew wouldn't want that," she whispered. "He would want me to put on my sparkly earrings, go get his Jasmine, and do anything other than sitting here, wondering if I will ever walk anywhere again."

She knew sleep would not come tonight again. She had listened to tapes of soothing earth sounds to try and help her doze off. She had opened the windows to her bedroom and listened to the ocean's midnight rumblings. She had walked a thousand miles inside her four walls and slammed a hundred doors. Still, it all came back to one thing. A hollow hole inside her heart.

The one thing she should have done she had not done. She couldn't find the strength to do it. She didn't even think she could.

She was so mad at him. But she knew that she would eventually. It was her only hope. She picked at her fingernails. She took cold showers. She thought about adopting a dog. She walked the malls and purchased things she didn't need, things she would never wear, picture frames that made her cry. Her stomach ached, but her new kidney kept on working. She was grateful for that.

She decided to go to Jasmine. It was time. They would go together to do the one thing that could start the healing of their mutually broken hearts. They would pray.

*****

Mona pulled into Jasmine's driveway. It was early, too early. She was probably still in bed. She hoped she was sleeping better than her. She decided to wait in the car. She began to twiddle her thumbs.

"This is crazy! I'm going to take a morning walk!"

She took the earring box from her glove compartment, opened it, and put the earrings on her ears. She opened the car door, put her feet one at a time on the pavement, and began her walk to the white sand of Sarasota.

*****

The house was not empty. Jasmine was there. She wanted to make it pretty. She had to make it pretty. Macaroni salad. She had boiled the "elbows" al dente. The pasta was cooling. She began slicing the celery and took the frozen peas out of the refrigerator. Too much green. She needed some orange. She put the carrots on the counter and nodded her own approval. Yellow and red peppers were next. It was going to be pretty. She demanded it.

She had been in therapy for a few months now. She kept hearing the counselor say, "Do something different from what you shared together. Put new pictures in old frames."

"Something different?"

She found the onion in her cabinet.

"Andrew hated onions."

She began to peel the sweet onion. It became an irritant to her eyes that were already tearing. She would do something different. She would add onion to her old frame. A new picture. She could hardly wait to tell her therapist about the successful attempt to move forward. She sat on the kitchen chair in that big kitchen of hers, staring at her now pretty salad.

"Mayo, I need mayo." That's different too. Andrew didn't like stickiness on his fingers. He didn't like mayo—just salt and pepper.

She took the mayo from the refrigerator, scooped a big spoonful out of the jar, and plopped it in the middle of the macaroni.

"Bring out the Hellman's, and bring out the best," she whispered to the bowl.

She knew she was doing strange things at 6:00 a.m. But people who were in the throes of grief did do strange things. Her therapist told her so. It must be true. Therapists were always right. Right? It all seemed surreal—trying to revitalize her body and her thoughts through such pain.

She walked to the window. She could feel the breeze coming from across the ocean. Echoes of memories came flooding through her mind as the waves crashed in the distance. Just when her tears threatened to fall, there was a knock on the door.

*****

She opened the door. It was Allie.

"I know it's early, but something told me not to wait, *to come now—*"

"Come in! Come in!" Jasmine exclaimed. "I never sleep, anyway." Jasmine held wide the door for Allie to enter. Jasmine attempted conversation. "I was just doing something 'out of the ordinary,' something different—something the therapist told me to do."

Allie followed Jasmine into the kitchen. The onion lay half peeled, half sliced on the cutting board. Allie looked at Jasmine. She saw both sets of tears. They seemed to be blending—one from a broken heart, the other from the half-peeled onion.

"You need to light a candle before you start peeling an onion."

Jasmine simply obeyed. Blinking back tears, she walked into the bedroom, retrieved a candle, and handed it to Allie.

Allie smiled sympathetically, placed it in front of the onion, and lit it. She looked at Jasmine and took her by the hand.

"Come sit."

She pulled out the chair for Jasmine. Jasmine sat. That's what grieving people do too. They follow the leader who has just walked into the kitchen, the one looking more in control. The one who would quite possibly have a plan. She needed a new plan. She needed a new leader, somebody to lean on.

She looked into Allie's eyes and saw how much she had loved Andrew too. She wondered if this woman was as strong as Andrew had taught her to be. She wondered if they could hold each other up when they cried together. She wondered if she should boil water. This was a crisis. That was what they did in *Gone with the Wind.* Allie took Jasmine's hands in her own and said, "Let's talk."

*****

"It's true that Andrew was my protector, whether it was in person when we were growing up or through the multitude of letters and postcards we wrote to each other through his military school stint. He always sent me funny cartoons while working my way through medical school and beyond."

Jasmine smiled.

"I remember when he came to me and asked me to become his doctor," Allie whispered. "I didn't know if I could do it, being a friend and all."

Allie sighed.

"He looked at me and told me that he didn't realize what a prophet he had been back in the day when he told me he would have to strip in front of me. We both laughed. I told him it might seem a little weird to me, but he insisted that I should be his doctor. He told me that I was the only one he would trust."

"He cared for you very much."

"He was the brother I never had."

Jasmine nodded.

Suddenly, out of nowhere, Allie said, "Let's walk the beach."

No answer was needed as both women walked to the door and down the path to the ocean. They walked along the ocean's edge, not noticing the woman sitting on the beach chair with the sparkly earrings.

*****

"Andrew loved those little birds, running along the shoreline," Jasmine said, pointing to the sandpipers who were escaping the waves that tried to catch them unaware on their delicate, tiny feet.

"He loved all types of animals and birds. He always looked at them as being defenseless in a way. He always cheered for the underdog and was a defender to those weaker than himself." Allie agreed.

"I know."

"He was so tenderhearted beneath that rough exterior of his," Allie said softly.

The two continued to walk. They didn't notice the woman who had gotten up from the beach chair and had begun to walk discreetly behind them. She kept her distance, not wanting to disturb their conversation. Allie stopped.

"Was this where it happened?"

This was the spot that was engraved upon Jasmine's heart. "How did you know?" Jasmine asked.

"He told me at his last appointment with me."

Both women looked out at the cresting waves.

"He wanted me to know that he was going to be okay. That he had done it. That he was ready to die." A wave built up in the distance. Both women looked at the crest surging toward them. Jasmine spoke. "Yes, this is the exact spot."

"Where he experienced the baptism of a lifetime?"

"Yes, it was quite dramatic for the both of us," Jasmine answered.

"Thank you," Allie said.

"It was a plunge into the deep that I rejoiced in getting so wet."

Allie looked at Jasmine. "I prayed for Andrew all the time that he would open his heart."

"He did."

And then they cried. It was then and only then that Mona walked over to the two and put her arms around them both.

"It's time we all grieved together, don't you think?"

Mona grasped the hands of both Allie and Jasmine.

"Where two or more are gathered," she began.

And then they prayed.

*****

The three women walked back to the house and choked down the macaroni salad with not enough mayo and too much onion. There was silence.

"People eat weird things when they grieve," Mona said. She wiped her hands with her napkin. "But you did make it look pretty."

For some reason, they all laughed. They couldn't help it. Tears and laughter just seemed to go together at that particular moment.

"I feed the ducks for you every time I go to the cabin." Allie volunteered.

"Let's go outside." Jasmine smiled. They took their cold drinks out to the patio and sat down. Mona looked at Jasmine.

"Andrew told me that one day you might meet another man just like him—a man with ghosts to chase, a man that might not be able to share certain things—just like when he was a 'runaway' man." She took Jasmine's hand in hers. Allie watched them both intently. "He was grateful that you had been the strong one—you never gave up on him, even when he disappeared. He asked me to tell you that if, indeed, you meet another man like him 'down the road' a bit *to try* to 'bring him out' like you did with him. He told me he fell in love with you when you asked him to allow you to see the hidden part of his heart that no one else had seen."

Mona sat back in her chair and sighed.

"His exact words were to 'try like the dickens.' He said that when certain ghosts were faced, you would have a relationship that would be as strong, if not stronger than the one you and he had."

Mona cleared her throat and leaned into Jasmine, taking her hands again. "Jasmine, he told me to tell you to fall in love again."

"That won't happen."

Mona leaned back in her chair. "He also said you would say that."

"It won't happen," Jasmine repeated. "Andrew was the love of my life. You never forget that. Not in a lifetime—not ever."

All three women talked into the wee hours of morning until their tears became dry. And all three women hoped for the dream of seeing Andrew's face just one more time. Not to be.

Chapter 20

Memories are strange bedfellows. Some are kind. Some make you smile. Others become nightmares. You wade through them. Sometimes you crash over them. After Mona and Allie had left, that was all Jasmine could think about. Memories. She sat there, numb. Her eyes traveled around the room when she suddenly remembered the secret place she and Andrew had built together to keep their "valuables" and cash—a place where no burglar could find.

"I wonder," she began as she started walking toward the bathroom where the secret place was located.

She bent down, looking under the cabinet. There it was, still there. No one had found it. She remembered Andrew saying it would probably be there long after they were gone. She hadn't looked in the box since Andrew had told her about his cancer. She had "bigger fish to fry," as Andrew used to say. She had a battle to fight.

She slid the box out of its place. One piece of paper fell to the floor. She took the paper to the living room, sat down, and began to read.

> My dear wife, my Jasmine. I have loved you since the first time I ever set eyes on you. We were really something, weren't we? By the time you read this, I will have made my way to heaven, and I am waiting for you to arrive one special day. I am saving your seat. Count on it. You will be wearing your sparkly earrings, and we will be

dancing well into the midnight hour—but then again, you always told me there were no clocks in heaven. I don't know how you always knew that, but I can tell you now I always believed you. You always said it with such conviction!

My darling wife, I have a favor to ask of you. Promise me in your prayers that you will move on with your life. I want you to do that. I know it will be hard forgetting me… (Yes, I am still full of myself!) I know you're smiling. Please continue to smile. That was the smile that made me become as a moth to a flame. It will attract others, I know. There are many moths flying around out there—wanting to get near the light. (Stop rolling your eyes.) Seriously, Jasmine, keep moving, find your way, and step into the future that God has planned for you, never to harm you, rather to give you hope and a future. (Remember when you used to read me that scripture?)

Do it now, Jasmine, for me. Always keep the joy that I hear in your voice. My heart lights up every time I hear it. Live each moment, and don't forget to feed the ducks. Those babies are probably grown by now. I love you. Move on. I'll be waiting for you.

Love, Andrew

Fresh tears filled Jasmine's eyes. Her Andrew. Wasn't it just like him to write a note, and wasn't it just like him to know her so well that he would know where to put it? He knew all along she would eventually go to that secret place. She would find it. Their connection had been that extraordinary. Their love never to be replicated. He was always writing notes. He even tried poetry—the "roses are red, violets are blue" kind.

Her little romantic, she had called him. But he was far from little. He was a big man with a voice as big as Texas. Her gentle giant. That's why it was so difficult to accept that a man such as he could fall so quickly and fade so rapidly. But only from her sight. Never her heart. Never her memories. Never.

Jasmine sat up a little straighter in her chair. Before she folded the note that had been so carefully written, she saw the tiny smudge at the very end. It was a stain. Yes, a stain. A tearstain. She knew. It had dropped there. He had cried. And now her tears were dropping in the exact same spot, mingling with his. Those tears would link in memory of a love never to be forgotten. Tears that would eventually find their way to an ocean of photographs yet to be taken. Andrew was gone, and a certain light had left her life. Only the shadow of his smile remained.

She retrieved the last tissue from the box and made the only promise she could keep.

"I can promise you I will feed the ducks. And, yes, the babies are all grown up."

*****

The days went by in a blur after Mona and Allie had said their goodbyes. Mona did not live far away and visited often, but the grief became its strongest at nighttime. Her body craved calmness. She drank Sleepy Time tea before bed. Didn't help.

Slowly she took little steps. She moved her fingers. Then her toes. She took deep breaths. She began doing little things. She looked in the mirror. She brushed her teeth. She fried an egg. She talked to the birds. She forced herself to lie in the bed that she and Andrew had shared. She found the smell of him still there. She didn't want to change the sheets.

She couldn't get the coffeepot off her mind. It was special. A time of quiet in the morning. A time of being together before the racket of the day began. She carried it to the curb with thoughts of buying a smaller one—one with no memories attached. Another goodbye.

She went back into the house, sat on the couch, and decided she didn't want anyone else drinking from that pot. She went back to the curb, got a shovel, and buried it. Seemed fitting at the time. Yes, she continued to learn that a person does strange things in the middle of grief. And that was okay. She determined to herself that she had to sort things out one day at a time. And if buying a smaller coffeepot was one of them, then so be it.

She muddled and mumbled through most days, and when another night threatened to loom over her, she forced herself back to the bed. She kept wanting the couch, but her feet always took her back to the bed. She thanked God every night for making it through another day. That's what Jasmine's life had become.

Just when she thought she had survived, the *other* goodbyes began to stare her down. Those *other* goodbyes hit her hard. Those were the mighty sucker punches that came out of nowhere with no signals of warning. They just happened. One by one, everything Andrew had touched disappeared. His shoes. His shirts. His golf clubs. His fishing poles. One by one, those goodbyes came and went.

She walked the beach, gazing at the tiny seabirds. Still there. She touched her toes to the surf and fell to her knees in the sand—the exact spot where she and Andrew had stood, confessed, and laughed. On her knees, she remembered the wave that had crashed over them, throwing them on the white sandy beach. They had clung to each other.

She remembered it all. Now she was alone. The waves continued their journey to the shore. The birds continued their dance in the sky, diving into the water, and circling back to the white clouds hanging overhead. The sandpipers remained ever so fleeting in their mad dash to escape the oncoming waves. Did they have a sense of impending danger?

She looked all around her. Everything was the same except her heart. She couldn't find it. The very core of her being had been shattered. She looked at the wide expanse of the beach. And it was on that beach months later that she made a decision.

She had to leave. A certain power began to infiltrate her very core. She would do it. She would leave. She would blend her past with her future. It would just take time. It would take time for her present to catch up with her future, and the blending would be difficult. But she would fight back. After all, she came from good stock. Her dad had been a fighter. He had been a Marine. Once a Marine, always a Marine. And his blood flowed through her veins.

Meanwhile, back in Brooksport Village

Jake couldn't sleep. He turned on his side and looked at the clock on the nightstand. Two o'clock in the morning. He wasn't used to not being able to sleep. Nothing worried him. He had the love of his life lying beside him. He was in a place he loved. He remembered the first time he had set foot in Brooksport Village. He smiled as he thought of Trudy. He couldn't believe his eyes when he first saw her—a woman dressed in purple eating extracrispy doughnuts.

He turned and looked at Kate sleeping soundly beside him. Yes, he had it all now. Life was good. So why was he wide awake at 2:00 a.m.?

He placed both feet on the floor and walked from the bedroom into the living quarters of Open Door. He looked into the dining area where Kate had carefully set the table for the early morning risers—the ones who took towels and blankets to the beach to save their seats.

Open Door was flourishing. The infamous bed-and-breakfast had become one of the main tourist attractions in Brooksport Village. Kate had made it so. She had survived so much in her lifetime. Losses had made her stronger. Storms had given her a resilience that could never be denied. And love had finally come full circle to claim both their hearts.

He walked over to the kitchen window, turned on the outside lights, and peered out at the lake. So peaceful. The bleeding hearts in Kate's garden were in full bloom. He looked at the bench and the bird feeder that seemed to feed more squirrels than birds. But that was okay with Kate. Oh, how she loved those squirrels! It all had to do with a man who had saved her life many years ago—Zack. Jake had been jealous of Zack for a short moment in time until he was told the whole story of how and why Kate had loved him so much. Now he was grateful for Zack. Because Zack had been the reason Kate had set down stakes in Brooksport Village. He would be forever thankful.

He walked out to the patio and looked up at the stars. "Whatever you're doing up there tonight, Zack, I thank you." He quickly reversed his prayer. "But God, I thank you first for that little rural New York church on New Year's Eve."

Yes, indeed, life was good for Jake now. He had quit running. He had helped Chip, the singer-songwriter down at the coffee shop to become a number one man in demand nationally with his number one hit "Hometown Girl" and many more that followed over the years.

He had friends from New York to Brooksport Village and all the area in between. But tonight, he was on edge. He didn't know why.

A shooting star streaked across the sky. Jake saw it.

Make a wish, he thought to himself.

But how could you improve on what his life was like now—perfect?

He couldn't.

He sighed, turned, and walked back into the kitchen. He poured himself a glass of orange juice, drank it, and went back into the bedroom. Kate was still sleeping. She and Trudy had things to do today after the breakfast crowd left for the beach. He had things to do too. He needed sleep.

But sleep did not come. Something was looming on the horizon, and it was not a beautiful sunrise. Jake's life was about to change, and it would be up to Kate whether it would make him or break him. Kate, loving Kate. Would she be the ever-compassionate one this time around?

"I don't really remember the day I first felt that all was not irremediably lost. Was it a child's smile that awoke me, or a sign of sadness exposed in a place I didn't want it seen? Or a sense of responsibility? Or had I finally given up on despair? Perhaps I was simply caught up again in the game of life."

(Anne Philipe)

Two years later…

Jasmine kept moving—one step at a time. She became malleable. She did not break. She did not crack. She had endured. She developed "garra." She had been forced to grow "claws." Claws to dig her feet in and hold on for dear life. Two years had passed. The decision to sell her house, well, she just couldn't make that a reality so quickly. She would also have a difficult time saying goodbye to Mona and all her friends. But she knew eventually she would have to face some hard realities—that a new beginning was going to force itself on her, whether she liked it or not.

She did not know about Brooksport Village *yet*—this little town that had survived many of its own mysteries, tragedies, and secrets. It had also endured the unexpected love stories that eventually ended happily.

The befuddled, bothered, and bewildered found refuge in this special town. And questioning minds found their answers.

A certain mending took place in that village town. Broken hearts that ventured there could be knitted back together by an unseen hand. Colors that were once black could be turned into a pastel, in spite of that dark thread that tried to weave itself between the soft yellows and greens when tragedy struck.

It was a town where people changed and became stronger. It was a town where people found a remnant of their life to hold on to as they kept moving forward into new scenery. It was a town that, when you arrived, you may not have known exactly where you were going; you just suddenly found yourself standing there, looking somewhat forlorn. You wouldn't know why you took the exit to Brooksport Village; you just, plain and simple, arrived one day. You would come to know down the road that an unseen hand had led you there. And you would never question it because you would be so glad that you came.

Jasmine would discover that town—the town that had lived through such grief as hers. It was only a matter of time. Little did she know that hundreds of balloons floating toward the sky would lead her down a path and through the door of Belle's Bakery.

The town waited as the mystery of the whats, whens, wheres, and whys began to unfold for her. There would be answers to all the questions that had sifted through her mind while she had sat on the white sandy beach of Sarasota.

PART 3

IN FLIGHT

"Faith is the bird that feels the light and
sings when the dawn is still dark."

(Rabindranath Tagore)

Chapter 21

Jasmine had asked Allie if she could stay at the mountain cabin before deciding what her next move would be. Allie did not hesitate, told her where the spare key was, and reminded her to feed the ducks. She was grateful for Allie, giving her this quiet respite where she could think clearly.

"Two years?" she questioned.

Andrew would be encouraging her to move forward. He told her that in the note. She didn't want to believe it, but it was true. She needed to hydrate her parched heart. She had to make some decisions. She jumped up, walked into the small kitchen, gathered some bread, walked out the door, and headed for the pond. The ducks were waiting.

*****

"I need to do something! What do you think I should do?"

She threw the breadcrumbs on the water. The ducks did not disappoint. They swam to her, quickly.

"Great"—she sighed—"I'm asking the advice of ducks!"

She looked up at the sky.

"What?" she again questioned.

She sat there for quite a while feeding those ducks and looking at the sky. She heard the rustle of the leaves. She felt the breeze on her face. She listened to the small waterfall in the distance.

"I cannot watch *Casablanca* one more time with a box of tissues on my lap! I need to regroup! I need to transition. It's time."

It was there in the mountains by that little pond that the first step was taken in her mind. Change was imminent. She knew it. She felt it. She was moving. The beach house by the ocean was on the market. She couldn't live in Allie's cabin. She had to move forward to a new beginning. She had the finances to do it. Andrew had made sure of that. She didn't know where she was going. She only knew she had to go.

She gathered the now-empty bag of crumbs in her hands.

"Goodbye, my friends. I'm passing the torch to Allie."

With that, she turned and walked away.

*****

With the mountain cabin behind her, Jasmine returned to her beach house only to pack the essentials for the road to nowhere in particular.

She remembered the conversation with the realtor.

"Sell it 'as is.'"

"Furniture and all?" the realtor questioned.

"Yes."

Major decision—done. She was ready. There would be hotels she could stay in before she would find where her heart would lead her. She became a woman on a mission but still fighting the memories. One day, she would be at peace with those memories. One day, she would find a certain solace in the very things that made her so sad in the present. One day, the smiles would return.

She drove down the highway remembering what her grandma used to tell her.

"You have to have grit, girl. Sometimes life is hard, and we don't like what is happening one bit, but God and grit will get you through."

Jasmine held tightly to the steering wheel.

She kept saying over and over two words, True grit.

And so she continued to drive toward her future with a gritty faith—a faith that would lead her to a little town, a town that knew how to grieve and heal with the best of them…

*****

Jasmine didn't know how long she had been on the road until her stomach began to growl. The exit sign for Carsonville caught her eye. She turned the car signal on and followed the exit into town. Immediately she was intrigued. She parked her car and looked around for a restaurant.

It seemed to be a quiet little town. A sidewalk sale was just packing up, and the sun was setting as she walked the street, looking for a place to eat. She discovered a family restaurant at the corner of town just across from a country bar and grill, featuring a sign, "Dancing on Thursday Night—Live Band!" It looked interesting. She ordered her food and gazed at the country bar again. It was Thursday.

"Well, I have to start somewhere," she told herself.

She took a bite of her sandwich and looked out at the sunset. It was a good view from there, on the edge of town.

There was just something about sunsets. The end of a day. The end of a chapter and a life, as she once knew it. She and Andrew used to watch the sunsets while sitting in the lanai of the house he had purchased. Those were the good days. She wondered if she would ever look at a sunset in the same way ever again. But this one seemed to touch a spot in her that had her thinking that just maybe she would be able to do that.

She left the restaurant and found a small hotel. She decided to stay in Carsonville for a while. She checked in and put what clothing she had brought with her in the small closet. She felt anxious. She sat down on the bed and looked out the window. She remembered the sign at the country bar, "Dancing on Thursday Night." She needed to stomp something. She decided that dancing was the thing to do. What better place to stomp than on a country bar dance floor with a live band?

There were some surprises ahead for Jasmine. Those surprises would come on a wing and a prayer when she least expected them. She didn't know it yet, but her pivotal moment would come in this little town called Carsonville, fifteen miles south of Brooksport Village. And it would be on the dance floor.

Meanwhile, in the not-so-sleepy town of Brooksport Village…

Chapter 22

While sitting on his porch, Gordy saw it—an inchworm. Amazing how keen your senses become when someone so close to you dies. It had been years, but he still felt the pain; he still could feel the chronic ache, especially when it came to celebratory times, like today.

He'd never thought about inchworms before, and today, he was analyzing them. His gaze did not leave that tiny worm's progress. It was maneuvering its way across the porch floor. He watched it as it worked so laboriously toward its goal—whatever that goal was.

"I wonder if inchworms think," he asked himself.

Inch by inch, that little worm made its way to the edge of the porch only to fall into the grass below.

"Oblivion?" Gordy asked. "Or inchworm heaven?"

He got up from his front porch swing and took his own "inch" walk toward his living room door.

Ever so slowly, it seemed he was continuing to trudge his way through the grief he thought he had left behind. He felt like the slowest fish in the ocean—a seahorse. What had the therapist said, "grief bursts," they come on you when you least expect them, and today was one of those days.

Today was his birthday. And he was watching inchworms and thinking of seahorses—of all things. "I'm really losing it!"

Suddenly, from around the corner, she appeared. "It's celebration time!" Trudy exclaimed. "Ted and I will pick ya up at seven o'clock! We're goin' to Carsonville for the night!"

"Carsonville?" Gordy questioned.

"Yep, Carsonville! Tonight, you're gonna dance!"

Trudy marched into the house waving a gift in the air, wrapped in birthday paper. Gordy sighed but followed her into his house.

"Trudy, I am not going anywhere tonight!"

She walked into the kitchen and opened the cabinet, taking out the whisky bottle and two glasses. "Oh yes, you are, cowboy! And you're gonna wear what I brought ya in this package!" She poured two shots, gave Gordy one, toasted him, and said, "Drink up! The party starts *now*! Happy birthday!"

*****

"Trudy, really?"

"Yes, really! Come on, Gordy! Do something silly and fun for a change! It's your birthday! Try it on!"

"I'll try it on. But I'm not wearing this!"

It was green. A green shirt. With green twinkle lights.

"Don't look at me as if I've grown horns, Gordy! And don't be a ninny! You're wearin' that shirt tonight!"

Gordy knew better than to argue with Trudy. He sighed and went into the bathroom to try on the ridiculous shirt.

"Come on out of that bathroom, cowboy! You've been in there long enough! Let me see you!" Trudy exclaimed.

Gordy walked out into the living room, where Trudy stood, sipping her drink. "I'm going to need another drink before I wear this anywhere, Trudy." Gordy moaned. Trudy obliged and poured another shot. "How do these lights twinkle?" he asked.

"I knew you would fall in love with it! Turn around." Trudy laughed. She searched near the hem of the shirt. "Here it is!" She flicked a tiny switch that was secured just under the fold, and those green lights began to twinkle, on and off, on and off. Just then Ted walked in.

"Nice," he said. "I'm not wearing this, Ted."

Ted shook his head. "So *you* say. Trudy says differently."

Trudy walked into the kitchen, retrieved another glass for Ted, and poured him a shot. "We'll be back to pick you up at seven, sharp, Gordy," Trudy began. "Be ready, and if you don't have this shirt on, I will dress you myself."

Ted downed his drink.

"Better do it, bro," Ted whispered over his shoulder before leaving with Trudy. "You know that's not a threat. It's a promise."

*****

Gordy knew she meant well. What was the harm? Make Trudy happy. Maybe it was time he got out and did some celebrating. Had a little fun. It had been years. He finally surmised, if he didn't do as Trudy requested, she would be trotting up his driveway with another casserole. And frankly, he was tired of pizza casserole. Or, heaven forbid, she just might attempt to dress him herself. It was only Carsonville after all. Not a fancy place. He would fit right in. He would wear the shirt.

*****

They arrived promptly at 7:00 p.m. Trudy was delighted when Gordy walked out of the house, donning the green shirt. They walked into the country bar just as the band was warming up. Trudy chose a table in the back corner of the bar because Gordy insisted. She would have preferred the front, where the music was good and loud, but she conceded. After all, he had worn the shirt. Tit for tat.

"I won't look so obvious back here," he told Ted.

Ted laughed. "Don't count on it. Not for what Trudy has planned."

Gordy turned to Trudy. "Don't you dare tell that band it's my birthday!"

Trudy looked smug. "Why would I do that?"

*****

Half an hour later, Jasmine walked through the double doors, immediately feeling out of place. How exactly would she go about meeting new people? How should she act? A woman alone in a country bar and grill with a live band? What in the world had she been thinking? She refused to run for the door. She had come this far.

"Walk in like you own the place," she reminded herself. Then she thought the place was probably full of "locals." Everyone would stare at her. Still, she summoned her courage and walked to the bar.

"I'll have a pale cosmo."

The bartender looked at her.

"Why the strange look?" she questioned him.

"What exactly is that made with?" he asked.

"Plain vodka and a mere splash of cranberry juice. A little triple sec."

"I can handle that," he said, walking off to make the drink.

She felt like a dunce. Of course, he was unsure about a "pale cosmo." This was a country bar and grill. She should have ordered beer, on tap.

He brought her drink and sat it on the counter. "Just guessing you're not from around here?" he questioned.

She couldn't help herself. She laughed. "What was your first clue?"

He gave her a wink and went to take care of other customers. Well, at least she had given him a new drink to add to his bar list—for city folk, when they sauntered into his bar. She took a sip. Strong. Well, she needed strong. This was her first night out in years. She slowly turned to look at the crowd. Dancers were on the dance floor. She was much relieved to see no one was staring at her, as she had imagined. She still thought of that imaginary big black *W* on her forehead. It seemed she was the only one who saw it. Nobody knew her or her story, and she didn't know them. It was better that way.

Her gaze went to the trio in the back corner of the bar. Two men and a woman. What was that on that man's shirt? Was the drink already making her see things? No, it was lights. Small lights, twinkling. What in the world?

It was then the band began to play "Happy Birthday" and pointed to the trio.

Oh, that explains it, she thought. It was a birthday celebration, and she ordered another drink.

She and the bartender became instant buddies after a few cosmos. She hadn't laughed in a long time. Tonight was a start. Then, again, maybe it was just the drinks. They did seem to get better and better as the night wore on.

"I think I shall be recklessly brave and go ask the birthday boy to dance," she said, looking at the bartender.

"Whatever happens here stays here," he replied. "Go for it."

Jasmine walked over to the trio, looked at the man in the green twinkle shirt, and asked, "Care to dance, birthday boy?"

The woman with him nearly pushed him out of his chair.

"Of course, he would love to dance!"

Gordy suddenly found himself on the dance floor with Jasmine. He knew she had been drinking some pink drink and a lot of them. He had watched her since she walked into the place. He thought that she could be trouble, but he finally eased into the dance and began to enjoy himself. After the dance, Jasmine thanked him and went back to the bar. He went back to the table where Trudy and Ted waited.

"Well?" Trudy asked

"Well, what?"

"Did you like it?"

"Stop it, Trudy! It was one dance."

Just then a slow dance was beginning. Jasmine walked back toward Gordy.

"Oh, here she comes again! Keep those twinkle lights glowing, Gordy!"

"Stop it, Trudy!"

"I'm not doin' a thing! I'm just sittin' here!"

Jasmine held out her hand to Gordy, and he took it.

"Well, I'll be!" Trudy said, grabbing Ted's hand. "Let's go spyin'! See if we can hear what they're sayin'!"

Ted held Trudy tightly and whispered in her ear, "The night was made for lovers, eh, Trudy?"

*****

Trudy was an excited mess as they drove back to Brooksport Village. "Well, did you get her name? Did you get her phone number? Did you—"

Gordy interrupted her. "None of the above."

"What? Why not?"

"I'm out of tune when it comes to this dating stuff, Trudy."

Trudy sighed. "Well, there'll be other dances. Keep that shirt in your closet. Keep changing the battery. Take care of it. Maybe the two of ya will meet up again someday. She'll remember the twinkle lights if nothing else."

*****

Gordy sat on his porch for a long time after Trudy and Ted dropped him off. Maybe he should have gotten her number. At least her name. Yes, he was out of tune. He was feeling a little like the inchworm. He walked over to the corner where the little worm had fallen after his long journey.

"Where are you, little fella?"

Inch by inch, Gordy was moving forward. He went inside and walked into his bedroom. So many pictures of Jessie in frames. So many tearful memories he still faced. Was it time to take the photos down? Put them in a photo album? Get them out once in a while and look at them? Slowly he began to take the pictures from their frames. She would want him to do this. He kept the photos of little Sam on the fireplace mantle. He missed them so much. But it was time to move inch by inch—forward. It would be a difficult journey—just like the slow crawl of that persistent little inchworm. But he vowed not to fall off somewhere into oblivion.

He tucked all the photos of Jessie in a plastic sleeve and put them in the drawer of the bedside table. He would buy photo albums tomorrow. He lay on his bed looking at the empty frames. He raked his hands through his hair and sighed. He stood and walked to the mirror, looking at the green shirt he still wore—the green shirt with the twinkle lights. He took off his clothes and hung them in the closet. He walked back to the bed and gazed at the empty frames once again. New pictures would have to fill them. If he had only learned one thing from his birthday bash, he had learned it was time for a new beginning. Old frames, new pictures.

*****

The next morning, Jasmine went back to see her bartender buddy. The bar was actually open. She sat on the same stool where she had sat the previous night.

"Lookin' pretty 'pale' this mornin', cutie."

"You know my grandmother always used to tell me, 'Pretty is as pretty does.'"

"And you don't feel pretty after last night?"

"No. She would have been real upset with me." Jasmine sighed. "She would have boiled a lot of water, that's for sure. That's what she always did in time of crisis."

The bartender smiled. "Well, I think you need a Bloody Mary. It'll clear your head. Always have 'em on special the day after our big dance of the week."

"I really think I just need a ginger ale, please."

He brought her ginger ale with lots of ice and placed it on the counter.

"I really blame it on the green twinkle lights on his shirt. Do you know him?"

The bartender knew exactly of whom she spoke. "Can't say that I do. Haven't seen him around here at all."

"Too bad, I feel I owe him an apology."

"Nope. He's probably thinking about you right now. Did he get your number?"

"No."

"Poor man, he's probably kickin' himself."

"I doubt that."

"I don't."

He walked off to wait on new customers entering with bloodshot eyes ordering their Bloody Marys.

Jasmine sipped her ginger ale. "Him" and "he" was all she knew about "him." Mr. No Name. She hadn't even asked his name. But then he hadn't asked hers either. She vaguely remembered someone saying something as she was leaving. Some nice woman had walked her safely back to her hotel room. Who was it? What had she said to her?

"Looks like Gordy is back to the land of the livin'."

That was it. What a peculiar thing to say, she thought. And what a peculiar name, Gordy—perhaps it was short for Gordon. Exactly who was that woman that had tucked her in last night?

"I'll lock the door behind me, sugar," was all she had said.

Purple. She remembered that woman wore a lot of purple.

"Weird, maybe I dreamed all that."

Green twinkle lights and purple. Really? She vowed never to drink another cosmo as long as she lived.

*****

Okay. Jasmine had gone back to the bar for her ginger ale and had watched all the people from last night order their Bloody Marys. All the time she was hoping no one recognized her as the maniac who danced with strangers—well, only one stranger. At least, nobody pointed at her. They were too busy shaking their own heads and questioning why they had done what they had done the night before. She was glad she had company—and that she had not been alone making a fool of herself.

Now it was time to explore the town she had stumbled upon due to her growling stomach. Was that only yesterday? Now was the time to apologize to anyone she might recognize as she walked the sidewalk. She hoped she had not offended anyone with her uncharacteristic behavior.

Honestly, what had happened last night? She had learned a lesson, for one thing—never to drink anything with the word *pale* in front of it. She remembered dancing with somebody. Of course, she did. She talked to the bartender no longer than thirty minutes ago about her mystery man. It seemed she had inherited more of her grandma's traits than she had realized. Now she had a mystery man too. Well, her mystery man had on a green shirt with twinkle lights. Had she really asked him to dance? She walked to a bench on the sidewalk and sat down.

"Yep, that's exactly what I did."

Sighing, she looked up at the sign on the retail shop directly in front of her: ANTIQUES.

Might as well go in and look around, she thought.

Jasmine truly got more than she bargained for inside the place that took her back in time. After the third floor of discovering the "pasts" of so many people, their possessions now discarded, she decided it was time to leave. She had bought nothing but had to admit she enjoyed the time she had spent there. Walking outside, she saw the manager, carefully placing a bowl of water on the sidewalk.

He looked up at her.

"For all the four-legged best friends who come to visit our fair town," he said.

"That's very thoughtful of you," Jasmine replied.

"What can I say? I'm a lover of dogs—cats too. Just seems that cats like the cooler indoors for their refreshment. They're more particular. They think they're royalty."

She smiled, remembering the cat lapping the cool water just inside the antique shop door. She actually pictured a crown on its head.

The shop owner was a kind, older man who had a knack of making people feel at home with him. Jasmine was no exception.

"Come sit with me for a spell, missy."

He pointed to the bench. "This old man needs to rest a bit—to get charged up for the evenin' rush."

Jasmine sat.

"Talk to me," he said.

"About what?"

"Anything. Good times you've had. Bad times you thought you would never get through. Joyful times when all your dreams came true. Anything. I like listenin'."

Jasmine looked in the eyes of that old man. "You've lived a lot of life, haven't you?"

He pointed to his chest and rubbed his hand over his face. "Oh, girlie, you wouldn't believe what this old heart has been through."

"I bet I would."

It was then he looked up at the sky. "Well, there they go again."

Jasmine followed his gaze, shielding her eyes from the sun. She had never seen so many balloons in her life. "I wonder what's going on over there. Does that place have a name?"

"Sure does. It's called Brooksport Village, 'bout fifteen miles north of here—not far."

"Have you ever been there?"

"Yep, I go up there with my grandson on some weekends. There's a fella there that owns a stable with horses. He lets young'ins come up there and ride those horses. Gives 'em lessons. Even lets 'em feed and pet those four-legged creatures. There's another man that works with the horses—a blind man. He has a 'reading hour' with the kids. He can't see to read, but he makes up his own stories to tell 'em. Those kids love that blind man!"

Jasmine smiled. "Seems you know a lot about that town."

"Pretty much."

Jasmine became lost in thought.

The old man kept looking at the balloons as they floated higher in the sky. "Crazy things happen in that town when people fall in love. Yep, ever since some New York executive came to that town, they've launched more balloons than I could ever count. Long and short of it is—he came, he left, he came back, he left again, he came back after 9/11 and left again—and then he came back for good. Seems he found his soul mate and couldn't forget her, after all his comins' and goins'. There's been balloons ever since. And not just on Memorial Day weekends. You ought to visit that town, missy. Just about ten minutes up the road, but then everything around here is just about ten minutes away."

He slapped his knees suddenly and said, "Time to get back to work, missy! Sure, enjoyed talkin' to ya!"

"You're all charged up now?" Jasmine questioned.

"Yep, plus I like sittin' beside pretty girls. I like to feed my ego thinkin' it makes my wife a little jealous. See ya on the flipside!"

Old and hep, Jasmine thought. He must have learned that "flip-side" thing from his grandson. Never too old to learn. She smiled and thought he must have been quite a character in his younger years. Probably still was.

She thought that his story probably ran pretty much parallel to hers, except when she turned to face the window both he and his wife were waving goodbye to her. He had his happy ending. She was alone. No Andrew.

*****

Jasmine found her way back to the family restaurant and ordered dinner. She vowed that tonight she would be a good girl. She would drink water, hydrate, and get to bed early. She would not be dancing with men who wore green shirts with twinkle lights, nor would she have women dressed in purple tuck her in bed and lock the door behind them. She would stay in her room and watch TV. Or she would go to the local bookstore after dinner, buy a mystery thriller, go back to her room, and read until the morning. Strange noises would not scare her in the dark. She would be locked in for the night. She would not go out to find more trouble for herself. She would quite simply "stay put."

Tomorrow she would have breakfast, get in her car, and drive fifteen miles north of Carsonville to another little town called Brooksport Village. One step at a time. One road at a time. One town at a time.

She remembered what her newfound friend had said.

"*Crazy things happen in that town when people fall in love.*"

Her curiosity was getting the best of her, not to mention all the balloons from just a few hours ago, that had floated through the sky. She thought that, just maybe, that little town had a story to tell; and she was in the mood for a good story. She was more than ready to hear about a happy ending. Maybe it was time she started believing in romance again. She decided to, at least, give it a second chance.

*****

It was more than ten minutes away. More like thirty minutes with all the windy roads and squirrels running in front of her car. She had never seen so many squirrels in her life. But she had never really looked for them either. Thankfully, she had missed hitting all of them. Even the ones that ran halfway across the road and changed their minds. Dumb squirrels. The sign told her when she had arrived: "Welcome to Brooksport Village."

It seemed simple enough once she was there. The village town appeared normal, if there was such a thing as normal anymore. And then she saw the woman going into a little bakery on the corner of the street—the woman dressed in purple. She had to follow her inside.

Belle was ready for Trudy's arrival.

"Hi ya, Trudy! How'd it go on Gordy's birthday? Did he wear the shirt?"

"Sure did." Trudy laughed. "I threatened to dress him myself if he didn't put it on!"

Belle laughed and put the doughnut dough into the fryer.

"Fresh oil, Trudy!"

"Gonna take these doughnuts and head down to the lake to reminisce that birthday night before openin' the salon."

"You don't reminisce unless something unusually exciting happened. Spill it, Trudy!"

Trudy began to tell the story about the woman who asked Gordy to dance when the welcoming bell rang on the door. Another customer.

Belle sighed and looked up. She wanted to hear the story. Trudy looked over her shoulder.

"Well, I'll be," Trudy whispered.

Belle poked her on the shoulder. "What is it?"

"The story just walked through the door."

*****

Jasmine took one look at Trudy, turned, and tried to walk away.

"No! No! Sugar! You come in here! I need to know your name! You may have gotten away from Gordy the other night without telling him, but you won't get away from me!"

Jasmine stopped in her tracks. This was the lady she thought she had dreamed about. She was real. She had not been hallucinating. Slowly, she turned.

"I thought I dreamed you," she said softly.

"Speak up, sugar. You're amongst friends here!" Trudy turned to Belle. "Give us two coffees, please, Belle. We'll take the corner table over there and share these doughnuts."

Belle obliged eagerly. She knew she would know the whole story soon. Trudy had a way about her that made people tell their story. It was about time they had some more excitement in this town. It had been quiet far too long.

*****

They sat at the corner table looking at each other. Jasmine looked at the floor.

"I'm sorry," she whispered.

"For what, sugar?"

"Dancing with your husband."

Trudy began to laugh hysterically. "You mean the man in the green twinkle light shirt?"

Jasmine nodded and finally looked up at Trudy.

"He's not my husband! He's a friend. It was his birthday, and I was bound and determined to get him out on the town. He's been cooped up at his ranch far too long!"

"Well, I'm sorry, anyway. I butted in where I shouldn't have during your own private celebration."

Trudy felt sorry for her. She took her hand. "No need to be sorry, sugar. No need at all. You brought that man back to life, if just for a few hours. I saw him on the dance floor and marveled at some of his 'moves.'"

Trudy continued, "You brought that man back to life, sugar." Trudy offered Jasmine a doughnut and continued talking, "But it's a long story. A long sad story for another time."

Jasmine was not so sure she should be here anymore. She didn't like sad stories. She had a whopper of her own she was still trying to deal with, regardless of how much time had passed. She should be back in her room reading her mystery thriller. She was questioning herself and her bright idea to explore this town by the lake.

"What's your name, sugar?"

"Jasmine."

"Like the flower?"

Jasmine's lips began to curve into a small smile.

"That's what I like to see!" Trudy let loose of her hand and scooted her chair closer to Jasmine. She took a sip of her coffee.

"Why did your mama choose the name Jasmine?"

"It means 'gift from God.'"

"And that's what she considered you."

"Yes, that's what she believed."

Tears were forming in Jasmine's eyes.

"Why are ya cryin'?"

"Because you're so nice—I mean tucking me in that night. Making sure I got home safely. Locking the door before you left my room. And now you're getting me to talk about my mother. I haven't been able to do that in a long time."

"Tell me your story, Jasmine."

"I don't really have a story," Jasmine whispered.

"Everybody has a story, includin' me," Trudy answered. "In fact, mine is still unfoldin'."

Jasmine felt she could actually talk to this woman. She just had a way about her. Kind of like the old antique store owner in Carsonville—only ten minutes away. Everything seemed to be only ten minutes away lately. That seemed to be how people lived in these small towns. It was either ten minutes away or just a little piece down the road.

"Maybe someday," Jasmine answered, "but my story is just life not turning out the way you planned."

"That's where new stories begin," Trudy said, squeezing her hand.

Jasmine took her first sip of coffee that was getting cold and looked at Trudy. "I like you."

"Most folks do."

Belle could not help interceding. "And that's the truth!"

Trudy drank the rest of her coffee and stood up. She changed the subject abruptly. "Why don't you come on down to my salon? I want to cut your hair!"

"Cut my hair? Whatever for? I like it the way it is!"

"I'm the best in the business, sugar. And believe me it's time for you to get a haircut!"

Jasmine looked at Belle as if to get her to plead her case.

"Whatever Trudy wants, Trudy gets. Best to learn that right from the start!"

"I'll just go down and set up the shampoo bowl and wait for you."

Even though Jasmine hesitated, she found herself asking, "Where is it?"

Trudy was running for the door. She was always in a hurry when it came to "doing" a new "do" on a new friend. And she felt Jasmine was going to be just that, perhaps even more—down the road—to a certain gentleman named Gordy. If she had her way, she was going to prove to herself once again how much she loved romance. Playing cupid was long past due.

"It's just down the street. You can't miss it. It's purple."

Jasmine looked at Belle. Belle smiled and winked. “Best be on your way, girlie. She’s right. You can’t miss it. But just in case you can’t see all the purple, it’s called Trudy’s Tresses and Tootsies.”

Belle had been right. There was no way on earth she would have missed Trudy’s Tresses and Tootsies.

*****

All that purple. But all Jasmine could think about was the kind lady beneath that purple who had seen her safely home and tucked her in, locking the door behind her. Surely, she could trust her with her hair.

She walked into the salon. Trudy had everything waiting.

“First, you go on over there and pick out the color you want for your fingers and tootsies.”

Trudy pointed to an array of pinks, reds, blues, yellows, and, yes, purples.

“Does everybody in this down obey you, Trudy?”

“Most.” Trudy ran her hands through her hair. “Except for Charlie—he could get sassy with me once in a while. He’s all grown up now. In school becomin’ a doctor. I’m prayin’ he comes back here to settle down. We need a good doctor just around the corner.”

Jasmine chose her color and took it over to Trudy.

“Figured as much, sugar. Pink.”

“What’s wrong with pink?”

“Nothin’, absolutely nothin’,” Trudy replied. She put the pretty pink polish on the counter and turned to Jasmine. “Now sit yourself down here. We’re gonna give you a new do.”

“Don’t get too carried away, Trudy.”

Trudy just smirked and began to wash Jasmine’s hair.

“How come you knew I needed a ‘fix,’ Trudy?”

“I can always tell when people like you come to town by their forlorn looks, sugar.”

Trudy became silent then, but her mind was going a mile a minute. This one was fragile, more fragile than Kate had been when she had arrived in Brooksport Village. *Handle with care, Trudy*, she reminded herself. *You don't want this little one to run like a doe, wet hair and all*—because that is what Trudy had pictured, if she pried too much.

"So what brings you to our fair little town?" Trudy asked.

"I saw some balloons."

"Ah, yes, the balloons."

"I was in Carsonville. I was walking out of an antique store and met a man who was putting a bowl of water down for all his four-legged friends. He's a lover of animals."

"I see."

"He asked me to sit down with him on the bench and started talking to me." Trudy began to rinse Jasmine's hair. "You kind of remind me of him, actually."

"How so?"

"When I sat down, he just said, 'Talk to me.'"

Trudy smiled as she began to towel off Jasmine's hair. "And did you—talk to him?"

"Yes, a little. He told me I wouldn't believe what his old heart had been through. He probably would have told me more, but that was when we saw the balloons."

Trudy began to cut Jasmine's hair.

"He told me that he comes up here with his grandson on some weekends, that there's a fellow who owns a stable with horses and a blind man that tells kids stories—some kind of 'reading hour' without the actual 'reading.' He said the blind man made up the stories and all the kids loved it."

Trudy began to smile. This fragile one was beginning to open up, and now she was talking about Gordy and didn't even know it.

"Then he told me that crazy things happen in this town when people fall in love. He said something about a New York executive that came to town and ended up staying after coming here, going back, coming here, going back. Anyway, it seemed he couldn't make up his mind to stay or leave."

Trudy remembered those days. She remembered them fondly. Seemed that old man in Carsonville knew a lot about the people in Brooksport Village. Well, what do you expect in small towns?

Everybody did know everybody's business. Trudy didn't mind. She kind of liked it. People were close.

"He said there had been balloons ever since that New Yorker came to town. He seemed to have started some kind of tradition."

Trudy plugged in the hair dryer and began to style Jasmine's new do.

"He told me I should visit this town. He said something was always happening here and that you all did a lot of celebrating and every time you celebrate something you launch balloons."

Trudy completed Jasmine's new hairstyle and gave her a mirror to look at the entire new look she had created. Jasmine took the mirror and gasped. She looked like a totally different person. But she liked it. She liked it so much she decided to change her fingers and tootsies polish to purple.

"Now you're talkin'!" Trudy exclaimed.

She motioned Jasmine to the footbath. Jasmine placed her feet in the warm water and began to think that this was the little town she needed. It seemed a certain type of healing balm had settled all around her. She felt peaceful.

She continued to talk to Trudy.

"So I decided to drive up here, take a look around, and see what you were celebrating."

"Well, I do believe that was our annual Memorial Day weekend balloon launch," Trudy replied.

"What else do you celebrate here other than holidays?"

"Weddings. We're a town that likes happy endings."

Jasmine's whole demeanor changed.

"You okay?" she asked Jasmine.

"It's just the word *wedding*."

"You have a broken heart, sugar?"

"You could say that."

Trudy decided there would be another time to talk about Jasmine's heart. She could still visualize that girl dancing on the dance floor with Gordy on his birthday, drunk as a skunk. She had a story. Yes, sir, she did. Trudy would find out just what it was, in time. For the time being, all she wanted to say was, "Well, sugar, you came to the right town. Brooksport Village has a reputation for mendin' broken hearts."

When all the "works" of hair, fingers, and tootsies had been done, Trudy stood back and admired her work.

"If you decide to stay in our little town for long, you may want to check out the Bed-and-Breakfast at the end of town. It's called Open Door. I know the owner."

Just then Kate walked through the door.

"Speaking of… Here she is now."

Trudy pointed to Kate.

"Jasmine, meet Kate. Kate, Jasmine."

*****

Jasmine left Trudy's salon and made her way to the Stumble In. She walked in and practically devoured the best burger in town. She thought that, yes, she would stay for a while. What else did she have to do? She decided to walk to the lake and then visit Open Door.

Arriving at the lake, she sat on a beach chair and thought about all the turns her life had taken. If anyone had told her she would be sitting on a lake beach today instead of wading in the ocean surf she loved so well, she would have laughed out loud. Her life had been near the ocean she loved. Her happy-ever-after had been with Andrew. And then it was all taken away. She was still pondering the question if she should stay in Brooksport Village or go back to Carsonville. She stood up and began to walk the path straight up to Open Door.

The closer she came to the bed-and-breakfast, she seemed more clear-minded than she had been for months. It seemed that she had recovered from her temporary anesthesia. Perhaps it was the air. Perhaps it was her new haircut or maybe the color of her newly painted nails. It didn't matter. She approached the front door and saw the note attached to the screen. "Come around back. I am in the flower garden."

She slowly walked to the back of the house and saw Kate sitting quietly on a bench in the middle of a sea of bleeding hearts.

Kate looked up. She had a welcoming smile.

"Jasmine, come sit with me."

Jasmine walked over to the peaceful setting and sat down. It seemed everyone she met lately was asking her to sit down and talk.

"You looking for a room?"

Jasmine did not answer right away. She took deep breaths and kept looking out at the lake. She listened to the birds and saw a robin splashing happily in the birdbath.

Kate perceived Jasmine's hesitant spirit.

"I come out here a lot," Kate ventured to say.

"I can see why," Jasmine whispered.

"Many of my guests come out here at dusk. They like to watch the sunsets."

Jasmine smiled. She was feeling more and more serene and at peace. "Do you have a room?" Jasmine asked.

Kate stood and held out her hand. "I have one vacancy if you would like to see it."

"I'll take it—unseen," Jasmine replied.

There was just something about this place that intrigued her. Now that she had found it, she didn't think she wanted to leave it so fast. She would go back to Carsonville and collect her things. She didn't know how long she would stay, but she felt a certain calmness about this place that she needed for now. And for now, this is where she would hang her hat.

*****

Jasmine made the trip back to Carsonville to check out of the hotel. She wanted to say goodbye to the two friends she had made there. Funny, she didn't even know their names but considered them newfound friends. She surmised that, sometimes in life, it's the strangers you meet along the way who may lead you to roads unknown. The bartender whom she taught how to make cosmos and the old man whose heart had been through more than she would ever know had been those special strangers to her. Angels unaware.

*****

Trudy was cleaning up, closing down the cash register, and debating about going to the grocery store for some low-fat cat food for Buddy before going home. Buddy—that sweet, adorable, protective cat of hers—needed *low fat.*

Ted was coming by, and they were going out to dinner. She would check his pockets before he took one step into her house. No treats! Buddy wouldn't like Trudy's pat down of Ted, but it simply had to be done. Buddy was getting too fat. The vet told her so. And Ted was the reason. She already had to buy a ramp for Buddy to walk up to the couch instead of jump. She ought to make Ted pay for it. She had to make sure she got home before Ted showed up with his pockets filled to the brim.

She wondered if Jasmine had taken her up on going to Open Door. She was kind of proud of herself, holding back, not mentioning that Gordy was the man who actually owned the stable and horses—and the name had been changed to being Dude Ranch, not a stable.

"She'll know soon enough," Trudy told herself. "If I have my way, those two will be together by Christmas!"

*****

On her way home, Trudy decided she needed lard. It would be a quick stop.

"So what do ya think, Belle?"

"About what?"

"Jasmine, that's what!"

Belle began to fry up Trudy's extracrispy doughnuts. "Probably from the city," Belle answered.

"Sure enough!" Trudy exclaimed. Trudy took the fresh doughnuts, smiled, and said, "That girl has a story, Belle."

Belle knew Trudy was on the hunt. This was going to be interesting. "I've been waiting for you to get back here and tell me what is going on! You certainly took your own good, sweet time!"

Trudy leaned into Belle and whispered, "Well, as you already know, it all started when Ted and I took Gordy out for his birthday."

Belle leaned closer to Trudy, wanting to know *all.* "Yes, go on!"

Trudy took one of the doughnuts out of her bag and took a bite.

"This Jasmine girl, this fragile one with the forlorn look?" Belle waved her on to continue. "This is the one that walked up to Gordy and asked, 'Hey, ya wanna dance?'"

Trudy turned and walked to the door. Before leaving, she looked over her shoulder and winked. Belle knew that wink all too well. Yes, siree, there was going to be some more matchmaking in this town. And it was high time there was! Belle could hardly wait for it all to begin. Whenever Trudy was involved, one could rest assured there would be fireworks.

*****

Trudy did not disappoint. She could hardly wait to track Jasmine down. The problem was where to find her. She wondered if she had decided to stay a few days at Open Door. Kate and Jake had decided to go to New York City for the weekend. He had to finish up some details for a new deal he was involved in, and Kate was going to visit with Sandra, Jake's very dedicated secretary. She couldn't question them about Jasmine staying there instead of going back to Carsonville to that hotel.

She kept looking out the window with the hope of seeing Jasmine walking up the street, to no avail. The salon had been quiet all day. She had no appointments scheduled.

"What to do?"

She decided to go in search of grease.

She put the "Closed" sign on the door and began her walk to Stumble In. A burger is exactly what she needed—with french fries and a side of mayo for dipping. She greeted everyone she knew along the way. She was thinking about how she could bring Gordy and Jasmine back together again. It had to seem like a "chance" meeting. She excelled in hooking people up. Just look at Kate and Jake. But this one, she had to be extremely careful with. Both she and Gordy still seemed a little ragged around the edges when it came to getting their life back together. She knew Gordy's story. She had to know Jasmine's. She had to know both their pasts before she could plan their future.

*****

Chapter 23

Yes, that was Trudy. Always planning someone else's future. She had a good heart. She always meant well. And she always did her "research." She was her happiest when she was on a mission. And this time, she had lasered in on Jasmine and Gordy. And besides, whatever Trudy wanted, Trudy got.

"Here she comes," Jasmine whispered to the server at Stumble In.

The server looked through the window and laughed. "Yep, here she comes. You know Trudy?"

"Yes. She gave me my new do and painted my fingers and toes the other day."

"Well, she's a master at what she does, I'll tell you that. She also knows everybody in this town, along with their personal business, if you know what I mean."

"I think I do."

"All I can tell you is if she sits down at your table and starts quizzing you, you don't have a chance. She'll get your life story out of you before you know what ever happened." The server looked up again and saw Trudy heading right to the door of Stumble In. "Prepare yourself, girlie, I think she's heading for you."

Jasmine waved to Trudy when she walked through the door. Trudy walked over to Jasmine's table.

"That's my cue to join you, eh, sugar?"

Jasmine motioned for Trudy to sit.

"Ordered yet?"

"Just getting ready to, Trudy. I could actually use some company. I would welcome yours if you're so inclined."

"I'm so inclined."

Trudy sat in the chair opposite Jasmine. She was elated. She had not left town. And Trudy had found her.

"You know, it wasn't so long ago there was another woman who sat in this burger place and decided to stay." Trudy waved to the server. "She came in my salon and asked for all three of my services."

"Just like you gave me the other day?"

"Yep." The two women ordered their burgers. Trudy looked intently at Jasmine. "She was the silent, private type, like you."

"I would probably like her."

"You know her."

Jasmine looked at Trudy. "Who?"

"Kate."

"So what was her reason for wanting all three of your services?"

"Somebody died."

"Oh."

That was all Jasmine could say due to the large lump that had formed in her throat. Seemed she and Kate had a lot more in common than most strangers when they met.

Trudy watched her.

"You've been hurt, haven't you, sugar?"

The server, bringing their burgers, saved Jasmine from having to answer Trudy's question. When the server left the table, Jasmine looked at Trudy and gathered up her courage to finally give Trudy an answer.

"I think you are the kind of woman that reads behind a person's eyes, and if you read mine, I may have to stay in Brooksport Village a little longer to get my bearings, to settle myself down, and balance myself out. I think you can help me do all of that."

Trudy took her first bite of her burger.

"Does that mean you're gonna check out of that hotel in Carsonville and come stay at Open Door for a spell?"

"Yes, I've already moved into the room Kate arranged for me."

Trudy sat up a little straighter. "If you have time tomorrow, I can show you around our little town. Think you might like that?"

Jasmine smiled at Trudy. "I would like that."

Trudy winked and thought of the plan that was already taking shape in her mind. She was bound and determined that Jasmine was going to come face-to-face again with the man who wore the shirt with the green twinkle lights.

*****

Trudy walked back to her salon, smiling all the way. First step, accomplished. Jasmine was staying at Open Door. If she had her way, that would be enough time for her to get those two together. Her plan was coming together very nicely, indeed.

Trudy thought to herself, *There's a man who needs you, sugar, and I do believe you are a woman that needs him.*

Trudy walked into the salon and sighed as she looked at all the mail stacking up on her counter. "I'll go through that heap of mail tomorrow." She shrugged. "Probably all junk, anyway." She headed for the door. She decided she deserved a big scoop of ice cream. She had some thinking to do.

*****

The next time Trudy saw Jasmine, she was walking along the lakeside. Trudy ran to catch up with her.

"Do you know when Kate and Jake are coming back, Trudy?"

"I think it's today, sugar. Why?"

"I want to extend my stay."

Trudy sat down on a nearby beach chair and patted the one next to her, motioning for Jasmine to sit. "You know what they say about small towns?"

"Everybody knows everybody," Jasmine answered.

"That's right. And it's time you knew something about somebody in this town since you are extendin' your stay."

"Whose that?"

"The man who wore the green shirt with the green twinkle lights."

Jasmine was astonished. "Don't tell me! He lives here?"

"Yeah, and sooner or later, you're gonna run into him."

Jasmine fiddled with the crease in her skirt. "Why didn't you tell me before?"

"I knew you'd probably hightail it out of town, that's why."

"Yes, I would have." Jasmine threw her arms in the air in disbelief.

"I think it's time you met up with him again." Jasmine got up and began to walk. Trudy jumped up to follow. "Does he know I'm in town?" Jasmine asked Trudy.

"Not yet, but I've been itchin' to tell him!"

"Don't!"

"For heaven's sake, why not?"

"Think back, Trudy, I made a fool of myself coming on to him. I'm embarrassed, that's why not!"

Trudy bent down, picking up a piece of sea glass. "You shouldn't be. Ya know, he regrets not gettin' your name and telephone number."

"How do you know that? And don't tell me it's his sad eyes!" Jasmine cocked her head, shading her eyes from the afternoon sun, looking at Trudy.

Trudy continued, "If you've heard people talk about me in this town, you must know by now that when I know somebody has a story, I find out what it is in no due order. And I'm gonna find out what yours is, sugar. You can count on it!"

"I have no doubt in my mind about that," Jasmine whispered.

Trudy, suddenly, stopped walking and stared at Jasmine. "You're not runnin' from somethin' you've done, are ya? Like the law?"

Jasmine laughed. "No, Trudy, I haven't broken any laws! I've always lived by the rules, actually bordering on boring."

They continued to walk. Trudy picked up a polished rock and tossed it to skim along the lake. "Spill it," Trudy nearly commanded.

Jasmine stopped walking, looked directly at Trudy, and said, "It's all about a man named Andrew."

*****

"Oh, a man," Trudy said with a shrug. It was more a statement than a question.

"Yes, Trudy, a man."

Trudy sighed. "Men. Don't they just give us the dickens? They make us wonder. They make us question. They make us laugh, and they make us cry. And yet we can't seem to live without 'em. I think women should rule the world. Less aggravation."

Jasmine did not reply.

The evening was closing in as Trudy and Jasmine watched tourists begin to leave the beach area.

"What kind of man is Andrew?" Trudy asked. "Did he leave ya? Is that why you were dancin' like a crazed woman that night in Carsonville? Because he left you?"

"Yes."

"Was he crazy?"

"Crazy in love."

"Then why did he leave?"

"I ask myself that question a lot—even after these past two years."

"Did you ever get an answer?"

"No."

Trudy dared to ask yet again, "Then why do you think he left? Was he a 'cowboy'? Ya know cowboys always leave. And, on the other hand, some of 'em do come back—like Jake. But ya have to find yourself a stable man, one that has stayin' power—"

"Trudy"—Jasmine interrupted—"my Andrew died."

*****

"He'd begun to wake up in the morning with something besides dread in his heart. Not happiness exactly, not eagerness for the new day, but a kind of urge to be eager, a longing to be happy."

(Jon Hassler)

"I'm so sorry, sugar. Do ya want to talk about it?"

"Not now. But someday."

"I'm here when ya do."

"I know."

Jasmine took Trudy's hands in her own.

"Look, Trudy, I know you mean well, but I don't know if I'm ready for a relationship with Gordy right now."

"I understand," Trudy answered. "I truly do. Gordy may not be ready either. I just took the bull by the horns and decided for myself what I thought was best for both of you. I apologize."

Jasmine looked up at the sky. "Why wouldn't Gordy be ready?"

"He lost somebody pretty much like you did—real sudden and all. But he didn't get the chance to say goodbye. It was tragic."

"What happened?"

"It was 9/11, Jasmine. He lost his wife and small son in one of those plane crashes."

*****

The very thought of that knocked the breath right out of Jasmine. "I guess he wanted to stomp something that night too?" Jasmine questioned Trudy.

Trudy took a deep breath. "I forced him to go to Carsonville that night. I threatened to dress him myself if he didn't agree. I think I scared him into going."

Jasmine could only imagine the scene and tried to repress her smile. "I'm glad you forced him to go. He actually helped me forget, at least for a little while, what I had lost."

"And you helped him too." Trudy shuffled her feet, standing in place, looking at Jasmine. "I think he would be glad to see you again. I really do."

"Trudy, I don't know."

"Well, why don't you think about it, and when you decide, you let me know? I'll take you to him."

*****

Jasmine did think about it. All the rest of that day and into the night. Could she? Should she? Open herself up to another man? She ached for his losses. She knew his heartbreak.

She walked over to the window in her bedroom. Kate and Jake had returned from the city and were overjoyed to be away from all the racket. Kate had said that the visit with Sandra had been delightful and Sandra had promised to come visit with them soon.

She knew she was avoiding thinking about meeting Gordy formerly.

"Well, how stupid!" she blurted out. "I'm not going to marry the man! I could at least meet him under normal circumstances and be friends!" What in the world was she thinking planning a future with him? It was all Trudy's fault, putting ideas into her head like that. Trudy told her she had not told Gordy she was in town—yet. What was it she had said, she was *itchin'* to tell him?

Jasmine had not known Trudy long, but she had known her long enough to know that she wouldn't wait much longer—not when she had an *itch*.

*****

Chapter 24

Trudy decided—against her own wishes—she would just have to sit tight until Jasmine was more in favor of Trudy's matchmaking in order to go forward. It made her feel antsy. But she would wait. That was hard for her to do, but she had to respect Jasmine's wishes, and she was not going to trespass all over Jasmine's memories of Andrew to get her own point across. Trudy knew there would be time to talk into more detail about Jasmine's late husband. She, of all people, knew that grief took time, sometimes it took years to peel back so big a raw hurt that was trying its best to scab over.

So it truly surprised her when Jasmine walked into the salon a week later, looked at her, and simply said, "I'd like to visit the stable now."

*****

They were walking toward Gordy's ranch when Trudy turned to Jasmine.

"I have to tell you, sugar, this is more than a stable. Gordy's place is now called Dude Ranch.'"

"Got it, Trudy. I just feel really uncomfortable about this. I really do."

"Oh, sugar, you gotta get over that! You gotta stop thinkin' you embarrassed yourself on the dance floor. It's been weeks now. Blame it on that girly pink drink you kept drinkin', and forget it!"

Jasmine stopped walking in the middle of the driveway that led to the ranch, while Trudy kept walking. Trudy looked over her shoulder. Jasmine said, "I think I'm changing my mind."

"Oh, come on! I'm just gonna show you the ranch. I heard he's not home, anyway. Talk around town is he went into Carsonville to interview a woman he wants to hire to help with all the expansions he's been doin'. See that new facility over there?" Trudy pointed to a building in the distance. "Gordy got the bright idea to have retreats here in our little village town. Of course, I was somewhat responsible for that to happen too. Seems a lot of city folks want to come someplace to relax and breathe fresh air. He needs a woman to organize things 'cause he already has a lot of bookin's."

"So you're sure he's not here?"

"I'm sure—someone told me that. But so what if he is? You said you'd like to see the 'stable,' right there in my salon, so I'm just showin' you the 'stable.'"

At least Trudy thought she was sure. She had heard that he was going into Carsonville. She had also heard that, at the last minute, he had to cancel his plans due to one of his employees calling in sick.

When they approached the stable, they saw him.

Jasmine turned to walk swiftly away just when Gordy looked up.

"Trudy, you bring me another casserole?"

As he stood to his feet and shaded his eyes from the sun, he could see another lady with her. It seemed Trudy was tugging at her to get her to move forward. He began to walk toward the two women.

"Smile, sugar, pretend you're on the dance floor and he has on his twinkly shirt."

It was too late to go anywhere, so Jasmine stood perfectly still. As Gordy got closer to them, a look of recognition came over him. He looked at Jasmine. She appeared to be speechless. He was caught off guard too.

"Where did you find her?" he stammered.

Then he thought what an idiotic thing to ask, as if he had asked Trudy to search for her. And he had done nothing of the kind.

Trudy feigned innocence. "Oh, you two have met?"

Jasmine tried her best to smile. She held out her hand. "I guess this is our formal introduction."

Gordy took her hand, looked at Trudy, and answered, "Yes, I guess it is."

Trudy beamed.

"Jasmine, meet Gordy. Gordy, meet Jasmine."

*****

All three of them were finally settled on Gordy's big wrap around porch when Trudy decided it was time for her to leave, after her second glass of sweet tea. Jasmine stood to join her.

"No, no, sugar, you stay here. You two get more acquainted. I've got errands to run and an afternoon appointment."

"I really should go," Jasmine began to insist.

"Don't be uneasy about Gordy." Trudy interrupted. "He's a good man with a harmless heart."

Gordy summoned up his courage. "I'd appreciate it if you did stay, Jasmine. Trudy's right, I do have a harmless heart."

Chapter 25

Gordy and Jasmine became what Brooksport Village called an item. Ended up that Gordy didn't need to interview anyone else for the job vacancy he had. Turned out Jasmine had quite a knack not only in hospital matters from her past but also at organizational skills, planning, and decorating. Just what he needed for the expansion he had made at his ranch. Bookings for summer retreats began to flood his mailbox from all the city folk within a two-hundred-mile radius, and Jasmine handled it all. He was beginning to think there was nothing that woman couldn't do. She was "purt near purfect," as Trudy would say.

They made frequent trips to Carsonville where they had met in that country bar with a live band. They became friends with the bartender who always had a pale cosmo for Jasmine, waiting on the corner counter where she had sat that first night.

"For you, my lady," he would say as he saluted her.

"Only one drink tonight, my friend, no matter how I may beg for another."

He would always wink at her. "I see you found the man with the green twinkle lights." Before he walked away to wait on another customer, he looked over his shoulder. "Glad you found him, little lady. Made you stay here a little longer."

Gordy would smile, take her hand, and lead her to the dance floor.

They would visit the wise old owner of the antique store. They bought a few things for the ranch retreat center. Homey things. Cozy things. They brought the past into the present with those things. They seemed to be blending without even knowing it. Old frames, new pictures.

"I see ya found somethin' up there in Brooksport Village," the antique store owner said to them on their last visit.

"Yeah, we just kind of stumbled into one another through a mutual friend that knew exactly what we both needed," Gordy had replied.

The old man looked up at the sky. "Probably see a bunch of balloons goin' up in the clouds before too long."

Jasmine would not forget Gordy's smile or her own. They both knew the significance of those balloons. She remembered one of her last conversations with that sweet old man while sitting on that bench in front of his store. *"Crazy things happen in that town when people fall in love."*

They would return to Brooksport Village, walk hand in hand to the lake, stop in at Belle's for extracrispy fried doughnuts, walk back to the ranch, saddle up a couple of the horses, and take an evening ride.

Trudy and Belle kept watching them.

"You're pretty proud of yourself, aren't you, Trudy?"

"Proud as a peacock, Belle, proud as a peacock!"

*****

Yes, Gordy and Jasmine's courtship was fast and furious. It was so good to be reawakened to feel again, to touch again, to be alive again. Mona and Allie met Gordy, saw the smile on Jasmine's face, and gave the thumbs-up sign of approval to the couple that had found each other after so much hurt the two of them had experienced in their past.

Allie met Kate and Jake while staying at Open Door. She convinced them to visit her cabin in the woods whenever they wanted to have a little getaway.

"I have a key hidden outside above the door. There's a little crevice there, and that key tucks in quite nicely. All I need to know is that you are there, so I won't intrude."

They made an arrangement that Allie would stay at Open Door whenever she wanted, at no expense, and they would make use of her cabin for their planned getaways. A tit-for-tat arrangement that worked for all. Friends, quite simply, did that for one another.

"There is only one stipulation," Allie told them. "You must feed the ducks."

*****

Yes, romance was in full bloom, just like the summer flowers. It didn't seem that anything would come between Gordy and Jasmine.

Jasmine had officially made Brooksport Village her home, and Gordy seemed happier than he had been in a long time. The stage was set with everything and every person in place. Everyone knew their parts with no interruptions and no intermissions. Life was going on without a hitch. Everybody was happy. Jake and Kate. Gordy and Jasmine. Ted and Trudy. Life was beautiful and good—until a series of unexpected events began to happen.

Jake's "inner voice" kept warning him of a gauntlet that seemed ready to fall. He was having trouble sleeping. Neither he nor his loyal secretary, Sandra, from New York, knew that she would be on her way to warn Jake of an uninvited visitor who would be coming to Brooksport Village. Sandra would try to steady him through it all.

No one knew that Jasmine would make a mistake that would lead to a very deep soul-searching for not only Gordy but for herself—a truth they had both tried to deny.

Ted would have to face his past in order to move forward into his future. He would have to come clean with Trudy, and in the "cleaning," he ran the risk of losing her.

And Trudy's failing to open the stack of mail on the counter in her salon would lead to something totally unimaginable.

Not too long ago, Belle had thought it was time for their sleepy town to have some excitement. It was about to begin. But all these things would snowball into a whiteout that no one would have ever expected. Whiteouts, where the sky became like steel, thick with clouds—not a sky that welcomed a burst of color.

All Belle had wanted was a happy ending to all the love stories that were playing out in front of her eyes. Not to be. Storms were rising. It would be a long time before any more balloons found their way upward. A very long time.

Chapter 26

Kate and Jake enjoyed their time together. They loved driving into Jake's old stomping grounds—the city. But, oh, how they enjoyed turning their faces toward the mountains and that little cabin that Allie had so generously offered them whenever they wanted to escape all the pressures of owning their own businesses.

So it was on this particular visit that they decided to stay a few more days. The mountains were so peaceful. The waterfall Allie had told them about was so beautiful. The television was never turned on. No radios. No phones. Only each other.

They drove into the nearest town for more supplies. Kate borrowed the grocery owner's phone to call her second-in-command to keep the home fires burning until they returned. Jake did the same. He knew he could always depend on Sandra and Butch, his right-hand man.

"Let's stay until the end of the week," Kate was saying when Jake came up from behind her, placing his arm around her shoulders.

All Jake had to do was nod, and it was decided.

They were happy in the seclusion of their little hideaway and wanted a few extra days to be alone.

*****

"You know, Trudy is pretty pleased with herself getting Gordy and Jasmine together," Kate said that evening while sitting by the firepit. The night had been somewhat cooler.

Jake poked at the logs before answering. "Trudy loves matchmaking."

"Well, it's only right they are together," Kate said.

"How so?"

"They are suited for one another." Kate smiled. "I'm glad they're together. Jasmine's story is pretty similar to Gordy's. They both lost their spouses quite suddenly."

Jake put more wood on the fire. "But Jasmine got to say good-bye. Gordy didn't."

"Grief is still grief."

"True."

"I just think they have suffered in their grief long enough," Kate said. "They need to be together."

"Plus, it looks like they want to be together," Jake interjected.

"Indeed, they do."

"Like us."

Kate snuggled closer to Jake. "We must remember to thank Trudy when we get home."

Jake finished her sentence. "For us."

They sat there in silence for a while.

"You know I love the lake, Jake, but I love the mountains too. I love the night sounds of the crickets."

"I love the high-rises in New York," Jake teasingly answered.

"Sure you do, cowboy."

Turning to face Kate, he touched her face. "Kate, you are my world. Lakes, mountains, oceans, or high-rises, I want you with me."

"Likewise, cowboy."

She settled comfortably back into the crux of his arm. Life was good. They both planned on keeping it that way.

*****

Little did either of them know that, upon their return to Brooksport Village, they would discover something that had been hidden in the secret depths of those high-rises Jake had teased Kate about while sitting comfortably in their own little cocoon that no one could destroy.

While listening to the crickets and the night sounds of the mountains, they had no clue of what was to happen, and it would be like a wrecking ball flying into their marriage out of nowhere. Isn't that just like life? Just when you feel the peace and the calmness of something so right, a storm begins to brew. And this time, it would come in the shape of a redhead.

*****

Chapter 27

She unlocked the door to her salon. She thought about how her matchmaking had become a huge success and smiled.

"Bound to be another weddin' here before too long!" Trudy walked into the reception area and looked at all the appointments that had been set for the day. "I'd better get crackin'," she said out loud.

She looked once again at her stack of unopened mail on the counter. Her first client of the day would be arriving soon.

"Tomorrow," she said, "I'll get to all that mail, tomorrow. I promise."

Sometimes procrastination can be deadly. For, once again, she missed something very important. Something she should have taken care of weeks ago. Something that could mean life or death.

*****

PART 4

THE REDHEAD

"Be strong and courageous. Do not be terrified; do not be discouraged, for the Lord your God will be with you wherever you go."

(Joshua 1:9)

Three months later in New York City…
Jake's office

Chapter 28

Sandra was humming her favorite song and watering Jake's plants when *trouble* walked through the office door. Turning, she saw her. The redhead.

She heaved a big sigh.

"I thought Jake was done with all you redheads. Which one are you?"

"Lydia, Lydia is my name."

"What brings you here, Lydia?"

"I need your help."

"For the life of me, I cannot imagine why," Sandra replied. She turned her back to Lydia and continued to water the plants.

"I have to find Jake."

Sandra rolled her eyes and tuned to face Lydia. "No, no, you don't." Sandra kept staring at her.

"I see you're still guarding Jake like a black bear with her cub," Lydia began.

Sandra turned away from Lydia once again and contemplated throwing the remainder of the water in the watering can at her before showing her to the door. Too impulsive. She thought better of that idea and kept looking at her out of the corner of her eye, waiting for the shoe to fall. Lydia probably wanted money. Why else would she show up at Jake's office? And if he were here, he would probably give her the money, asking no questions.

She walked over to the small plant with one mere bloom.

"This is the most fragile one," Sandra said without looking up.

Lydia walked over to where Sandra was standing. "It looks like it's dying."

"Oh, it's not, I can assure you. It may look fragile, but it's very strong. It survives. You see that little bloom shaped like a heart?"

"I do."

"Do you see that little teardrop at the tip of the bloom?"

"I do."

"It's called a Bleeding Heart."

Lydia ran her hands through her hair. "Look, I'm not here to make Jake's heart bleed, believe me."

Sandra dashed her hand across her face. "And I'm just the woman to make sure you don't. You're right. I am the black bear," Sandra retorted. She turned away from Lydia and walked across the room. She wanted some distance between them. She needed to take a deep breath before she dared to speak again.

"I'm not going to let you come in here and turn Jake's world upside down. He is one happy man now—married to the love of his life, *and* you are not—"

Lydia interrupted. "Jake's married?"

"Yes," Sandra replied vehemently, "and it's not to you!"

Lydia smiled and walked over to Jake's desk. She continued to watch Sandra. "I thought he would never marry," she began.

Sandra looked at her. "Time changes things, Lydia."

"Believe me, I know."

Sandra put the watering can down, walked over to Jake's desk, and sat down in his chair. "Would you like to sit?" she asked, not as if she meant it.

Smiling, Lydia took the chair across the desk from Sandra. "This is not going to be a 'face-off,' Sandra."

Sandra could smell trouble. She replied with only a stare, no words were necessary, because if looks could kill, Lydia would have keeled over on the spot and been buried in ten seconds.

"I'm not here to mess up Jake's life. In fact, I never wanted this day to ever happen."

"What do you mean?"

Lydia continued talking as if she had not heard Sandra's question. "I'm trying to find Jake to warn him."

Again, Sandra stared at her. Drumming her fingers on the arm of the chair, she fought the urge to actually strangle the woman. "About what?"

"There's someone who wants to find him, and, believe me, when this guy sets his mind on something—well, he's just like Jake—nothing will stop him."

"Exactly who is this guy, and why does he want to find Jake?"

Lydia got up from the chair and walked to the window. She gently touched the fragile flower resembling a heart and looked down at a group of teens working on their computers and their phones. They were sitting on park benches. They were searching for—who knew what?

"Young kids these days know a lot about computers. They can find anybody."

Sandra spoke. "Don't change the subject, Lydia. I'll ask you again. Who is this guy that wants to find Jake?"

Lydia turned to face Sandra. "I'm here because the guy who wants to find Jake is named Joshua. Joshua is Jake's son."

*****

Sandra jerked her head up. "What!"

"Joshua is Jake's son."

Sandra jumped from her chair and walked over to face Lydia. Lydia had lied. This *had* just become a face-off.

Lydia was the first to speak, with a calmness that surprised even her.

"It wasn't just a fling with Jake, Sandra, at least, not for me. But he wasn't one to get too close to anyone back then. He told me the day he left me standing in Central Park that he had—what did he call it?—'emotional limitations.'"

Sandra could only stand and continue to stare at Lydia.

"What will it take for you to believe me—that I'm not here to hurt Jake? Nor am I here to take his newfound, happy life away from him. In fact, I'm glad he got over his 'emotional limitations.'"

Sandra threw her arms in the air. "And you think this information will not disturb his newfound life in any way!"

"Let's go for coffee," Lydia said.

"No," Sandra replied. Lydia was becoming frustrated. Sandra surprised her. "All of Jake's auburn-haired women liked dirty martinis. Let's go get one."

"I don't drink anymore."

"Why is that?"

"I'm a mother now."

*****

That was the one comment that had Sandra beginning to believe her—that she wasn't here to turn Jake's world into a chaotic series of events that could possibly end his happy life with Kate. And if not end it, at least put a huge cog in the wheel.

Becoming a mother changed a woman usually for the better. Sandra hoped that was the case with Lydia.

The coffee shop was busy, but they managed to find a corner table out of the racket swirling around them.

"Talk to me," Sandra said.

Lydia looked down at her hands. "I did love Jake," Lydia began.

"Everybody loves Jake."

"I know."

"What's not to love about Jake?"

Lydia thought for a moment before answering. "His back—when he walks away."

Sandra took a deep breath. "Please go on."

Lydia took a deep breath. "Jake never knew about our baby."

Sandra stirred sugar into her coffee.

"I was going to tell him that day we met in the park. It was such a beautiful spring day. I remember it so well. But he didn't give me a chance. He spoke first. He was a man of few words that day. He simply looked me right in the eye, told me we were done, and walked away." Lydia snapped her fingers. "Just like that. He was gone. He never looked back, and I was forced not to as well."

Sandra leaned back in her chair, taking a sip of her coffee.

"I'm only looking back now because Joshua is so hell-bent on finding his dad."

Sandra urged Lydia to keep talking.

"I was hurt when all I could see was Jake's back walking away, but reality didn't keep me there for long. I had a lot of thinking to do, decisions to make. So I left the city. I found myself a white sandy beach. I rented a little house right on the water. I walked a lot. I heard it was good for pregnant women to do just that—walk."

Sandra did not speak. She kept listening.

"I looked for shells. I watched the seagulls, flying so free, and I went back to the house, sat on the couch, and cried rivers. It was in that beach house, in a tiny bedroom, that I made my decision. I came home vowing to have my baby and raise Jake's and my child on my own. I vowed Jake would never know."

"Your pivotal moment?"

Lydia smiled. "Yes, there was a pivotal moment."

Sandra stirred her coffee and fiddled with her napkin. She looked at Lydia and smiled. "You have to know the only reason I'm still sitting here and listening to you is because I'm starting to like you."

"As I said before, you always were very protective of Jake. I admire that in you actually."

Sandra nodded. "I'm dedicated to that man. He's special."

"Yes, he is."

Lydia decided to answer Sandra's question. She remembered her pivotal moment.

The crowd was beginning to leave the coffee shop, but the two of them lingered.

"That evening after I had walked the beach, I came back to the house and went into the bedroom after my good long cry. I began to unpack my suitcase, opening drawers, putting things away. That was when I found it."

"Found what?"

"A Bible."

*****

Sandra ordered another coffee—this time pulling a small flask from her purse.

Lydia gave her a look of surprise.

Sandra shrugged.

"What can I say? My husband drove me to work today. I always carry this in my purse when he drives. He scares me to death, especially in the city!"

She shrugged again and poured the whisky in her coffee. "Sorry, I need this."

Lydia smiled and continued talking. "I sat on the bed and opened that Bible."

"Your moment?"

"Yes."

Sandra's demeanor began to soften.

Lydia's voice was soft as a whisper. "I opened that Bible—didn't know what I was looking for exactly. It just seemed to be a beacon of hope to me."

Sandra understood.

"It just fell open to Joshua 3:4. It told me I would be going a way I had never gone before. At least, that's how I interpreted it for my own life's situation. And then my eyes went up to chapter 1, and I read how he would never leave me—ever."

Both women looked at one another.

"One of my Ebenezer stone moments"—Lydia smiled—"my turning point. I've had several since then."

Sandra motioned for the server to bring the bill. "Sounds like you've done some studying of that Bible you found in that drawer, Lydia."

Lydia sat back in her chair. "I have."

Sandra paid the bill and stood up. "Oh, we're not done," Sandra said, looking at Lydia. "I just can't sit still anymore."

Lydia rose to her feet. "I understand. This is quite a lot to comprehend."

"Look, Lydia, I'm a mother, too, and I just want you to know it is okay to have a little liquor once in a while. I still love my children." She grabbed her purse, looked at Lydia, and urged her to follow. "Let's please go to the bar."

They arrived at the bar. Lydia had coke. Sandra had a martini—a dirty martini.

*****

Lydia could not help but smile, remembering the comment Sandra had made earlier in Jake's office about redheads. "Seems like brunettes have an affinity for dirty martinis too."

Sandra took a sip of her drink, leaned into the table, and asked, "So let me get all of this straight. It was that moment in that beach house that you decided to keep your baby? When you opened the Bible?"

"Yes."

"And you've raised him on your own to this point?"

"I plan on continuing to do that."

"But you have to find Jake so he will be prepared when his son comes looking for him?"

"That's right."

"Nothing else?"

"Nothing else."

Sandra became very pensive, taking another big sip of her drink. "Joshua 3:4?" she asked.

"Yes?"

Sandra looked straight through Lydia. "Is that why—"

Lydia answered the question forming on Sandra's lips. "Yes, that is when I decided if my baby was a boy, his name would be Joshua. It means 'Jehovah saves. Jehovah provides.' It was in those words that I found new strength and courage." Lydia sat a little straighter in her chair. "And our God did save us many times. The check always arrived on time for any emergency that came our way. Bills were always paid. Joshua excelled in school and had lots of friends, still does. He pitches for the school baseball team." Lydia reached for her purse and retrieved a picture, handing it to Sandra. "This is Joshua."

Sandra took the photo. Except for the auburn hair, he was the perfect image of Jake, especially his eyes. She nearly gasped at the resemblance.

"No doubts?" Lydia asked.

Sandra shook her head and answered, "None."

Lydia continued, "Well, all is still well. It's just different since the trip he went on last summer."

Sandra continued to listen.

"It was a mission trip. I thought it would be an experience for him that would be meaningful. His friends were going. I thought it would be good for all of them."

"What happened that changed his life on that trip? What made everything different?"

"Sandra, I didn't tell him about his father. The seed was planted by a counselor there. He thought he looked like Jake and told him so, even showed him a picture of Jake he had taken at some Memorial Day celebration. He didn't mention the name of the town. That's why I came to you first. I knew you would have my answers."

"Who was the counselor on that trip?" Sandra asked.

"It was a man named Phil."

*****

Sandra remembered Phil from Brooksport Village. She had met him at Jake and Kate's wedding. It was there she learned all about him. He had told her his story. She had listened with tears in her eyes. Not one word had she missed of his personal tailor-made conversion. And that conversion had led to a changed life. Being a counselor on missionary trips had become his passion. Helping young boys and girls find their way in life had become a top priority for Phil.

"I know Phil," she finally answered. Sandra defended him. "I know he meant well. I know he didn't intend to cause trouble."

"Oh, I'm not blaming Phil. I've lived long enough to know that the truth catches up with you sooner or later. Eventually, the piper shows up to get paid."

"When were you going to tell Joshua about his dad?"

"I was never going to tell him. I had fabricated another story to tell him, one that wouldn't set him out on a search that might not end well. I was all set to do just that. I had rehearsed and rehearsed what I was going to say. He had become old enough to understand certain things. My son is very smart—just like Jake. After that mission trip, he started putting two and two together, and here I sit now telling you." It was nearly dusk when the two prepared to leave the bar. Lydia dared to touch Sandra on the shoulder. "Can you help me find Jake?"

"I can do better than that," Sandra said. "This mama black bear can take you to him."

*****

Sandra couldn't just show up in Brooksport Village with Lydia. Jake would have a heart attack. She couldn't broadside Jake like that. She had to protect her "cub."

She remembered her words to Lydia, "Everybody loves Jake." She had to give him the first heads-up. Sandra believed that when Lydia appeared in Brooksport Village, the knowledge of him having a son would not give so hard of a punch if he knew what was coming. Forewarned was forearmed.

Perhaps he could process all this information before she brought Lydia to Brooksport Village. He would figure it all out, and he would find a way to tell Kate.

She had to talk to Trudy first.

Trudy would know what to do. Trudy loved both Jake and Kate. She would know how to make this as painless as possible. She picked up the phone and called Butch, Jake's right-hand man.

"I need you," she said when he answered.

"Do you know how long I have waited for you to say those three words?" Butch teased.

"I'm still married."

"Unfortunate for me."

"Still madly in love with him, too—my husband."

"Again, unfortunate for me."

"I need you to come into the office. We need to talk. I have to persuade you to do something."

Butch put on his sexiest, most deep voice. "This is getting more interesting."

"This is serious, Butch. Get into this office!"

*****

"I can't do that!" Butch shouted.

"All you have to do is answer the phones, take the messages, and water Jake's plants."

"You make it sound easy."

"It is easy."

"That's a woman's job."

"I'll pretend I didn't hear that."

"I won't be gone long."

"Where are you going?"

"None of your business."

"If I'm going to sit in your chair and answer these phones while you are going to God-knows-where, it *is* my business."

"No, it's not."

"Does Jake know it will be me answering the phone when he calls?"

"He will know soon enough, but it won't matter."

Butch shoved his hands into his pockets. "Whatever that means."

He gave Sandra his meanest look but knew all along he would do as she requested. He had always had a soft spot in his heart for that woman, and he would do whatever he could to help her out in whatever situation she was in.

"Oh, okay." he finally agreed. "But you owe me a dinner."

"I'm married."

"I know. You keep reminding me."

"Happily."

"I know that too."

Butch winked at Sandra. "Just messin' with you, little miss. You know that."

"Yes, I do know that, but I will do dinner!" Sandra walked to the door, looking over her shoulder. "Don't get your hopes up, big fella! I'll bring my husband along to chaperone our dinner of a thick steak, baked potato, and salad with double ranch dressing!"

She heard his laughter, along with the first ringing of the phone he was to answer, as she walked down the hall and out of the building. She was headed to Brooksport Village; and it wasn't for steak, baked potato, and salad.

*****

"What are you doing answering the phone, Butch? Where's Sandra?"

"Oh, hi, Boss."

"Where's Sandra?"

"All I know is that she said you would know soon enough and it wouldn't matter once she got there."

"Got where?"

"Don't know, Boss. She just left."

"Well, hold down the fort, Butch. Have her call me when she gets back. She can explain the mystery."

*****

Trudy was in her office, trying to sort through the stack of mail that kept getting bigger, when she heard the bell on the front door of the salon ring of a new arrival—a walk-in. Good. She could put the mail off for another few hours.

"Trudy! Please be here! Are you here?"

Trudy walked out of her office from the back of the salon. "Sandra! My goodness, child, it's good to see ya!" Both women embraced. Trudy looked at Sandra, cocking her head. "What's wrong, child? You have that forlorn look—been in the city way too long."

"I am forlorn."

Trudy put the "Closed" sign on her door, walked over to her, and linked arms with Sandra. "Come on, my friend, let's walk. The lake is beautiful this time of day. Let's go."

*****

Sandra told Trudy the whole story.

"How are we going to handle this, Trudy? Without anyone getting hurt?"

"Well, that cowboy sure has his plate full now, eh?" Trudy questioned.

"He doesn't know about this. He's minding his own business and living happily, and then up jumps the devil!"

"I don't think Lydia is the devil, after what you've told me about her," Trudy replied.

"Oh, I don't either. It's just an expression I picked up from Jake a long time ago. He seemed always on guard when things were going too good in his life. 'Up jumps the devil,' he used to say. But somehow, he always managed to fix the problem. Well, this is going to hit him hard. No, she's not the devil, but she very well could be that left ball that comes out of right field or the shoe that's going to drop like a hammer in the middle of his marriage."

Sandra bent down, picked up a flat rock, and skipped it over the lake. She sighed and said, "After hearing her story, I cannot help it, I like her! No wonder I look so forlorn! I don't know how to handle this!"

Trudy looked at her, took a deep breath, and agreed she felt pretty inept herself at the moment.

"Not sure how to handle it yet, but I'll think of somethin'."

Trudy didn't know what that somethin' was going to be. She kept thinking, *If I were a man and just found out I had a son I knew nothing about, what in the world would I do?*

She had no idea. Maybe it was time for her to go to the city and find some answers for her friends in the middle of all the racket that the city brought. She could think it out over some comfort food and a few shopping sprees. She did need a new pair of flashy shoes.

Stop! she thought.

She didn't have time for all that! She needed to take action—soon.

She made up her mind in an instant. After Sandra left, she headed straight for Open Door. A plan was forming in her mind, and it wasn't about buying flashy shoes in New York City.

*****

Trudy walked into Open Door.

"Come on, Kate! Get your purse! We're leaving!"

"Where?"

"To shop for things we don't need, things we'll never use or wear and will probably give away by this time next year!"

"You're crazy!"

"I've been told that before!"

Jake wandered into the kitchen.

"The darndest thing—"

He saw Trudy.

"What are you two up to?"

Kate looked at him. "We're going shopping for things we don't need."

He would never understand women. And to think he was the one that had given Charlie advice about girls several years ago. He shrugged his shoulders. "Okay."

Kate playfully pinched his cheek and said, "We'll be back after dinner. What were you going to say when you came in here?"

"Oh, just that I called the office and Butch answered, said Sandra had gone somewhere. Didn't know where. That's not like Sandra, not telling me, putting Butch in charge of the phones—of all people."

"Well, I'm sure she has an explanation," Kate replied.

Trudy feigned looking through her purse, mumbling to herself, "Boy, does she ever have an explanation!"

Jake turned to go back outside, grabbing an apple as he left the kitchen. "Have fun buying things you don't need."

"Where are we going, Trudy, for this shopping spree?"

"Carsonville."

Kate did not hesitate. "Love the antique store there. Let's go!"

Trudy knew the jovial mood Kate had going on at the moment would take a mighty turn within just a few hours. But this was Trudy's plan. She had to tell Kate first. In private.

*****

Carsonville was a great place to shop. Trudy knew the town well.

"This is where I hooked up Gordy and Jasmine. See that little country bar down there?" Trudy pointed to the end of the street.

"I do."

"Well, that's where we're gonna eat after we do some shoppin'. They serve great margaritas."

After they had bought the things they would never use, need, nor wear, they found themselves sitting across from one another eating chips and salsa. Trudy decided a pitcher of margaritas was called for. She needed a prelude of a relaxing potion for the conversation that would follow.

Trudy kept taking big gulps and deep breaths.

"Trudy, what's wrong with you? Do you need a paper bag to breathe in? It sounds like you're hyperventilating." She kept wondering if she was doing the right thing. She took another deep breath and another gulp. "Trudy, you're scaring me!"

Trudy grabbed Kate's hand. "We're women, right?"

"Yes."

"We've been through a lot together, right?"

"Yes."

"Woman to woman, we stick together, right?"

"Yes, Trudy, what is going on?"

"Sugar, we have to talk."
"About what?"
"A boy. A boy named Joshua."

"Life only demands from you the strength you possess.
Only one feat is possible—not to have run away."

(Dag Hammarskjold)

Chapter 29

Jake was looking out the kitchen window when he saw Phil walking up the path to Kate's flower garden. He walked out the door and greeted him.

"Hey, Phil, what brings you to Open Door?"

Jake motioned for Phil to sit. Phil waved to Jake and took a seat. "Just planned on sittin' here a spell." Phil dragged his hand over his face. "Need time to think. I know this is where Kate comes when she has to think about things. Brings her answers. Thought maybe she wouldn't mind if I did the same. Didn't know you'd be here, Jake. But to answer your question, it's a boy. A boy brings me to this flower garden."

"Charlie?" Jake asked. "I hear he's doing so well, getting that medical degree soon."

"He's not a boy, anymore, Jake. He's a young man, and I am so proud."

"So who is the boy you're talking about?"

"It's one of the boys I was counselor to on the last mission trip I went on." Phil dragged his hand over his face. "I wasn't gonna say anythin' to ya before I did some thinkin' about it up here—but here goes." Phil reached in his pocket and took out the picture he had taken of Joshua and the "prized fish" he had caught while on the mission trip. "I wanna show you somethin', Jake. It's just a feelin' I have. I may be all wet about this. Goodness' sakes, I hope I'm wrong, but—"

Phil handed Jake the photo. Jake held the photo and did a double take.

Phil fumbled for his words. "I know. First time I saw him at the retreat, I thought I was seein' a younger version of you. He sure looks like you, Jake, 'cept for the red hair."

Jake couldn't find his voice.

Phil shrugged his shoulders and sighed. "This boy, Joshua, started tellin' me his story after I had shared my own experiences one night around the campfire—me being a single dad and all, some of the things Charlie and I went through. All he did was listen to me that night, but the next day, he came up to me and said his mom was a single mom raisin' him."

Phil took the photo from Jake and put it back in his pocket. It looked to Phil that the photo was burning holes inside a heart that had just seen a truth of something Jake had known nothing about.

"He told me he hadn't asked his mom about his dad. He just felt she would tell him when she was ready to tell him. He looked so much like you, Jake. I made the mistake of tellin' him he looked like a man I knew. I've been ponderin' it since then. I think I should have kept my mouth shut, ya know?"

Jake looked down and then stood up very slowly. "Let me see it again."

Phil handed him the photo.

Jake flinched, looking at the photo. Could this possibly be? Of course, it could. Before Kate. Long before Kate. Which one? Which redhead had it been?

"Can I keep this, Phil?"

"Of course." Phil stood, looking at Jake. "I'm sorry, Jake. I just wanted ya to know I probably stuck my nose where I shouldn't have. I guess, in a way, I wanted to warn ya. He may come lookin' for ya to see for himself. These days ya can find just about anybody you're lookin' for. All ya need is a computer and a few 'smarts.'"

Phil looked up at the sky. "God help ya, Jake. He's only twelve years old, which means that single mama of his may be comin' with him."

Jake said nothing.

Phil rubbed his neck, searching for something more to say and wondering if he should apologize again.

As Phil began to walk away, he kept repeating to himself, "I should have kept my mouth shut, puttin' ideas in that boy's head—that I may know his daddy."

Jake stopped him. "It's not your fault, Phil. Don't you think that for one minute."

Phil put his hand on Jake's shoulder and squeezed. "Sorry, man."

Jake watched Phil walk back toward town. He turned and walked toward the kitchen door.

"The hen has come home to roost," Jake said to himself. "And I didn't even know there were hens looking to roost."

*****

Jake felt numb. He was glad Kate had gone with Trudy to shop for things they didn't need. How could this happen? He was happy. He loved Kate. He sat in the kitchen, trying to remember exactly which woman it could have been and asking why she hadn't come to him long before now. He reasoned that most women would have done that. Twelve years? Why wouldn't she have come to tell him? Forget that! Why hadn't she told him in the beginning?

How was he going to handle this? Should he wait for the two of them to just show up? Then he would know which one. He wasn't proud of this. How could he even ask, "Which one"? Had he been with that many women? No, he wasn't proud of that either. What was he going to say to Kate? How was he going to tell her he had a son? Maybe the boy wasn't his. For a fleeting moment, he thought it could be a mistake. He looked at the photo once again. No, there was no mistake.

He suddenly knew why Phil had blurted out that he knew a man who looked like him. The resemblance was uncanny. He would have blurted it out too. The "surprise factor" made you blurt out things you wouldn't do ordinarily.

He had to leave. He had to go somewhere to think before Kate got back home. He couldn't stay here. He went inside, packed a few things, and walked out the door. He didn't even think of leaving a note for Kate. What would he have said, anyway?

"I have a son. I'll be back later?"

Ludicrous.

His thoughts were imprisoned behind his sad eyes. Leaving was his first mistake at facing the cold, hard truth. Old habits die hard. Seemed Jake still had those running shoes packed away in the closet of his mind. He had to be alone. He turned the car toward the highway. He knew exactly where he was going.

When he pulled onto the dirt road that led to Allie's cabin, he realized he hadn't even asked Phil the boy's name. He called himself a jerk, got out of his car, and went to look for the hidden key.

*****

While Jake was starting his car engine, Trudy was telling Kate what Sandra had told her.

"You're telling me Jake has a twelve-year-old son?"

"That's what I'm sayin'."

Kate grabbed her packages and stood up. "Let's go." Kate took off running for the car; Trudy was close behind.

"Slow down, sugar. Jake knows nothin' about this to my knowledge. I wanted ya to know so ya could get a handle on it!"

They arrived at the car, Kate heading straight for the driver's seat.

"You're drivin' now?"

"Get in and hold on!"

"I don't like this, Kate!"

"Neither do I! All I know is I have to tell Jake. Nobody else! Me! And I want to get home as fast as I can!"

"Did I do the right thing? Telling ya first? Please tell me that I did!"

Kate pushed the gas pedal, and the car sped down the road. "You did, Trudy. You just took me too far away from home to tell me!"

*****

Kate arrived to an empty house. Guests were still at the lake. No Jake. She walked into their bedroom and noticed dresser drawers open. She walked over to the closet. Clothes missing.

"He knows, he ran."

She walked in the kitchen where Trudy stood, opening a bottle of wine.

"After all these years, he still ran, Trudy."

Trudy looked around the room. Speechless, she looked at Kate. She didn't know what to do or say.

"Somebody told him before we got home, but who? Who else knew?" Kate questioned.

"Only Sandra, as far as I know," Trudy replied.

Kate took her glass and sat down at the table. "Why, why did he run, Trudy?"

Trudy drank a big gulp of wine. "He just needs time to think, sugar. He'll be back."

"I know he'll be back! That's not the point! The point is he didn't have enough faith in our marriage to work through this together! To talk this out, together! Instead, he runs off to goodness-knows-where! I wanted to be the first one to tell him! He, on the other hand, decided he couldn't face me and ran off! No note! No nothing!"

Kate slammed her hand down on the table. "That is what hurts more than him having a son, Trudy! He has a past! So what? We all have a past! What he has to realize is that his 'past' was before me! He seems to have forgotten that I had a daughter before he even knew I existed! But we worked through it and so much more because I believed in 'us.' After everything we have been through, why couldn't he believe in 'us' the way I do?"

Trudy continued to sit silently, drinking her wine.

Kate filled her glass and looked at Trudy with her sad eyes. "What hurts the most is that he didn't trust me enough to love him through it!"

*****

Trudy looked at Kate. "I'm stayin' the night," she said.

"You don't have to do that, Trudy."

"Yes, I do. Settle yourself down. Go get on your pajamas. We're gonna camp on this tonight and try to figure out where in the world those cowboy boots took him this time."

Under her breath, she called him a jerk.

Kate got up from her chair and did exactly what Trudy had instructed her to do. After all, everybody always obeyed Miss Trudy. Charlie had told her that the first day she had set foot in Brooksport Village. And Trudy always knew best. Kate was grateful for the company.

*****

Undercurrents in life can prove treacherous when they pull us under. We cannot breathe for what seems like hours. Truth hits hard when it becomes a two-edged sword, cutting both ways.

So the two women "camped on it." They thought about where Jake might go. Back to New York? Back to ask Sandra some questions? They called Sandra. No, he was not there. Where?

"He's just somewhere thinkin', sugar. I repeat, he'll be back. You gotta remember he just found out about this. He's in shock. He'll tell ya when he gets back. He just doesn't know how to tell ya yet."

"He shouldn't have run, Trudy! When he was mixed up about us, he ran! But now we're married! He shouldn't run away from me. I'm his wife! I'm the one who is supposed to help him hold steady through thick and thin. He's not supposed to run anymore to God-knows-where! After all these years, he still doesn't trust me to love him through the good and the bad?"

She kept hammering away at the trust issue. It was driving her crazy.

Kate jumped up from her chair.

"I would love his son! Why? Because he's a part of Jake! He loved me when he found out I had a baby that tore my heart out when I had to give her up. He loved me when he found out that baby, all grown up, was Sarah. Can't he see, in that pea brain of his, that I would do the same for him? Can't he think beyond his nose? Can't he know in that dimwit mind of his that I will love him—no matter what?"

Kate kept marching around the room as if on a mission.

"He's just mixed up right now," Trudy tried to calm Kate. "He'll get it all together, and you two will talk it out."

"All I know is he better get his ass back here soon! I have a lot to say to that cowboy and his seemingly chronic wanderings! I'm going to hit his ass with a two-by-four!"

Trudy nearly choked on her wine. Kate had actually said the word *ass* not once but twice without taking a breath.

*****

Kate decided she wanted to be alone, after all, and convinced Trudy to go home. It was late. She poured herself another glass of wine, set it on the table next to the couch, and promptly knocked it over. With hands shaking, she cleaned it up.

She could understand him needing to think. But she couldn't understand him feeling the need to think *alone*. Didn't married people *think* together? That was the way it was supposed to be, wasn't it? Didn't married people work things out while sitting beside one another in the same room? Weren't married people supposed to trust each other to the point that their love could survive even the toughest of circumstances? Weren't they supposed to share feelings, doubts, and weren't they supposed to help guide one another to the answers of questions that would arise in a marriage? Well, weren't they?

She turned down the bed.

Those were the thoughts that kept running through Kate's mind while trying to sleep.

"How long will you be gone, Jake? Where are you? And why aren't you here with me?"

Her anger had turned to sadness when sleep finally overtook her. It seemed that all she could hear was the bottom line shouting in the distance: trust—he doesn't *trust* you enough to stay with him through the bad and sometimes the downright ugly. That bothered her. That bothered her a lot.

*****

Chapter 30

Allie saw him unlocking the door to her cabin.

"Oh, I'm sorry, Jake, I didn't know you and Kate were coming up!"

Jake turned. "No, I'm the one that's sorry. I didn't phone you first."

Allie looked around. "Where's Kate?"

"I'm alone."

"Your look is making me think there is 'trouble.'"

"Yeah, you could say that."

Allie sighed. "I'll leave you alone, then—to think." She turned to go.

"No, it's your place. I have no right to assume I can just drop in whenever—"

He sat down on the step, leading to the path where Allie stood.

"I want you to stay."

She looked at him. He seemed so hurt, so in need of a friend.

"Go get the bread," Allie said.

"What?"

"We're going to feed the ducks."

*****

The day was quiet. A gentle breeze skated down the path to the pond. They reached their destination in silence and sat down on the ground next to one another. The pond was like glass, and the ducks were hungry. It was that kind of day when you could whisper secrets and no one would hear, except for the one person who sat beside you—someone you trusted. He had come here for some peace of mind and for some answers. He had not expected to see Allie. He trusted her. And perhaps, it was providence that she was here. She just might have some answers. She was smart and a *doctor*.

Jake was first to break the silence.

"It seems that I'm reverting to some of my old habits."

"What do you mean?" Allie asked.

"I tend to run when a crisis pops up." He smiled. "I do that instead of boil water. I should boil water. Then I'd be standing in my own kitchen with my own wife."

"Crisis have to do with a woman?"

"Yep. A redhead."

"Oops." Allie threw a piece of bread to the ducks. "Rest easy, soldier. It's not running when you come to a place like this. You've simply arrived to think. Your car just led you here."

She threw another chunk of bread to the leader of the ducks.

Jake decided to just blurt it out. "You see, I have a son. He's about twelve years old now."

"Oh."

"I didn't know I had a child—until a few hours ago."

"Oh."

"That's all you have to say?"

"Uh, huh."

"I'm asking for some advice here."

Allie patted him on the shoulder. "You're right about one thing, soldier. You should be home in your own kitchen, talking to your own wife. It's her you need to trust, not me."

"I can't right now. I have to think. I have to know how to talk to her, what to say to her."

"In situations like this, I do believe that honesty is the best policy."

"But where do I start?"

Allie stood up and looked Jake in the eye. "At the beginning." She stood up and began walking back to the cabin. She turned, facing Jake once again. "Come with me. Let's go back and cook some lasagna."

"What?"

She remembered that was what her own mom always did when there was a question looming that she had no answer to. She didn't bake. She didn't reach for Clorox to clean. No, she cooked lasagna.

Allie remembered a time when her mom had made so much lasagna she could have fed the whole neighborhood—the time they were helping Mona make sure Andrew was safely out of his father's sight, to a place that his father would never know. Somehow it worked. Lasagna was magic.

"You heard me."

Jake stood up to follow. Allie was ten feet ahead of him, trying to think. All she could think about was that she had to boil water—for the noodles. Indeed, what was she supposed to say to him? He was married to Kate. She had only known the two of them for a short time. She knew Kate had a daughter, which was no secret. But this son? Obviously, this twelve-year-old boy had been a secret for a long time—even from Jake, since he was just now finding out about him.

Oh, my, she thought to herself. *I'm an oncologist—not a therapist.* She walked into the cabin with Jake not too far behind.

"What now?" Jake asked.

She reached for a pan, poured water almost to the brim, and turned to Jake, who wore that ever so forlorn look.

"Time to boil water." That was all she could think of.

*****

Jake remained at Allie's cabin for a week. He did a lot of thinking and ate a lot of lasagna. He fed a lot of breadcrumbs to the ducks. For once in his life, he listened to everything around him. He thought of the little church where he had sat next to a little old lady who had motioned for him to remove his hat. He smiled, thinking of her. He thought of the pastor who had told him he was being pursued. He smiled again. He thought of the snow angel he had made that New Year's Eve. And then he thought of the decision he had made back then—to go back to Brooksport Village and claim Kate as his own.

Allie had brought all those memories full circle for him.

"Sometimes, you have to think back to the beginning and look at how far you have come," she had said, "to see the numerous blessings that you have and to realize you want to keep them. Then you fight hard for it. You dig in. You become fierce to save what you have. You become a victor instead of a victim."

It seemed, whether Allie liked it or not, she had become his therapist. She also became a good friend, sort of a "tamed-down Trudy" kind of friend. If someone had told her that her medical degree would have automatically thrown her into on the couch therapy, she would have laughed. She tried not to get too close to patients, but there were some—well, you just couldn't help yourself. Had Jake become like one of her patients? In a way, she determined.

By the time the week was over and the ducks had gained a few extra pounds, Jake decided that it was time to go back to Brooksport Village to face Kate.

He had gone back to the beginning with the help of Allie, and his mind was much clearer than it had been when he had arrived. He surmised that, sometimes, a person just needed a once-upon-a-time stranger who had become a friend to talk to—somebody who could see the forest, in spite of the trees. Allie had become that person for Jake.

"Thank you, Allie. Sometimes you can find answers in the most unlikely places."

"I hope I helped you in some way."

He threw his suitcase in his car. "You did. And what better place than these quiet mountains?" He gestured to all the beautiful scenery surrounding him.

"True."

Jake got in the car and rolled the window down. "One question," Jake began.

"What's that?"

"Why do you call me 'soldier'?"

Allie smiled. "Because you remind me so much of a guy I used to know who went to military school. You're a lot like him—in many ways."

"Good ways?"

"Yes, very good ways."

Jake started the engine. "You're welcome at Open Door anytime, Allie."

Allie shielded her eyes from the sun. "Kate is waiting for you, soldier. See you on the flipside."

*****

With that, he was going back—coming and going, coming and going had been his life. Seems it still was when something threatened the lifestyle he loved. After all these years, he had still felt that stronghold around him—tying him in knots—just run. No more! He had learned a lot from Allie that week, not to mention the pleasure he had found in feeding those ducks. What had she said to him before they started cooking all that lasagna?

Rest easy, soldier. You're not running when you come to a place like this. You've simply arrived to think. And you've come to the right place.

Yes, indeed, he had gone to the right place. And he had found the right "doctor."

Allie watched Jake leave. When she could see his car no more, she walked back into the cabin. It seemed empty now. No Jake. But she smiled, remembering how that man could fill up a room with his presence. Nothing more. Hands off. He was a husband.

Odd how a good-looking man can become just a friend to a woman looking for love. She had to admit, she was looking.

But that's what Jake had become to Allie, a friend who knew the woman, Jasmine, who had married her childhood, tumbling, rumbling Andrew. Funny how life always seems to come back around full circle.

Allie looked at her watch thinking this had been quite an unusual week for her. Unusual and gratifying. But it was time to pack up and go back to the city. Time to save some more lives—or, at least, try.

*****

It had been a long week for Kate. Trudy had tried to calm her but admitted, even to herself and Ted, that Jake had done the wrong thing. Every day they waited for a phone call. None came. Every day they waited for Jake to come driving up the street. Every day Kate became angrier and yet concerned.

Kate was walking out of Trudy's salon when she saw him coming. She pretended she did not see him. She didn't know what she was going to say to him. She was livid. "Concern" had suddenly disappeared. And besides that, there were a couple of guests waiting for her at Open Door.

Jake slowed the car as he approached Kate. Trudy did a double take when she saw his car.

"Oh, boy," she murmured to herself. "Fireworks, gonna happen, and it's not the good kind. I smell it in the air!" Trudy continued to watch as the car continued to slow down.

"Hey, Kate," Jake said.

Kate did not stop walking. "That's all you have to say to me—'Hey, Kate'! You've been gone a week with no calls to let me know if you're alive or dead! And that's all you have to say to me—'Hey, Kate'!"

"I know I have some explaining to do, and I will. We have to talk."

Kate stopped walking and looked directly at him. "Talk? I'll say we have to talk! We had to talk before you ran off to God-knows-where! You ran and left me here to clean up your mess!" She began walking again.

He kept up with her while driving the car. "Kate, can we just go down to the lake and discuss something?"

She gave him a look of disdain.

Then it hit Jake. "You already know, don't you?"

"It's been a week, Jake, an entire week! How would I not know? News like you having a son travels pretty fast!" She began to walk up the sidewalk to Open Door.

He parked the car and ran after her. "Kate, I know I have a lot of explaining to do. I grant you that—"

She interrupted him. "Don't! Don't grant me anything! You owe me more than 'granting' me something! You disappeared! You owe me an explanation. You owe me answers! But most of all, you owe that little boy and his mama sitting in our living room right now some answers! They've been waiting for you to show up! Just like I have! I gave them a room to stay in until you got home. I figured it was the least I could do. Go to them first, Jake. Then, and only then, will I listen to you!"

Jake pointed to the front door. "They're in there?"

Kate kneaded her forehead, pinched the bridge of her nose, and said nothing. She did not trust what would come out of her mouth anymore. She merely turned and walked to the flower garden.

Jake looked at the entry door from the front yard. He mumbled to himself, "They're in there."

He didn't know which redhead was waiting. He didn't know exactly what he was going to say. What he did know was that he had to face them both. He had no plan. He looked up at the sky. "Is this another one of my personal Jerichos, God? Please help the walls come tumbling down."

*****

Lydia and Joshua had already seen Jake from the living room window. Lydia motioned for Joshua to come sit beside her. Both mother and son were nervous. Soon another nervous soul would join them. What do you say at moments such as this? Indeed, what do you say?

Jake walked into the living room and saw them sitting there. He recognized Lydia right away. He looked at his son and saw his own eyes looking back at him. Jake spoke first.

"I'm sorry. I didn't know."

Joshua looked at his mom, who merely nodded. In a flash, Joshua was running to Jake and held his father for the first time. Jake's arms went around his son, and from across the room, Jake heard the relieved sigh of Lydia.

Slowly, his son pulled away from him, looked up at his dad, and said, "My name's Joshua."

*****

Kate sat in the garden for what seemed an eternity. Ted had convinced Trudy that this was to be a private moment for the four of them. He told her she should sit on her hands and find something productive to do—like go through that stack of mail that kept staring her down every time she walked into the salon. This was a moment that Jake, Kate, Lydia, and Joshua had to work through for themselves. Trudy knew Ted was right; it seemed tangled at the moment, but she also knew the tangles would get untangled. At least she thought they would. But things like this took time. Sometimes a lot of time. She would talk to Kate. She would talk to Jake. She would help make it all right again. She fixed things.

*****

It was Lydia who joined Kate in the garden. Jake had taken Joshua to the lake. Father and son had left holding each other's hand.

Lydia walked over to Kate, who was sitting on a bench in the middle of all those heart-shaped flowers with the tear on their tips.

"I've seen these before." Lydia touched the fragile heart with ease.

"They're fragile," Kate said.

Lydia looked at Kate. "But strong enough to survive the winter storms?"

Kate smiled. "Yes."

"Strong—like you, Kate." Lydia sat down beside Kate on the bench. "I was never going to tell Joshua about Jake. I was going to make something up. I told Sandra all of this—"

Kate interrupted. "And then the mission trip happened, and Joshua met Phil."

"Yes."

Kate sighed. "Lydia, it's okay. You're a mom. You tried to protect your son. That's what moms do. Believe me, my own story proves that." She took Lydia's hands in her own. "Everything always has a way of working out. This will work out too."

"I would never want to cause trouble between you and Jake. You have to know that."

"I do know that." Kate took a deep breath. "And besides that, Jake has always been able to cause enough trouble by himself."

Lydia smiled. "You're right about that. Jake never loved me. You have to know that, Kate. It's you he loves. Sandra and I had a long talk about you and Jake."

Kate smiled, still holding Lydia's hands. Lydia looked up to face Kate.

"I will admit I cared more for Jake than he did for me. I knew that all along. But I thought that maybe one day—but that day never came."

"I'm sorry, Lydia. I know firsthand how Jake can break a heart. I'm sorry he broke yours."

"I survived. I'm raising my son. We're doing quite well, and, believe me, I want nothing from Jake."

"Well, let me tell you something, Lydia. The one thing I do know about my husband is that he will—in some way—make this right for you and Joshua *and* for me as well. I don't doubt that for one minute."

Both women looked out at the lake. They saw Jake and Joshua walking, skipping stones across the glassy surface.

"Oh, I'm mad as a hornet right now at him! But it's not because of this sudden change in our lives. I've adjusted to change all my life. It's the fact that he ran away!"

Lydia squeezed Kate's hand. "But, Kate, he came back."

That was Jake. Always coming back. But Kate was not going to live like that. There was going to be some changes, and Jake was going to listen to her. She had a lot to say, and she was going to say it.

The right time came after Lydia and Joshua had gone back to their own home, promising that Joshua would come back for frequent visits and they would stay in touch from this point on. A line of communication had been set. Now there was business to attend to with Jake and Kate. Serious business. And Jake would see a side of Kate he had never seen before.

Jake found Kate sitting in her garden, a cup of tea in her hand.

"I see you boiled some water."

"I did."

"Can I sit with you?"

"You're my husband. Of course, you can sit with me."

Jake sat down beside Kate cautiously. Kate looked at him.

Sighing, she began to speak. "Don't treat me with kid gloves, Jake. I've survived much worse than this."

"I know you have. I'm just sorry I'm the one causing you so much hurt now."

"I know you are, Jake. But you have to stop running when life throws you a curve." Kate took a sip of her tea. "And as it has turned out, it's not been so bad after all, has it?"

"No." he agreed.

"You have a son."

"Yes, I do."

"A fine son."

"Lydia has done a great job with that boy."

"Yes, she has."

Jake tried to put his arm around Kate, but she pulled away. "What about us, Kate? Are we okay?"

"I want to say we're okay. But the truth be known, I'm not okay. I'm not okay at all."

*****

Jake stood up and walked over to the bleeding hearts, touching one of them. "You know I bought one of these plants and put it on a shelf in my office window in New York. I thought I had left

Brooksport Village for the last time. I thought I would never see you again." Jake sighed. "It always made me sad to look at it."

"Why?"

"Every time I looked at it, I thought I had made the biggest mistake of my life, leaving you behind." He walked back over to Kate. "Sandra finally got tired of me looking so lost and not really communicating with anyone. So she told me to go back to wherever I had come from and find you. She got tired of me 'mooning' over a plant that would never survive in a windowsill. She told me it was too delicate to survive. She said plants like that needed a big garden with a sky full of fresh air. But she kept tending to it. You know, it's still there."

"Maybe it's time to bring it back here, Jake, with the rest of them."

"What can I tell you now, Kate? I want to make everything right again. I had our life all planned out. Lydia showing up was not a part of it."

"I know that. But the fact is—it is a very big part of our lives now."

Jake raked his hands over his unshaven face.

Kate looked at him. "You look awful."

"Thanks."

"You're welcome." Kate sighed. "Jake, it's not about Joshua. He's your son. We will do right by him. It's about you not trusting me enough to stay here and talk this out. It's about you doubting my love for you. It hurts me to think that you would run somewhere else and talk to who-knows. Did you do that, Jake? Did you run and talk to someone else? You were gone for a long time."

"A week."

"That's a long time when a wife doesn't know where her husband is."

Jake thrust his hands in his pockets, saying nothing.

Kate blasted him. "Don't try to shelter me from your problems, Jake! It's time you learned I'm made of sterner stuff! You better start talking!"

*****

Kate stood up. "I want to go to the lake."

"I don't want to."

Kate looked at him. "And why is that?"

"Depends."

"On what?"

"If you're going to tell me to jump in or not."

Kate shook her head and walked over to him, taking his face in both her hands. "Humor won't save you this time, Jake, but love will. I love you. I want you to get that through your thick skull and your—from time to time—dimwit brain. Honestly, I don't understand how in the world you run a big business but, somehow, you manage." She sighed. "When it comes to common sense, you don't even get off the batter's mound."

He began to feel like he could breathe. "You still love me?"

"Come on." She took his hand. "Let's go to the lake. I'm not going to tell you to jump in. I won't even push you in."

They walked slowly toward the lake's edge. They found two beach chairs that had not been stored away for the night, pulled them through the sand, and sat down.

Jake let Kate begin the conversation. And besides that, he didn't know what he was going to say, anyway. *Emotional limitations*, he reminded himself. He thought he had better try to be willing to fix that in his life.

"Before we were married—when you were still trying to find yourself—I had to let you leave."

"I know. You told me I had to find my own Jericho."

Kate couldn't help but smile. "Yes, I remember."

"Trudy told me I had to find my own pharmacon."

"I remember that too."

"And I did. I found them both."

Kate ran her hands through her hair. "Jake, why did you run this time?"

"I was scared."

"Scared of what?"

"That I wouldn't be able to cope. That I would end up not being a man you could look up to, a man you could respect, and then, after all that, I was afraid I would lose you. A man who loses the respect of his wife loses everything. Even love can't glue the pieces back together."

"Running away was not an option, Jake."

He shrugged. "I didn't know what to do, Kate."

"Not knowing what to do just proves you are truly a dimwit when it comes to love. Common sense should tell you that you don't walk to your wife, you run to her, you *talk* to her."

"I know you're right. I just have these 'emotional limitations.'"

"Cut the crap, Jake! And get over your excuses! You're a good man, Jake, a real good man. You have a good heart. I see that every day we are together. You have to stop running." Kate stood up and held out her hand. "Let's walk."

They began to walk hand in hand.

"We're married now, Jake. I simply will not allow you to run anymore. We owe each other that. You know me inside and out, and I'm finding out some different things about you—*granted* just lately. But, Jake, I know you had a life before you met me. So did I. You've accepted my past. I want you to know that I accept yours too. What matters is that we're together now. The present and the future matter to me—not your past."

She turned and faced him.

"Some of the past just caught up with you. That's all. Yes, you have a son. Yes, Lydia is now in both of our lives. Notice I said '*our* lives'? And I've talked with her. I like her. She's not looking to cause trouble. She's a mother who wants the best for her son. I accept that. I understand that. You need to accept and understand too."

She turned to keep walking. Jake placed his hands on her shoulders and turned her to him. "I do accept that. I accept my responsibility with Joshua too. I don't begrudge any of that." He kept looking intently at the face he loved so much. He cupped her face in his hands. "I don't want to lose you, Kate, because of this. I don't want anything to come between us. I want us to agree on my responsibility that I have for Joshua. I want you, Lydia, and I to work this out together and all the decisions that need to be made concerning my son. Can we do that?"

She placed her hands on his face. “I fell in love with this face many years ago. I’m not going to stop loving it now. Of course, we can work together for Joshua’s best interest. I’ve talked with him, too—during that dreadful week you were gone. He helped me in the kitchen. He helped me in the garden, always asking questions about you. Lydia and I had a lot of tea while sitting on the porch, talking about you. You seemed to be the topic of conversation day in and day out of that awful week. I learned that they’re good people, Jake.”

“So you boiled a lot of water?”

Kate couldn’t help it; she chuckled.

“Yes, we boiled a lot of water. Opened a few bottles of wine too. Trudy came over with a case of both white and red. Lydia didn’t drink. But Trudy and I made up for that. More for us, and I don’t mind telling you, we needed it! We couldn’t let ourselves think that something awful had happened to you!”

The sun was beginning to set. They looked out at the horizon together.

“Jake, you have to promise me your running days are over, no matter what. You have something that comes to light, you come to me first, and I will promise you the same thing. We have to talk about these things. We can’t run.”

“Kate, I promise, but—”

“No buts—”

“But someone called me a soldier and told me to rest easy. I wasn’t running. I was thinking.”

Kate waited.

“I need to tell you about the woman I was with for that week I was gone.”

*****

Kate held her breath. A woman? He was with another woman? For the week he was gone? Kate felt weak. She thought her knees were going to buckle from under her. “Should we go back and open a bottle of wine? Am I going to have to be drunk to listen to this?”

"No." He held her close. "No, you see I discovered that a new-found friend can show you the forest in spite of the trees and that another beautiful woman in my life can be a friend and nothing more. And besides that, you know her. While you boiled a lot of water, she and I fed a lot of ducks while I was away. And we made a lot of lasagna. It's magic, you know?"

"Allie's cabin?" Kate questioned.

Suddenly, the weight of the world vanished. Allie. Oh, thank goodness. Allie. She must remember to thank her.

"Yes, Allie's cabin. I didn't call ahead. I had no idea she would be there. We just kind of bumped into one another."

Jake told her everything. From the time, he arrived at the cabin until the day he found his way back home—after he had spilled his soul to the oncologist he had now given the title of therapist.

He concluded with a statement that had Kate right back to the first day she had fallen in love with him.

"I've had my eyes set on you since the day I tipped my hat to you on that Memorial Day Weekend. You were the 'runner' then. Remember? I love you more than I have ever loved any woman in my entire life. You're the only one I want to be with. I'm not going to run anymore—no matter what. I will boil water, or I will find my quiet place nearby to sit and think. Just look for ducks. You'll find me there."

"You know we have ducks on this lake, too, don't you? And I'll make sure we have lots of lasagna."

She put her arms around Jake's neck. "Oh, and just so you know, I still respect you."

*****

Trudy listened to everything Kate shared with her about "the talk" she and Jake had at the lake.

"Oh, sugar, I'm so glad! It sounds like everythin' is gonna be just fine, and Joshua is such a sweet boy!"

"Yes, yes, he is."

"Well, I'm happy for ya. I knew you two would talk it out. And like you said, we all had a life before we met the 'others' we're with now."

Trudy walked over to the stack of mail still on the counter.

"Someday I have to sort through this pile," she exclaimed. "But not today. Come on! I have to talk to you about Ted. Talkin' about secrets, there's somethin' he's keepin' from me. He's becomin' too distant with me lately. Now that your love story has come to another happy, sweet end, I need to concentrate on mine. And it's your shoulder I need."

PART 5

STAR BRIGHT

Chapter 31

It seemed that love was back on track in Brooksport Village. Someone once said, "What doesn't kill you makes you stronger," and that was true with Jake and Kate. Those two came out of Jake's past stronger than ever. Things settled down once again in their little town.

Charlie would be graduating from medical school soon with Sarah not far behind. Phil was continuing to go on mission trips, hoping not to uncover any more secrets; Belle was making up new recipes, bringing new flavors to her extracrispy doughnuts; and Trudy continued to let her stack of mail get higher and higher. Oh, she paid her bills, but the other stuff could wait. Or so she surmised.

New summer romances were budding with the tourist teens, and the romances that seemed to be weathering the tests of time were galloping along smoothly.

It looked as if Gordy and Jasmine would be Trudy's next success story. She was glad because she had a few worries of her own and couldn't concentrate on anyone else.

Why was Ted becoming so distant? She couldn't wrap her mind around it. He was becoming more and more secretive. He was going on more and more business trips. And he was always coming to her place irritated and somewhat sad. He seemed to have changed overnight. He was not the Ted she used to know. She had to ask him some questions soon.

Yes, she had made up her mind to find some answers, even if she didn't like what she might hear.

But then "life struck" once again, and an emotional storm cloud was forming on the horizon—like a thick blanket of fog—big, densely white, and ominous.

Trudy's questions to Ted would have to wait.

*****

Chapter 32

Gordy was humming as he walked the path to his ranch. Jasmine had planned dinner, and he was looking forward to it. Early summer always lifted his spirits. He was beginning to think that life was good again.

He stopped walking to pick a flower along the path. Jasmine loved flowers. He kicked himself for thinking too late; he should have stopped at the florist on the way home. When he looked up, he saw something that caused his heart to tumble and his knees to buckle.

No! Absolutely not! She was not riding that white horse! That was Jessie's horse and only Jessie's! Star Bright. The horse Jessie had nursed back to life—no, the horse that she had loved back to life. That was not Jasmine's horse to ride!

He began to run toward Jasmine. She saw him and guided Star Bright to his side, giving him a welcoming smile.

"Welcome home! I have dinner in the oven and a bottle of wine chilling!"

She patted Star Bright's side.

"Look! I think he likes me! He's a pleasure to ride! He's not wild at all, like you told me!"

Gordy stood there, arms flailing around, grabbing for the reins of the horse.

Jasmine's smile became a look of shock.

"Get off that horse!" Gordy shouted. He managed to grab the reins but kept shouting. "Now! Get off that horse!"

Jasmine jumped down and saw the fury behind Gordy's eyes. She had never seen him act this way. She felt as if she had been slapped. "Gordy, what's wrong? Is there something I should know? Is Star Bright not well—he can't be ridden? What is it?"

"It's none of your business, is what it is!"

Gordy turned Star Bright around and started walking toward the stables, leaving Jasmine in the middle of the road not knowing what to do or where to turn.

*****

"You may my glories and my state depose, but not my griefs. Still I am king of those."

(Richard II)

Gordy walked into the kitchen after unsaddling Star Bright and brushing him down. The first thing he saw was the table set for two, candles ready to be lit, and a bottle of wine being chilled in the ice bucket. He felt no remorse. She had no business getting on that horse! Why had she done that? He had never told her the history that surrounded that white horse. He felt there was no need to. Rather than tell her it was a memory for him, he had told her that Star Bright was wild and crazy with his riders and never to saddle him up for any rides. He had lied. Star Bright was the most gentle horse he had ever known. That horse was like Jessie. Gentle and kind. It was Jessie he missed. It was Jessie who was supposed to be riding that horse—not Jasmine!

He took the half-cooked dinner out of the oven and threw the pan on the counter. He took the chilled wine and threw it in the trash. He wanted no part of it! He was angry. Jasmine had trespassed upon his own personal holy ground, and in that one instant, she had become an interloper. He had felt like he had nowhere to hide from the memories that came crashing in at that exact moment he saw her from a distance.

He shoved his hands into his pockets. What gave her the right to saddle up Jessie's horse?

Why couldn't he have seen this before? Jasmine was going to blow away all his memories of his beloved Jessie. He wouldn't have it! This was his private place! Some things he just kept reserved in his own private space for Jessie. No one was allowed in. No one was going to take that away from him! Not even Jasmine.

Gordy kept thinking over and over; she should have never gotten on that horse! That was Jessie's and his memory—she had not been invited to intrude upon that privacy.

He found himself at 2:00 a.m. sitting with feet on the floor on the side of his bed. Looking across the room, he continued to stare. Jessie's shoes were still there, neatly tucked behind the closet door in a box that no one opened but him. He knew where they were. Nobody else did. He knew the color and each little sequin on top of those sandals. She had worn them often. Those shoes were yet another memory he would not forfeit, would not forget.

He walked to the closet and found the soft warm blanket that had covered him through the most devastating time of his grief. He swung it around his shoulders. After all these years, he thought he had conquered his grief. He hadn't. One foot still in the past and one foot in the future since he had met Jasmine. Everything was Jasmine's fault.

She had not followed him to the house. Why should she? He had acted like a raving lunatic. But now he would take deep breaths. He would deal with his anger. He would continue with his life before he put on that green shirt with the twinkle lights. He would break it off. He had to. Jessie had been the love of his life. It wasn't fair to Jasmine, and it wasn't fair to him to continue what he now looked at as a charade. This had to be dealt with—soon.

*****

Grief is unpredictable. You stumble. You gain your ground and decide it is time to walk over the line. You look back, and you see that the line has disappeared, making you think that it is, indeed, time to move forward. Or is it? How does one ever know really? How can you move forward when you begin to set boundaries on where a relationship with another person is to go and make your own set of rules as to where it can't go? Moving on seems to be the goal, but it doesn't happen that way. It has to be a moving forward instead. Like walking into the sunset—an ending and yet a beginning when the sun rises again.

One must not turn around to look back at the shadows. But that's what Gordy did; he looked back.

The dominoes began to fall when Jasmine got on that horse. All the work he thought he had done while ploughing through his grief had ended with a girl saddling up and riding toward him with a smile on a streak of white. Or was it more? Was it something deep down in the core of his being that he wasn't quite over yet? Perhaps it wasn't the saddling up of Star Bright at all. Could it be the plain and simple fact that Gordy needed more time to grieve? Could it be that he had become a captive to his memories?

*****

It was 2:55 a.m. when Jasmine sat straight up in bed. She put her feet on the floor and walked into her kitchen. She had been in Brooksport Village long enough to seemingly fall in love again. Gordy reminded her of Andrew in many ways. But was that good or bad? Was she trying to replicate what she had with Andrew? She was a fool to ever think she could. Andrew would have never spoken to her the way Gordy had. He would have never flailed out at her. He would have never frightened her the way Gordy had, with his eyes flashing out in an anger she did not understand.

What was it about that horse that caused Gordy to show so much agitation toward her, an agitation that was filled with anger? He had always treated her with gentleness. He had understood her loss. He had been through it himself. Why was he so angry with her now? They had both been through so much, their lives running parallel in so many ways.

She poured a glass of orange juice and looked toward Open Door. Only the porch lights were on. Everyone seemed to be sleeping but her. She wondered if Trudy was awake. She opened her computer and stared at the screen. She looked at her message board. She began to type.

"Are you awake?"

There was a slight pause, and then she heard the ping of her computer.

"Yes."

"Are you alone?"

"Yes, Ted is on assignment. It's just Buddy and me."

"Can I come over?"

"What's wrong, sugar?"

"Everything."

"I'll boil the water."

*****

Trudy opened her door, and Jasmine nearly fell into her arms, sobbing her heart out.

"I don't think I boiled enough water," Trudy said. "Come in here, child, and sit down. What in the world is going on?"

Trudy poured the tea and motioned for Jasmine to sit down.

"Tell me about him, Trudy," Jasmine began. "You know Gordy so well. You have a history that he still won't open up to me about. I need to know."

Trudy placed her cup of tea on the table beside her.

"First, you tell me what happened that has caused you to be in such a tizzy."

"I think it all comes down to Star Bright."

"What makes you think that?"

"I had prepared a dinner for Gordy and myself. After everything was in order, I decided to saddle up that magnificent white horse and go meet Gordy halfway to his ranch. I thought we could ride up to the house together. He told me once that Star Bright was too wild to ride and I should never saddle him up, but I thought he seemed so gentle, so—"

"You got on 'Star Bright'?"

"Yes. When I saw Gordy, I rode up to him, and he nearly literally jerked me off that horse! He was so angry. He was yelling at me. I dismounted. He turned his back to me and walked away with Star Bright."

Jasmine's hands were shaking as she sat her teacup down.

"I can tell by the look on your face that I did something wrong. What was it?"

"Getting on that horse, sugar, getting on that horse." Trudy stood up. "It's late, sugar. You stay with me tonight. In the mornin', I'll fix you a good breakfast, and we'll walk down by the lake. You'll think more clearly after some bacon and eggs. Grease helps."

She took Jasmine's hand. "Come on, now, you know I'm right. It's late. I always have the guest room clean for such moments as these."

Jasmine went with Trudy. She knew she was right. As she walked toward the guest room, she thought this was the second time Trudy had taken her by the hand, tucked her in, and made sure she was safe.

"Thanks, Trudy," Jasmine said as she turned to walk into the bedroom.

"Soothing lavender, sugar, the walls here are soothing lavender. Ya sleep well, ya hear?"

*****

Trudy sighed and picked up Buddy as she walked to her own room.

"Some things just tie ya up in knots, Buddy. Grief is one of 'em." She put Buddy on the pillow next to her. "Gordy sure did lose the love of his life when Jessie died," she continued talking to Buddy. "And his son on top of all that!" She patted Buddy's head. "So glad I can talk to you, little man. Thanks for listenin'."

With one final pat of Buddy's head, she whispered, "Let's get us some shut-eye. We've bacon to cook tomorrow."

Buddy stretched, looked at Trudy, yawned, and laid his head back down. In a mere minute, he was asleep.

*****

Jasmine awakened to the smell of bacon.

"She meant it. She's cooking." She walked into the kitchen and found Trudy opening a can of cat food. "None for me, thanks."

"Sit down, sugar! Bacon's for you. This, this is Buddy's own filet. You'd have to fight him over it."

Jasmine sat down while Trudy served her. "Thanks, again, Trudy."

"I never turn away a wounded warrior, sugar."

"Does that mean I will live to fight another day?"

"Yep, that's exactly what it means."

She looked sideways at Jasmine. Deciding the dust had settled somewhat, she decided it was time to tell Jasmine some facts about Gordy she didn't know. Obviously, he hadn't told her. Now it was up to her.

"Is the bacon grease helping to clear your mind a little?"

"It's working wonders, Trudy."

"Okay, when you're done with every last piece, we'll go for a walk. Eat those eggs too. You need protein." Trudy poured herself a cup of coffee. "We're goin' down to the lake."

*****

They walked along the water's edge. Jasmine kept staring ahead. Trudy began picking up stones.

"What are you going to do with those?"

"Put them in jars. They're polished." Trudy held one small stone out to Jasmine.

"What are you going to do with the jars?"

"Not sure yet." They continued to walk. "For now, I just keep pickin' 'em up but only the ones that speak to me."

"You're weird."

"I know." They both laughed. Then Trudy just blurted out, "He's not done grievin' yet. I thought he was, but he's not."

Jasmine said nothing.

"His Jessie was somethin' else."

Jasmine stopped walking and looked directly at Trudy, tears flooding her eyes, threatening to fall at any moment. "So was my Andrew!"

They sat down in the middle of all that sand and pebbles. Trudy looked at Jasmine. "You're not either, sugar."

"What are you saying? Not either, what?"

"Grievin'."

"Are you saying Gordy and I met too soon?"

"Yep, that's what I'm sayin.'"

"What do I do now? Just leave?"

"I'd hate to see ya go."

"I love this town, the people—you."

"And the town welcomed you, kind of lured you in, I guess. Brooksport Village has a tendency to do that."

Jasmine remembered the first day she had walked the streets of Brooksport Village with a hangover she thought no bottle of aspirin would cure.

"But it's not about just leavin' a town, is it?"

"What do you mean?"

"Sometimes you gotta go back to pick up some pieces you lost along that grievin' trail."

Jasmine began to draw lines in the sand as she listened, thinking of a decision she would soon have to make.

"Sometimes we think the grievin' is over. We meet someone like a Gordy and share a dance or two. We share a meal. We meet for coffee. We go back to the place we met, and we say to ourselves, 'Done.' Ready to move on. *Then* all hell breaks loose. In your case, you got on a horse."

Jasmine leaned her head on Trudy's shoulder.

"Tell me about that horse, Trudy. I need to know."

"You know how Jessie and little Sam died."

Remembering what had been shared with Jasmine, she felt as if the breath had been knocked out of her. There were no words to speak.

"Our town grieved with a hurt that was untouchable. Gordy had lost two precious souls, and so had we. It was a dark time, a real dark time for all of us. We cried a lot of tears behind closed doors that seeped onto the streets those horrible days after the tragedy. Days turned to weeks, weeks to months, and months to years. I didn't think Gordy would ever get over it."

Trudy sighed. "I thought he was learning to live with it when he met you." Trudy paused before her next question. "That horse you were riding?"

"Yes."

"That white horse was Jessie's horse. Gordy had purchased it at an auction. It was very sickly. He felt sorry for it. He brought it home, and Jessie fell in love with it. They called in the best vets from all around. Jessie nursed that horse back to life with her love and all that tender care she gave everybody she met. She even slept in the stable with it on the nights they didn't think Star Bright would make it through. But he did. That animal was very special to both of them."

Jasmine could only nod and look down at the pebbles at her feet.

"It's not your fault, sugar. Gordy just hasn't been able to make it through certain things."

Jasmine became deep in thought. "There's certain things I still have trouble with myself, Trudy."

"Like what, sugar?"

"Only things grieving people would understand."

"Try me."

Jasmine ran her hands through her hair.

"One night, Gordy thought we should watch a classic movie. He popped popcorn, and we settled in to watch what he told me was one of his favorites. It was *Casablanca*. I jumped up from the couch and ran out the door. That was Andrew's and my movie. I couldn't share it with anybody else. I never explained that to him. I told him I hadn't felt well and had to leave in a hurry."

Trudy looked at her and took both her hands in hers.

"So it seems you did your own kind of holdin' certain things back, too, eh?"

Jasmine had not looked at it like that at the time. She had felt she would be betraying Andrew in some way—watching that movie with someone else. Trudy was right.

"Looks to me that you two haven't 'come clean' with each other about your past loves. Too hung up on not wantin' to hurt somebody's feelins'. Oh, how it hurts me to tell you this because I think you and Gordy would be perfect together, but I have to say it."

"What, Trudy?"

"Maybe you both need more time, sugar. You can't put a time frame on grief. There's no boundary lines of when and where it begins or ends. Sometimes it's an endless circle. It seems to never disappear. It never falls off a cliff and disappears. It just keeps visiting when you least expect it, and it's not the kind of visitor you bake a cake for."

Jasmine kept looking at her, her eyes brimming with tears.

"But there does come a time when you don't linger there with it. You start talkin' to it. You open the door. You greet it with a sigh, tell it that you expected it to come calling on this day—this birthday, this anniversary, this Christmas—this horse, this movie. But you remind it not to get too comfortable because it will have to be on its way soon. You give it what time you need and tell it to move on. Then you take a deep breath and move forward yourself."

Trudy retrieved tissues from her pocket and handed one to Jasmine after taking one for herself.

"One thing you and Gordy both have to admit and stare down, if you have to—pray with it, cry about it, sleep with it, eat with it, have a sip of brandy with it—"

"What's that, Trudy?"

"The relationship you had with your Andrew, the relationship he had with his Jessie—neither will ever be replicated ever again. They were special. They were no ordinary relationships. They were most likely one in a million relationship that very few people ever find in their lifetime. You found it. Gordy found it. Wrap those memories around you like a cocoon, but don't let them imprison you. Stay warm in it awhile, and then work your way out of it. It will be a struggle, but you will be stronger because of it." Trudy stopped, caught her breath, and continued, "Ever see a butterfly leave its cocoon?"

"No," Jasmine confessed after dabbing at the tears rolling down her face.

"It's really somethin' to behold. You want to help 'em. You think it would be so easy to help 'em fly sooner, but you don't dare. They have to struggle. They have to build their strength. They have to be able to fly on their own. The very struggle makes them stronger. It's not supposed to be easy for anyone—learning to fly on their own, but the sooner you and Gordy realize that, the quicker you can start your new chapters." Trudy stood up. "It's gonna be more of a struggle than you ever realized. Both you and Gordy thought you were done with the hardest part, but you're not. It's the 'other goodbyes' that are gettin' to ya."

"Other goodbyes?"

"When all the fingerprints start to disappear one by one. *Casablanca* was yours. Star Bright is Gordy's. When someone else seems to take over the memory."

Jasmine could not contain the tears any longer.

Trudy put her arms around her. "I know you've had a tear-filled past, sugar. So has Gordy. Bad as I hate to admit it—he's bein' chased by ghosts, sugar. He's got more cryin' to do." Trudy looked out at the lake and then back to Jasmine. "You do, too, sweet girl. I knew that the first time I saw you on the dance floor in Carsonville. It was your sad eyes. I knew you were one hurt little puppy the very night you walked over and asked Gordy to dance."

"You're one special lady, Trudy."

"I know that, sugar."

"Does everybody tell you that?"

"Yep. But it doesn't matter to me what people think. Only one I want to please is him." Trudy pointed upward to the sky.

"What does he tell you, Trudy, exactly?"

"He tells me I'm royalty, sugar, I'm royalty. And right now, he's tellin' ya the same thing. You still have some roads to walk down, but you'll make it. Ya surely will."

*****

Jasmine went back to her own little house around noon. The talk with Trudy had explained so much to her own heart. She was thinking of *Casablanca*. She was thinking, of all things, macaroni salad. She remembered the day in July when Gordy had asked her to bring macaroni salad to the July picnic. Everyone was bringing a dish to pass. She had been standing in his living room when he had asked her. What had she done? She had run out of the room, just like she had done the night he wanted to watch *Casablanca*. He had followed her.

"Hey, kid, it's okay. Bring whatever you want."

She had taken apple pie instead.

She couldn't blame Gordy for nearly dragging her off Star Bright. She understood. It seemed she and he were running more parallel than she could have ever imagined. Neither of them had come to grips with the anger that lay just beneath the surface of their separate griefs for Jessie and Andrew. That anger of feeling Jessie and

Andrew had been taken away too soon. And there were some memories they were refusing to give up.

They both had giants in front of them. Giants that only they could fight alone. They had hurts that had to be stopped from whispering in their ears, those hurts that kept intruding upon where they had hoped to be with each other. They couldn't lean on each other. They had to stand alone, first, before they could be with anyone else. They had to settle down and figure it all out. Alone.

She realized that she must go to Gordy. She had to apologize. The sooner, the better.

*****

Trudy walked into Crabby's Bar. It didn't take long for her to see Gordy sitting in the corner nursing his ginger ale. No words were needed. One look from Gordy said it all. She began shaking her head.

"Nothing to say, Trudy?"

"Nope, looks like I've got some cookin' to do."

Then she walked out the door.

*****

The next thing Gordy saw when he had gone back to his ranch was Trudy, walking up his path with a casserole in her hands and that purple scarf in her hair. She marched right up his front steps and into his kitchen.

"Trudy, why are you bringing me a casserole? Nobody died."

She gave him a look that stopped him cold in his tracks.

"That's where you're wrong, blue eyes," she replied. She walked across the room, placed the casserole on the counter, and sat down at the kitchen table. She just stared at him.

"Jasmine was at my house cryin' her eyes out last night, and you have the most miserable look on your face—that, my blue-eyed wonder, says it all."

Gordy walked to the window. In the distance, he could see Star Bright. He poured himself a glass of water.

"She rode Star Bright," he simply said.

Trudy sighed.

"She didn't know that horse was special," he continued, "I never told her."

Trudy kept listening.

"I guess I should have told her. It was just that it seemed something private between me and Jessie—a boundary no one should have crossed, I didn't want to share with Jasmine." He sighed and walked to the table, sitting across from Trudy.

Trudy's eyes softened. She understood.

"When I saw her on Jessie's horse, well, it was like an explosion in my mind." Gordy got up and looked out the window, once again. "That wasn't her horse to ride. It wasn't right. It didn't fit." Again, he sighed. "Star Bright was okay with it. I wasn't."

Trudy finally spoke. "That special horse of yours felt another gentle touch, a touch he had missed for a long, long time." Trudy took a deep breath and continued, "That special horse let her in."

Gordy looked at her.

"You've missed that touch too," Trudy concluded.

He knew she was right. "But—"

Trudy interrupted him. "I know, but, Gordy, you have to realize you will never ever find another Jessie. There are no substitutes for her."

His face fell, as if a shadow had suddenly covered him.

Trudy continued, "That relationship will never be replicated. It was way too special."

She walked over to Gordy, putting her hands on his shoulders, forcing him to look at her.

"Listen to me, blue eyes. I know you. I know you don't like breakin' hearts. Handsome men do it all the time, sometimes without realizin' it. But you listen to me, and you listen good. I've known you a long time, and I know that heart of yours is big enough for two women in your life. Two special women. You don't let go of the memories. Nobody's askin' you to, especially Jasmine. Neither are you forgettin' Jessie. It is not a betrayal of Jessie—if that's what you're thinkin'! But do you think you can put those memories in a 'memory room'? A secret place in your heart only you visit from time to time?

And do you think you can let another woman in on the other side of that room?"

Gordy looked long and hard at Trudy before answering. "No, I don't think I can."

Trudy took a deep breath and turned to leave. She took one last look at Gordy before saying, "That's why I brought you the casserole, blue eyes. You're grievin', all right. You're grievin' the death of a hand you refuse to grab."

*****

He watched her leave. Maybe she was right. It had been years since 9/11. He thought he had turned a corner when that feisty Jasmine had asked him to dance. But then she had to saddle up Jessie's horse. And it all came back like a flood. That day. That horrible day he had lost Jessie and Sam. That day he had closed himself off to anything more in his life.

He was learning another lesson from the hand of God. Trudy didn't know, but he already had that secret place in his heart. Grief had built it, and the walls were strong. Grief is like that. It never quite goes away. That secret place in his heart—that was where his grief sat, always waiting for him to come visit. And if he didn't go through the door, grief burst through it to him, leaving him speechless. Grief never seemed to let him rest—not for long. It was like a recurring bad dream. He admitted, even after all these years, there were some nights he slept on the couch. When he visited that secret chamber in his heart, he couldn't drag his feet to his bed. He wasn't over Jessie. He would never be over Jessie. It was not fair to Jasmine to even think that he could. He had to let her go. She would find another dance partner. A woman as vibrant as her always did. Men gravitated to her. She just had that certain innocence that men couldn't resist.

*****

Jasmine had to sort out her thoughts before going to Gordy. She also knew that she had to make a decision, a major decision, one that would change the direction of her current path, one that would change the direction of her life once again.

She spent many restless nights struggling with that decision, but, in the end, she knew she had to leave Brooksport Village.

She packed her belongings and left the final month's rent on the bedside table with a note. She had rented the house when she had decided to make this village town her home. Open Door had been her respite for a few weeks when she first arrived, but now the little bungalow she was leaving had formed a special place in her heart. It saddened her. In fact, everything and everyone she was leaving behind saddened her.

Isn't that just like "life"? Just when you think you have reached a new beginning, something happens that makes you turn around and stumble. For her, it was getting on a horse. She had to question herself, as well as Gordy. Neither one of them was ready for their relationship to blossom into something more than it already had. She had to admit that she had come nowhere near to picking up the pieces of her life since Andrew's death. Neither had Gordy. They had both been in denial. There was much more digging to do. Getting on that horse proved that truth to him and to her. She was grateful Trudy had shared the memories about Star Bright. It forced her to think about her own memories and how she kept protecting them.

She carried her suitcases to her car and thought again of Gordy's reaction when he saw her on Star Bright. She had been so stunned and, yes, shattered by his behavior as she rode down the path to greet him, a smile as big as Texas on her face. His reaction was not a greeting of warmth and welcome. He was irritated and raw. He was cruel. He may as well have slapped her across the face. That's what it had felt like. She couldn't say a word. Her smile had faded, and all she could do was look at him and retreat.

But that was before she knew the reason he had reacted so uncharacteristically. That was not the Gordy she knew. That was not the Gordy she thought she was falling in love with. That was not the Gordy she wanted to be with. He was fighting a ghost that had to be dealt with; for that matter, so was she. She just didn't realize it until his own "giant" stood between him and that magnificent horse that Jessie had loved and brought back to life.

She took a deep breath and decided to visit the lake before her departure. She had to clear her mind. She needed to find some ducks to feed. Ducks calmed her, another memory she and Andrew had shared when they knew their time together was short. Both she and Gordy needed time to come to terms with their still lingering grief. The bottom line had entered their gentle and seemingly comfortable relationship. It was now a matter of seeing one another face-to-face and admitting it.

*****

She became stronger with each step she took toward Gordy's ranch. She did not hesitate when she arrived at his door. She knocked. Gordy answered within a few short minutes.

He looked at her.

"It seems strange—you knocking on my door like we're strangers."

"Maybe we are," she replied. "May I come in?"

He motioned for her to enter and stepped to the side when she walked past him.

"I owe you an apology, Gordy."

"Would you like to sit?"

"No, I won't be staying long. I just want you to know that I didn't know about the memory that Star Bright held for you."

He ran his hands over his unshaven face. "How would you know? I never told you. I should have told you. I don't know why I didn't."

After a brief hesitation, Jasmine answered, "There were things I should have told you, too, Gordy, but I didn't."

"Why do you think that is, Jasmine? Why did we both hold certain things back from one another?"

"Because we considered them private. Things that were just between Andrew and me. Things that were just between you and Jessie. Precious things that we denied anyone else the privilege of knowing—our secret memories with my Andrew and your Jessie. We didn't want anyone trespassing on them."

They continued to look at one another.

"Like someone intruding on an unhealed heart? Is that how you would describe it, Jasmine?"

"Yes, and I'm so sorry."

"Who told you about the horse?"

"Trudy."

"Well, it was no secret. Everybody who lives here knew about Star Bright. I should have told you the truth instead of making up some lie that he was too wild for anyone to ride. I'm sorry. And I'm sorry for the way I reacted. I truly am. You didn't deserve that."

"It's okay now. I understand." She seemed to fumble over her words. Looking sheepishly at him, she finally admitted to her own special memories of Andrew. "It's kind of like *Casablanca* and the macaroni salad."

Gordy remembered both days. "When you ran out of the house?"

She nodded.

He began to put two and two together. "Andrew? A memory?"

She could only nod.

He walked over to her and took her gently in his arms. "I understand too."

She looked up at him and sighed. With an effort, she pulled away from him. "We both have more grieving to do, Gordy. That's why I'm leaving—for you and for me. We thought we had come out on the other side, but it took a white horse to tell us we haven't."

"Where are you going?"

"You don't need to know."

Gordy steadied himself. She looked away from him. "I'll miss you, Jasmine. I really will."

"I'll miss you too."

They both knew they were doing the right thing, even though it felt so wrong. They both had to let go. They had shed many tears already, but God's shoulders had proven strong. They would remain strong through the rest of the battle that remained to be fought.

"Grief is a strange bedfellow, eh, Gordy?"

All conversation had ended with that question as Jasmine began to walk away. Gordy was crushed, like trying to breathe on a hot, humid day.

Jasmine looked over her shoulder to the stable as she walked down the path, away from a future she could have had, if only...

Star Bright was watching too. One foot stamped the ground as she left. Somehow, he knew that she was leaving, just like his Jessie had done years before...

*****

She had one more stop to make before leaving town. Trudy. That wild woman who had taken her under her wing when she was a mere stranger in town. She had to say goodbye. She found her at Belle's, exactly where she had met her formally for the first time.

With one look, Trudy surmised what Jasmine had decided to do.

"Hey, sugar, ya goin'?"

Jasmine nodded.

Trudy shuffled over to the corner table and sat down. She motioned for Jasmine to join her. "You can't run, sugar."

"I'm not running away, Trudy. But I have to go back in order to move forward. Do you understand?"

"I think I do actually. You've got some rememberin' to do. You've got more tears to shed." Trudy looked at her bag of doughnuts. "These help."

Jasmine smiled. "I have to go back and pick up some 'things' that grief seems to always leave behind. I tried to go around it. I was only halfway through that battle when I met Gordy. I forgot to finish the trip."

"He did, too, sugar."

Jasmine gave Trudy a hug. "Tell that Buddy of yours I said goodbye."

"I will."

Jasmine turned to go.

"When ya get to where you're goin' find some water, pick up a rough stone and throw it in. It will resurface a beautiful, polished piece, just like you will, sugar."

Jasmine walked back to Trudy and hugged her, whispering in her ear before leaving.

Trudy watched her go. What a fragile flower she seemed. When Trudy needed answers, she always went to the city. But this one, this one needed a quieter place to be alone. She had to find that secret garden of hers, wherever it was. She had to sit awhile. Wait in the stillness. Somehow, she would find her answers. Fragile flowers like her always did.

She looked away from the window.

"Tell me somethin', Belle. Why does love sometimes make people so sad?"

Belle shook her head. "Don't know, Trudy, just don't know."

Trudy knew that Jasmine had made the right decision. And she understood why. All the talking in the world was not going to do any good until both Jasmine and Gordy had shed their last tears for the tragedies that had hit them both. Sad. Oh, so sad *when* love made people afraid.

Trudy faced Belle.

"She'll be back."

"How do you know that, Trudy?"

"She didn't whisper goodbye. She whispered, 'So long.' That's how I know."

Belle wasn't so sure.

*****

Riding down the interstate, Jasmine was off and running once again. But she did know exactly where she was going. She was going back. Back to her hometown, back to look at the house that was once hers and her grandma's. Back to the flower garden. Back to Polly. She just didn't want to tell Gordy.

She drove to the first rest stop, pulled over, and parked the car. There was an ice cream truck serving kids whose parents had stopped for a brief stretch of their legs. She bought a cone—vanilla. She wanted simple now. No nuts. No toppings. She smiled while thinking of nuts. Kate was always feeding those squirrels nuts. Kate never told her why she loved squirrels so much; she just figured that everybody had their own reasons for liking or loving what they did. She walked to a bench close by and watched the kids running and playing. She saw the parents gather them back into their car to continue their journey. Everybody was going somewhere.

She continued to sit there, watching the ice cream melt, dripping between her fingers. The last time something had trickled through her fingers was sand, on the beach. She remembered the beach house she and Andrew had shared. Oh yes, she had some more remembering to do. She had some letting go to do. But how could she do it? She looked up at the sky.

"Tell me, again, Andrew. Tell me somehow, someway. How do I move on with my life when I have one foot in the future and keep dragging the other foot behind me that wants to stay in the past?"

Yes, Jasmine had a lot to think about. There was no way she could love anyone else until she learned to put new pictures in old frames. Until she could keep the wonderful memories that she had of Andrew and bring them with her into the present with no reservations—until she could blend the two together. Was it possible? And if so, how long would it take?

Both Gordy and Jasmine faced parallel ghosts. How in the world could she ask Gordy to face his own when she had so many of her own in front of her? Only God knew how long it would take. Only God knew the answers to her questions. And only God could bring her to the place she needed to be. Only God could bring her to her own special garden.

*****

"In our sleep, pain which cannot forget falls drop by drop upon the heart until, in our own despair, against our will, comes wisdom through the awful grace of God."

(Aeschylus)

Chapter 33

Jasmine did not go to Polly's place right away. She took a drive downtown first. Hearing the train whistle, she sat down on a nearby bench. Maybe she should have gone to the ocean. Water seemed to calm her more than train whistles.

She sat in silence. She knew Polly would be surprised to see her. She thought she should take her a gift, since she was barging in on her in hopes of staying with her for a while.

"She always loved Evening in Paris perfume," Jasmine whispered to herself, "or was it just the pretty blue bottle she loved?"

She concluded it was both and decided to stop at the department store and buy it. She could imagine it all now. Polly would look at her and question.

"What's wrong?"

She would then fall into Polly's arms and weep uncontrollably.

No! Forget the Evening in Paris. She decided on chocolate instead.

She got in her car and went to the convenience store on the corner and bought M&M's. She would eat them all on the road heading toward Polly's house. Chocolate had caffeine in it. She needed caffeine.

"They melt in your mouth, not in your hand."

True. Some things never change—except for matters of the heart.

*****

One always goes back. If not to stay, to remember…

Jasmine pulled over to the side of the road before taking the final turn to Polly's house. She ate the rest of her M&M's and took steady breaths—long, steady breaths. She needed a moment before going that final mile. Her grandma's house had been sold, but Polly would stay in the house next door until the day she died. At least that is what she had told Jasmine. But Jasmine thought if Polly met the right man, she would be off and running. Then again, maybe not.

She hadn't thought to call ahead of her arrival. What if Polly wasn't there? She couldn't stay with the people who had bought her grandma's house. She couldn't just walk in and say, "I used to live here. Can I sleep in my own room for a night or two—until Polly gets back?"

She could always turn around and go back into town to one of the hotels if she needed to.

She breathed a sigh of relief. Why was she so anxious? She was in her own hometown, for goodness' sake. She knew her way around. She had always had a Plan B. The hotel would be her Plan B. Again, she took steady breaths, long steady breaths, as she charted her course toward Polly's.

The first thing she saw was the flower garden with the backdrop of her grandma's house. Everything was in order; everything was flourishing. Polly had kept her promise. Not one weed to be found. Not one rose bush left untrimmed.

The sun would be setting soon. The old swing on the porch was still there, too, freshly painted.

So the new owners still sit on that swing, she thought.

Many memories began to take shape behind her eyes that were brimming with tears. She wondered again if anyone ever got over losing people so dear to them. She thought not.

She gazed over to Polly's house in the distance. Polly was at her clothesline carefully taking clothes down before the dark settled in. She breathed a sigh of relief and thought how life seemed so simple here. She wondered why she had ever left. Maybe she was meant to be here and nowhere else after all.

Polly looked up and began to walk back to her house when she spotted Jasmine. She dropped the laundry basket and shouted,

"S——t fire, girl! Am I having a reaction to my new medication, or are you really and truly standing over there next to that flower garden of your grandma's!"

"It's me, Polly!" Jasmine shouted back.

Polly took off running, and it was mere seconds before she had Jasmine in her arms. It was then, and only then, that Jasmine finally burst into tears.

That's what happens when someone comforts you in a time of need. You cry and you can't stop. Like a pressure cooker releasing its steam. You explode in the arms of love.

*****

Polly gently pushed Jasmine away from her embrace to look at her face.

"You're still as pretty as a picture! You look fine. Your color is good. So why do I feel you are in such organized disarray?"

"I don't feel pretty, but I do thank you, Polly."

Polly grabbed her once again and held her closely. "Come on," Polly said.

"Where are we going?"

"Back to my house. We're going to climb the stairs to what I declared to be your room whenever you wanted it when you went away, and we're going to get you settled in."

Jasmine let Polly lead her to her car.

"Then"—Polly kept talking—"we're going to open a bottle of wine, pop popcorn with lots of salt, and watch *Miss America*."

"Just like the old days?"

"Yes, my sweet, just like the old days."

They drove the short distance to Polly's, retrieved the suitcases, and walked to the front door and up the stairs.

"You get settled. Then you come downstairs and tell me your secrets."

*****

Polly sensed that Jasmine needed a moment. She needed some silence within her familiar territory. She needed the security inside the room that had been declared hers from the moment she had left after her grandma's funeral.

She wondered what had happened. Everything had seemed good and happy after Jasmine had met Gordy. At least, it had seemed so in all the letters Jasmine had sent her.

She decided to have a first glass of wine before Jasmine came downstairs. She had a feeling she was going to need it. And besides that, Ellie always told her she seemed to think more clearly with a glass of wine in her hand.

*****

Jasmine entered the kitchen.

"Now I've caused you to drink," Jasmine mumbled.

"Stop mumbling, child! No one causes me to drink! I do it of my own accord!" She poured Jasmine a glass and handed it to her. "Now tell me what's wrong."

"I got on a horse."

"Oh, dear! Did you get knocked off? Did you get hurt?"

"In a way."

"What do you mean 'in a way'?"

Jasmine took a sip of her wine. "I didn't see the guillotine coming."

Polly sat back in her chair, staring at Jasmine. "Honey, you are definitely in disarray. Perhaps you better start at the beginning."

*****

Jasmine told Polly the whole story. Polly was just relieved she had not injured herself from her fear of thinking Jasmine had fallen off a horse. Yet her heart ached for the emotional wound that was etched upon her face.

"You know, I always had hopes that you would find another man like Andrew. And I thought you had found him when you met Gordy. Both of those men were the kind that when they fell in love it would happen fast. But life can still get pretty complicated around men like that. Seems like you've discovered some of those complications."

Polly got up from her chair. She walked to the cabinet and pulled down another glass. Taking it back to the table, she sat it between them. She pointed to the wine. "This helps, and so do hissy fits." She took a sip from her own glass. "I used to throw hissy fits when I was young," Polly confessed. "Don't remember *you* ever throwing one growing up. I think it's high time you did. You deserve a hissy fit, and I'm here to help you."

Jasmine looked at Polly, wondering if she were kidding.

"You do know what a hissy fit is, don't you?" Polly took another sip of her wine. "You know—it's when you slam doors, scream, and throw things." Polly handed her the empty glass. "Go ahead. Throw it!"

Jasmine looked doubtful. "Really?"

"Yes, really! Go ahead, honey. It's amazing how good you're going to feel afterward!"

Jasmine did not hesitate. She threw the glass against the wall.

"Good! Now go slam the door!" Polly pointed to the front door.

Jasmine walked to the door, opened it, and slammed it hard.

"Good! Now scream!"

Jasmine looked doubtful.

"Don't worry, honey. Whatever happens in my house, nobody ever questions."

Jasmine screamed.

Polly walked over to her, gave her a heartfelt hug, and whispered. "You have just had your first hissy fit. How do you feel?"

It was a total surprise when Nora, the next-door neighbor, knocked on Polly's door. "Is everything okay over here?"

Polly laughed a laugh that was full of mischief. "Oh yes, thank you for checking. My best friend's granddaughter just had her very first hissy fit."

"I've had a few of those myself!"

"Then you understand."

Jasmine held out her hand. "I'm Jasmine. You bought the house my grandma and I lived in for many years."

The neighbor took her hand and introduced herself. "I'm Nora."

Polly retrieved another glass from the cabinet. "Please sit down, Nora. We were just having wine and hissy fits in here."

"I suppose these fits are centered around men." Nora sat, joining them, lifting her glass in a toast. She took a sip. "I came over to ask you a favor. I heard the screaming and thought I better check on that too."

"What's that?"

"My husband and I are going on a little trip for a long weekend, and I was wondering if you would watch the house and feed our cats." Before Polly could answer, Nora looked at Jasmine. "You lived in the house? Would you like to stay there while we're gone?"

Jasmine hesitated.

Nora quickly continued, "I'm sorry. I'm the sentimental type and just thought you might like to stay and remember old times."

Jasmine fumbled with her emotions but finally questioned, "That's actually very kind of you. What do you think, Polly?"

"Looks like you have two attractive offers while you're here, honey—with me and also the house you grew up in."

Jasmine looked at Nora. Maybe this was where she could begin to pick up some of the pieces that had been missing in her life for so long. "I would love to take care of your cats, Nora."

"Wonderful!"

Nora rose to leave, suddenly remembering. "I almost forgot! I found a box of things that belonged to your grandma. While you're there, you might want to go through it."

Before leaving, she said, "Oh, also, the guest room is the room where the jasmine plant sways outside the window. It has a nice fragrance at dusk. I think you'll enjoy it."

Polly and Jasmine looked at each other in complete silence. They were remembering when that jasmine plant had been planted beneath that bedroom window and the little hummingbird that had been buried there.

"Who was he, Polly? The man who planted that special plant? I remember him vaguely."

Polly cleared her throat and poured another glass of wine. "That's for another time, sweet girl, another time. Besides that, we have popcorn to pop. We have to get ourselves settled in for *Miss America*."

*****

The first night in her grandma's house found her remembering...

Her grandma had always had a welcoming lap. Jasmine climbed upon that lap when she was a toddler. She took her grandma's face in her hands.

"Laugh for me, Grandma."

"Why?"

"Cause your laugh makes me laugh! You laugh funny!'

Soon they would be laughing together just because everything seemed funny when her grandma laughed.

Jasmine sat propped up in the bed thinking of yet another time—she had been eight years old when she asked her grandma a very important question.

"Grandma?"

"Yes, child?"

"Did you ever kiss a man?"

Ellie ran her fingers through her hair and looked at Jasmine with a smile. "Yes."

"How many?"

"A few."

"More than one?"

"Yes."

"Why?"

"I was looking for the right one."

"How many of them did you have to kiss before you found the right one?"

Ellie heard her heart sigh. "Quite a few."

"A hundred?"

Ellie laughed. "No, not that many."

"Wow." Jasmine sighed.

"Why the big sigh?" Grandma asked.

"I think kissing a boy would be yucky." Jasmine sighed again.

"As you get older, child, you just may look at it a bit differently."

"It doesn't matter, Grandma. Kissing will probably go out of style before I have to kiss a boy."

"Does that make you sad?"

"A little."

"Why is that?"

"Because I'll never know what it was like."

*****

Jasmine got up from the bed and walked over to the window. A slight breeze had brought the sweet fragrance of the jasmine plant into her bedroom—just like the old days. She breathed deeply. She had found out what it was like—kissing a boy.

"Sorry, Grandma, I beat your record. I made it up to at least a hundred before I met the right one."

Once again, Jasmine thought of the man who had been a part of their lives during her younger years and wondered if he had been the right one for her grandma. She was determined to get Polly to talk about him. She remembered him being a big part of her life for a short time when she was very young, and then he had gone away. She knew the stories that Grandma had told her. But for some reason, she just couldn't accept that he had disappeared and never come back. Or had he?

*****

The next morning, Jasmine fed the cats and let them out on the fenced in deck to sit in the sun. She, too, wanted to enjoy the brightness of the day but chose first to go down into the basement where she discovered the dollhouse she had been given as a child. The new owners of the house had sat it upon one of the shelves and told her about it before they had gone on their trip. They had assumed it had been hers. She was glad.

She walked over to it. It looked a little rusty now. But once upon a time, it had been shiny. She remembered when the mystery man had given it to her. How old had she been? Five, maybe.

*****

"I can't touch it!'

"Why?" he questioned her.

"It's too beautiful!'

He stooped down until he was eye level with her.

"You're beautiful too. You don't break when I touch you."

Grandma walked into the room.

"You can touch your dollhouse, child. You can arrange the furniture. You can make up stories with the people that live there. They won't break."

The man hugged Grandma, smiling as he pulled her close.

"Jasmine, what do you say we carry the house and all the furniture, plus the people up to your bedroom?"

"Can we sit it in front of the window so the people can smell the jasmine flower at night?"

"Of course, we can," he said

Slowly, Jasmine reached out and touched the dollhouse. Now she was grown up. Now she was not afraid to touch it. She would carry it upstairs and place it in front of the window once again. And she would wait for the sweet fragrance of jasmine to float through her bedroom window that night.

*****

The memories of childhood enfolded her when the evening came. She remembered her nights of crying over a teenage breakup. She thought her world had ended.

"When do the tears of a high school breakup turn into an adult weeping?" she asked herself.

She wondered, *When does a door close gently—a click—and dry tears shout, "I'm alone"? When do tears change their meanings?* She had caught her grandma crying one day. Had it been for the loss of her own daughter? Or was it when the mystery man left? Jasmine couldn't remember. What she did remember was that when her grandma began to cry or feel sad, she would sing. Troubled? She would sing. Happy? She would sing. It got to a point where you didn't know when she was troubled or happy, because she was always singing.

"Sing, child, sing!"

She could almost hear her grandma commanding her to do so.

She remembered—when her grandma burned the beans, she would sing. When she forgot the grocery list, she would sing. She'd burn her finger and sing. She would trip on the steps with groceries in her hands and sing.

"Let's make cookies, child!" And they would sing.

"Singing takes away the sting of disappointment, child!"

Should Jasmine sing now? She had lost everything. She had lost Andrew, and now she had lost Gordy. She couldn't bring herself to sing one note.

Suddenly, it was very important to her to clean up that dollhouse. She would arrange the furniture. But the people had disappeared. A house with no people. How could that be? Sometimes it happens. She thought of her house on the ocean. Still empty. No people. Not yet. Maybe never. What would become of the house Andrew had purchased?

He, that mystery man, had told her that she was beautiful and she would not break. He was wrong. She did break. And now she found herself crying on the floor, completely shattered, for what was and was no more.

It was the next morning that she found the letters. Jasmine read every one. Love letters. Everyone signed: Love, "Me." Who was "Me"? She wanted a name. She was more determined than ever to have Polly tell her about who this man was.

*****

"How many chances does a person get to start over?" she asked Polly while working in the flower garden, after Nora and her husband had come back home.

Polly looked at her and, without hesitation, replied, "As many as they want."

Jasmine pulled at a stubborn weed.

Polly pursued the conversation. "Do you want to start over here, in your hometown, child?"

"I think I do."

Polly stood, shading her eyes from the sun. "I don't."

Jasmine could not believe her ears. "What do you mean, Polly? Wouldn't you like to have me back here?"

Polly smiled. "There is nothing I would like more, child, but this is not your future, not anymore. Moving forward is what you need to do. Ellie would tell you the same thing. I know that in my deepest of hearts, that is exactly what she would tell you. There's a life out there for you to find. You've had some hard knocks, but you come from good stock. You're strong. And you're going to become stronger."

"Move forward to where, Polly?"

"Brooksport Village."

"That's not forward."

"Oh, but it is, child! That's where you belong. You and Gordy have some sorting out to do, and if I know you and Gordy like I think I know you and Gordy, especially from what you've told me about him—well, the two of you are going to do it!"

"That's ridiculous, Polly. I've thought and thought about it, and it's over. The timing wasn't right."

Polly got down on her knees and turned Jasmine to face her, eyeball to eyeball. "S——t fire, girl! I don't believe that malarkey for one minute! You need to go face that man and find out if you need to put a period where a comma has sat dormant for all these months! Can you do that?"

Jasmine could not answer.

"What color are his eyes?" Polly asked.

"Blue."

"All the more reason."

Eight months later…

Chapter 34

Jasmine and Polly were seated on the front porch. It was a lazy, hot afternoon when she decided to finally ask the question.

"Who was he, Polly?"

Polly was fanning herself. "Lordy, child, I don't think I'll ever get used to how hot summers get down here!"

Jasmine sighed. "Don't act as if you didn't hear me, Polly! I found the letters."

"What letters?"

"The ones he wrote to my grandma. The ones he always signed, 'Love, Me.'"

"Oh, those letters."

"Who was he? I really want to know. It makes me sad to think Grandma gave up a most important part of her life to take care of me. I really want to know who he was."

Polly got up from her chair.

"Where are you going?"

"To uncork the wine, child. We need wine for this conversation."

*****

They sat on the porch in silence, sipping their wine. A gentle breeze began to blow as dusk was drawing near. The sweet fragrance of jasmine was floating around them when Polly began.

"He was a good man. A real good man." Polly took another sip of wine and fiddled with the folds of her skirt. "He had three women in his life, child."

"Three?"

"Yes, one was like a sister to him, one was a friend, and the other, well, the other was the woman he loved."

Jasmine looked out at the flower garden that was once her grandma's.

"The one that was like a sister"—she took another sip of wine, a bigger sip—"well, her name was Mona."

Jasmine sucked in her breath. "You mean Andrew's mother?"

Polly nodded.

"They met in a support group. She was there, learning how to live with an abusive husband, and he was there learning how to live with a—what they call—a 'functioning' alcoholic wife."

It was beginning to get darker with the breeze becoming cooler.

"Nice when the sun goes down, eh, child?"

Jasmine had to agree and poured herself another glass of wine. "Andrew mentioned that a friend of Mona's helped her financially in order to get him into military school, away from his father."

"That was him." Polly helped herself to more wine. "I learned all of this when you and Andrew were planning your wedding. Mona and I met at that time, and during one of our conversations, we both discovered we had a major thing in common, and that was him. You see, I was the second woman in his life. I was his friend."

"And the third?"

"Ah, the third. The third was the woman he loved." She placed her glass on a nearby table, turned to Jasmine, took Jasmine's wine glass, and placed it beside hers. She looked straight into her eyes. "And that woman, dear child, was Ellie, your grandmother."

"Did Grandma love him?"

"Oh, child, she loved the dickens out of him!"

"But she didn't marry him. Was it because of me?"

That question seemed to always be a commanding force in Jasmine's life. Had her grandma given up so much of her own life because of her?

"Child, her top priority was raising you after your mama died, but it wasn't because of you she never married him! Don't ever think that! She would not be happy if she thought you were thinking like that! It wasn't you at all!"

"Then why? Why didn't she marry him?"

Polly picked up her wine glass.

"Oh, wait, please tell me he wasn't already married!"

"No, child, he was divorced when he met Ellie. After his divorce, he took to the road and found our little town, and Ellie right along with it. He and I became buddies. Oh, I could see the spark between those two a mile away. Shoot, I was afraid I would get singed just standing next to them when they merely looked at one another."

Jasmine smiled. She knew of which Polly was speaking. She had the same sensations just having been in the same room with Andrew. "So she could have married?"

"Yes."

"Just when I thought it might happen, life got in the way." Jasmine pondered that answer as she remembered. "I must have been around five years old."

Polly looked out at the sunset. "Yes, you couldn't understand why he was leaving."

"I remember Grandma said that his family needed him."

"Yes, his daughter mostly. And then the years kept slipping away. Ellie and he wrote lots of letters. But then, one day, Ellie just called it off. I guess she felt that was best. I do know it broke her heart."

"And he never came back here—to try to change her mind?"

"No."

"Why not?"

"More 'life' happened, and the world got in the way."

"What do you mean?"

"Nine-eleven happened."

Jasmine looked at Polly. "And his family needed him again?"

"Oh yes, but not his daughter. It was his grandson that needed him in a mighty way. At least that's what Mona shared with me during one of our conversations."

"Mona had stayed in touch with him?"

"Yes, she knew he had met someone, and she encouraged him to *go get her*. I believe those were her exact words."

"But he didn't."

"No, he didn't."

"Did you tell Mona who that woman was?"

"No, I didn't."

"Why not?"

"That had always been a subject between Ellie and me. She was my best friend. I didn't feel it was right. I felt I was still within her confidence, even if she wasn't here anymore."

Jasmine reached for Polly's hand. "I understand." Blinking back tears, Jasmine whispered, "He did come back."

Polly reached for the wine. The bottle was empty. "Another bottle?" she asked Jasmine.

"I think we should."

*****

"I saw him."

Jasmine continued.

"At Grandma's funeral."

It was dark, and the stars were beginning to appear one by one.

Polly looked up, whispering a silent prayer.

Jasmine continued to speak. "I saw him sitting on the last pew of the church when I gave the eulogy for Grandma." Jasmine remembered him. "I saw tears running down his face. I wanted to run after him when everything was concluded, but he was gone too quickly. I wanted to talk to him. I wanted to rediscover him." Jasmine looked up as tears threatened to fall from her eyes. "I remembered that face. It was a little older. But it was the same face that left us when I was five years old. It was him. He came back too late." Jasmine looked at Polly as she poured more wine. "What was his name, Polly?"

Polly was lost in her own thoughts. He *had* come back—too late. "Carson, child, Carson was his name."

"Do you think I could find him?"

"These days you can find just about anybody you want to, child."

"I wish I could find him, Polly. I wish I could look him in the eyes and tell him how much my grandma did love him and how she should have never let him go."

Polly sighed. "If I had one thing I could have changed for Ellie, it would have been for her and Carson to have been together, that they could have built their white picket fence, prepared their Sunday dinners, worked in that flower bed of hers together. I would have never gotten tired of watching them sit on that swing on her front porch as the stars came out. They were meant to be together." Polly threw up her hands. "Not to be, I guess!"

Polly stood up and took a step toward the door. Before entering, she turned to Jasmine. "If Ellie were here, she would be telling you exactly this. Don't let your past have so much control over you that you are forgetting your present and the hope for your future. Don't do it, child! Reach out. If it's you who has to take the first step to Gordy, then you do it. Ellie would not want you to make the same mistake she did by not reaching out to Carson."

Polly took one last look at the horizon. "You simply cannot move from place to place and keep the pain. You'll never find 'home' if you do that! The pain will always be with you. Time to settle the pain, child. Time to settle the pain. Think about it."

Lightening the mood, she slapped at her arm. "Time to go inside. Those mosquitoes are pretty big out here in the country, as you know! And besides, you have to go in and start packing. I'm kicking you out. Go get him, child. Go get Gordy."

*****

Later that night, Polly looked out her bedroom window and up at that great big sky with all those stars, and she began to question her "buddy."

"Why, Carson, why wouldn't you have stayed and talked to me after Ellie's funeral? We had memories to cry over. We had comfort to give. We had hugs to embrace and tears to blend. Perhaps we could have answered the questions all of us ask from time to time. We could have eased our minds, shown gentleness, been gracious to one another and compassionate. Why did you slip away? I was your second woman. I was your friend. Aren't friends supposed to help friends through difficult times? You helped your family, way back when. Why couldn't you help the friend and the granddaughter of the woman you loved? I don't understand."

She turned the covers down on her bed and climbed in. As the wine was lulling her to sleep, she finally reasoned to herself.

"I guess some things in life are just unexplainable. Love hurts sometimes. Love just downright hurts."

And then she was out like a light as the moon cast a brightness across her bedroom floor.

*****

Jasmine had her own thoughts, preparing for bed. Polly was right. She had to settle the pain, but she was not packing. She wasn't going anywhere. Could she ease out of the pain she felt by looking at her own grandma's life and the choices she should have made when it came to Carson? The letter she should have written. The mystery man had not really ever been a mystery. She had known him through age five. She knew he deeply loved her grandma and her grandma loved him. She needed time to think. How had the conversation blended into the subject of her and Gordy? This was supposed to be about her grandma and Carson.

"It must run in the family," she whispered. "We supposedly strong women in this family keep losing the men we love. Why is that?"

She had no answers. She walked to the window and looked up. "Do you have a plan, God? If so, can you please tell me what it is?"

Oh, he had a plan, all right—a plan that was set in motion the minute those moonbeams streamed across Polly's bedroom floor.

A few days had passed when Polly came bursting into the kitchen, where Jasmine was sipping her coffee.

"Well, I see you haven't left yet, so I packed! But I see you are in deep thought! That's good. I'm going on a little trip! Can you take care of your grandma's garden until I get back?"

Jasmine looked up from her coffee. "Of course, you know I will. Where in the world are you going? You never go anywhere. You're a homebody. At least that's what you keep telling me."

"Well, after our conversation of a few days ago, I've decided that maybe I need to move forward too. I won't be gone long. Just long enough to take care of some business, you know, some personal stuff."

With that, Polly loaded up her car with what she would need for her journey and was on her way. Jasmine waved her goodbye and went back inside. She had some serious thinking to do herself. Perhaps it was best that she was alone with her thoughts. Polly was right in so many ways. But was she right about Gordy? Should she *go get him*?

*****

Polly was going on a trip all right. It was time she took the bull by the horns. And there was no doubt in her mind that she was doing the right thing. It was time to settle some things. And she was making it her business. Ellie would have agreed with her. She was sure of that. They had always done wild things together when they were younger. Sometimes preposterous things. She assured herself this would be wild, but that was her middle name when she was younger. Now she was going to be young again and do something preposterous.

"Homebody"? Really? Had she really said that? Well, now she was older. Maybe she was becoming more of a homebody. But she simply was not going to allow her best friend's granddaughter to make the same mistake her best friend had made in not reaching out to Carson. No, siree, she was headed straight to Brooksport Village.

PART 6

TED

"So, when a raging fever burns,
We shift from side to side by turns;
And 'tis a poor relief we gain
To change the place, but keep the pain."

(Isaac Watts)

What was happening? Everything was unraveling. Thank goodness Jake and Kate were back on track.

Gordy had slipped back into the grip of grief. And Jasmine was gone.

"I seemed to have made a mess of things," she mumbled to herself. "I tried to 'get ahead' of God and take things into my own hands with those two!"

Trudy sighed. There was nothing she could do—with one gone, who-knows-where, and Gordy "holed up" in his house. She was tired of making pizza casseroles. Besides that, she had some problems of her own; in one word—*Ted.*

She looked up at the sky.

One thought was on her mind now. Ted was acting more and more peculiar. There had been a time when she could always bring him back to her side with her humor. But lately, all that had changed. He had not thought of her as "funny" at all. She didn't know what his problem was. She didn't have time for all this nonsense. Why couldn't people just fall in love, build their white picket fences, plant their flowers, get a dog, have some children, and get on with it?

She needed to get her crochet hooks out again. People wouldn't believe that she crocheted. It seemed too tame for her. But Trudy had a quiet side too. And crocheting gave her peace. She knew exactly what she was going to make. She also needed lard. She strode over to Belle's. After her doughnut fix, she promised herself to tackle the pile of mail on her counter at the salon. It was way past due. But first she would crochet. She had to have a calmness about her to tackle that stack of mail.

*****

Trudy sat in the corner of her salon in the old rickety chair where so much forgiving had taken place in the past. She stared at the mail she had put on her lap. She began sorting through it one envelope at a time, one magazine at a time, and more junk mail than she could ever imagine. Some other things had been tossed there, old receipts and invitations that needed an RSVP. She determined to be more conscientious with her mail.

"What's this?" she questioned.

She sighed. "Should have sent this in weeks ago."

It was a warranty for the new dryer she had purchased for the salon. She picked up a pen and began to complete the form, vowing to drop it in the mail on her way home. She had always been a stickler about things like warranties. She had paid too much money in her lifetime on appliances. She wanted refunds and parts replaced for free if something went wrong. And most often, something did. Completing those warranty cards seemed to guarantee her some satisfaction, especially if a part broke, they would fix it for free, not to mention notifying her personally if there was a recall for some reason.

Ted was on assignment again. Seemed lately he was always on assignment. Something was wrong. She just couldn't put her finger on it.

She thought about going home to her empty house, a thought that did not appeal to her at all. She gazed around the salon with all the laundry that had to be done, and she really needed to order more supplies.

"I'm gonna go home to get Buddy," she said to herself and the salon walls. "Might as well do some work around here while Ted's 'on assignment.'"

In the past, he had told her the time and place he was going to be. This time, as well as other times recently, he had not. He had been gone almost three weeks, this time with no calls, no messages. Maybe another woman? She remembered their last conversation. She had not been very diplomatic.

"What is it with you?" Trudy questioned.

Ted answered with another question, "Does something have to be going on with me?"

"Look, somethin' keeps naggin' ya, and to tell ya the truth, your moodiness is gettin' a little tiresome for me!" Trudy walked over to Ted and stared him eyeball to eyeball. "That gum you've been chewin' on lost its flavor? Time to stick it on the bedpost and get on with your life? If that stick of gum is me, well, I'll deal with it. It's best you be on your way!"

Maybe that was when he decided not to tell her where he was going or when he was coming back.

Trudy questioned where he was. "On assignment? I doubt that."

With the way Gordy and Jasmine's love life had gone south, she couldn't rule out anything. She had thought they were the perfect couple. Oh, well. If Ted had found someone else, she would merely join the throngs of the brokenhearted and get on with life. Maybe somebody would bring her a casserole for a change.

She ran her hands through her hair, and with another big sigh, she walked out the door toward her house to get Buddy. He was the one that never, ever let her down.

This night would be no exception.

*****

"Come on, Buddy. Let's go."

Buddy sauntered into the living room, tail pointed toward the ceiling, and meowed.

"That's right. It's you and me tonight, my man! We're gonna go do some work at the salon. Lots of laundry—towels and such. Gonna get organized. Got your treats packed, got your food packed. We're gonna spend the night on the couch over there."

With one final check around the house, she picked Buddy up and walked out the door.

*****

Trudy made the bed on the couch. It was still early. She grabbed dirty towels from the basket and started to go downstairs to her laundry room.

"Maybe he was just too 'vanilla' for me," she said aloud. "Maybe I was just too peppermint for him—you know, with green and red candies all swirling together."

"There's something to be said about vanilla, Trudy," Kate said.

She hadn't noticed Kate standing in the doorway of the salon. "Oh, sugar! Where did you come from? You caught me talkin' to myself!"

Kate walked over to Trudy. "I know a lovesick fool when I see one. And usually, they're talking to themselves. Kind of like what I used to do. Remember?"

Trudy shrugged, dropped the towels on the floor and sat down. She stared at Kate.

"Speechless, Trudy?"

"I think my last words to him sent him packin'."

"Why?"

Trudy sighed. "I couldn't wipe the forlorn look off his face, and it was gettin' to me. And what I said to him before he left—well, it wasn't too kind."

Kate tried to make Trudy feel better. "We all say things at times we wish we hadn't said, Trudy. Don't feel guilty about that. Ted knows you love him. How long has he been gone?"

"Going on three weeks."

"But who's counting?" Kate walked over to the window and put the "Closed" sign on the door. Walking back to Trudy, she said, "Talk to me."

*****

"Ted was gettin' distant from me long before he hightailed it out of town." Trudy took a deep breath. "You know I have to find out why people are so 'closed' with their hearts. I want to know why they laugh too loud and fidget too much—the people who don't look at you when you talk. They have secrets. I have to know what's goin' on inside their heads."

"How well I know that."

"Well, Ted kept gettin' more and more like that lately. I would ask questions, and he would avoid me. He's not the fun man in the purple chapeau anymore. Somethin' is hauntin' him, Kate. Some ghost from his past. He did tell me that, lately, he wakes up sweatin'."

Kate needed to give Trudy some encouragement. "It's just a bump in the road, Trudy. Relationships aren't always fun. Jake and I sure learned that truth."

"I know love takes work. I know sometimes it's a struggle and an uphill climb. I'm willin' to work at it. I didn't think I'd ever open my heart again after Frank, but I have." Trudy ran her hands over her face. "But I can't make that climb if he's not willin' to talk. I'm no mind reader."

"I wish I could wave a wand over you and make it right, Trudy."

"I know, sugar."

Kate flung her arms in the air. "I don't want you running off to New York City! Like you did before, and not let anyone in this town know where you're going. You remember?"

"Yes, I remember. Don't worry. I'm not goin' to the city this time. Rest easy, but I do have a lot of thinkin' to do." Trudy looked at Kate. "I have laundry to do—lots of it, so Buddy and I are stayin' here tonight. I might as well get caught up with everythin' around here while Ted's gone. Practice what I preach. Busy hands keep ya outta trouble and help ya not to think too much. Now you go on! Get outta here! You have a man to go home to! Don't be worryin' 'bout me!"

*****

Trudy put the first load of towels into the washing machine and walked back upstairs. "Time sure goes by slow when you're not around, Ted," she said to herself.

She was going to have to face the fact that she truly loved that man. Why else would she be in such a hot mess over him not being here?

She gazed over at Buddy, sitting on the couch that would be their bed for the night.

"All ready to snuggle, eh, Buddy?"

Trudy sighed and looked out the window where she saw Charlie walking toward the salon. Home now from that big university with a medical degree in his hand. He was bound to find a hospital soon that would be the perfect fit. A visit from Charlie before he went off to greener pastures. Just what she needed—a dose of Charlie. They hadn't had a long talk in quite a while. She smiled as he walked through the door.

"Hey, Miss Trudy, want to grab some dinner with me?"

"I would like nothing better, Charlie! Where do ya wanna go?"

He held out a bag of burgers he had already purchased from Stumble In. "To the lake."

"Grease?" Trudy questioned.

"I know how you like your grease and salt, Miss Trudy!"

"Just give me a minute!" She had to mail that warranty in, late or not.

They stopped by the post office to send off the warranty and then walked toward the lake. They settled into two beach chairs. Charlie unwrapped one of the burgers, put it on a paper plate, and looked at Trudy.

"Looks like you're gonna make some kind of an announcement," Trudy said.

"I am."

She didn't think she could stand one more smidgeon of bad news. She nearly choked on her words. "You've done well for yourself, Charlie. I'm proud of you." She took a bite of her burger and, with a perplexed look, asked the question. She dreaded his answer. "Are you goin' to leave us, Charlie, now that you have your degree? You know we need good doctors in this place. I hope ya consider stayin' here, *but* I'm not tryin' to make up your mind for ya."

Charlie took a sip of his drink. "Sarah and I have talked. She has one more year of school left."

Trudy nodded. She wanted to delay his answer to her because she felt in her bones he would be moving to a bigger place, a bigger hospital. She quickly changed the subject. "Ya know I was gonna be an astronaut until I flunked arithmetic. Then I was gonna be a secretary until I realized I had ADD and couldn't sit still."

Charlie began to laugh.

"What's so funny?"

"You being an astronaut!"

"It's not so outrageous!"

"Oh, but it is!"

Trudy took a deep breath and looked out at the lake, the wind playing with her hair, the sun on her face. She looked up at the sky. "Yes, an astronaut." She sighed. "My daddy knew that would never happen. So one year he took a trip to one of those hair and beauty surplus stores and bought me a hair salon kit with blow-dryers, combs, brushes, and all kinds of shampoos and conditioners. He knew how I loved to fiddle with hair. He also found me a tutor for math so I would be sure to graduate."

"And the rest is history," Charlie said.

"Yes, the rest is history."

"You found your calling, Miss Trudy."

"You'll never stop calling me Miss Trudy, will you?"

"Nope, that's how I grew up. You taught me manners. Remember?"

"I remember very well."

Charlie gazed out at the beach where he used to work, bringing chairs in and storing them for the off-season. "I do know what I'm going to do. In fact, I've already done it."

"You're moving, aren't you?"

He avoided her question. "When I was younger, I thought I wanted to be a therapist."

"I remember."

"Then I realized Brooksport Village is therapeutic enough for everybody who lives here, so I decided to be a doctor."

"And a fine doctor you're gonna be!"

Charlie put his burger down and looked at Trudy. "Well, like I said, Sarah and I have talked."

Trudy took a gulp of her soft drink. "Okay, I'm ready for what you're gonna say next, but I may need a shot of liquor to get over the aftereffects."

Charlie laughed. "Oh, Miss Trudy, Sarah and I have both decided we're staying here! Right here! I'm going to work at the hospital!"

Trudy could not contain her excitement. Jumping up from her chair, her hamburger now in the sand and her soft drink spilt all over the ground, she grabbed Charlie and pulled him to his feet.

"Oh, Charlie! Do you know how wonderfully excited this news makes me feel! I am thrilled! And this news is just what I needed to hear today! You have brightened my spirits and my day!" She kept hugging him over and over.

"I thought you might like the news," he said.

She couldn't let him go. A ray of sunshine had just pierced the darkness.

*****

As they walked back toward town, Trudy was almost dancing a jig.

"Settle down, Miss Trudy. People are going to think you've lost your mind!"

"They already think that! They've known that for years! You remember how I used to be the topic of conversation around all the dinner tables in this town every evening!"

"True!"

As they neared the salon, Trudy swung around and asked, "When do you start your new career, Charlie?"

"Already have! Everyone kept the secret until I told you. I wanted you to hear it from me." Charlie wasn't quite ready to say goodbye to Trudy. He walked with her into the salon. "I never did thank you for all you've done for me through the years, Miss Trudy."

Trudy squared her shoulders and looked at him out of the corner of her eye. "Awww, shucks, Charlie. You don't have to thank me."

"Oh, but I do. You were always there for me." Charlie looked at Trudy with admiration gleaming from his eyes. "You never lied to me. You always told me straight up how things were. You always told me the truth."

"That's the only way to live life, Charlie."

"With the truth," Charlie said.

"Yes."

"Well, one day maybe I can repay you for all the truths you've helped me see."

"You want to thank me? You already have, by sayin' you're stayin' here—here where your roots are, here where there's always romance, well, kind of." Suddenly she thought of her own "romance." Then she continued, "You stayin' here in this little town where you can depend on people never lettin' ya down. That is thanks enough for me."

Charlie got up to leave.

Trudy touched his shoulder. "Thanks for dinner, Charlie, and there is one other thing you can do for me."

"What's that?"

"You can call me Trudy now. Leave off the 'Miss.'"

He blew her a kiss as he walked out the door. "Never. You'll always be Miss Trudy to me."

*****

"Well, Buddy, looks like you're already asleep. You've already cozied up, haven't you?"

Trudy remembered the towels still in the washer.

"Well, I'll join ya after I get those towels in the dryer, little man."

For some reason, she couldn't take her eyes off that sweet cat of hers. She began to walk toward the stairs going down to the laundry room.

"It's gonna be a long night, Buddy. At least, for me."

Before going down the stairs, she looked once more at Buddy.

"Well, at least you will lose some weight without Ted around givin' ya all those treats he hides in his pockets—that I asked him not to do."

Buddy looked up, yawned, stretched, and promptly went back to sleep.

Trudy kept murmuring as she walked down the stairs, "No Ted. No Ted."

"Whoever wishes to keep a secret must hide
the fact that he possesses one."

(Goethe)

Chapter 35

Ted was angry with himself. How could he leave Brooksport Village without saying goodbye to Trudy? Without asking Trudy to trust him while he was away? Trudy would expect explanations. She would ask questions. He wasn't ready to answer those questions. Not yet. And besides that, he didn't like goodbyes. He was not a man who could give explanations because his explanations never made sense in his own mind—much less trying to explain things to another person. Trudy was always full of questions when it came to matters of the heart. That was why he hadn't said goodbye.

He thought she deserved more than what he was capable of giving her. He had tried to leave her a note, but his words fell flat. They were not good enough. She deserved more. He wanted to turn the car around and speed back to Brooksport Village. He wanted to tell Trudy the truth. How else could he set himself free from his secret? He had to tell the woman he loved.

It had happened so long ago, and he had managed to move forward. Or, at least, he thought he had. The investigation had been short, not so simple, and definitely not so sweet. The guilt remained. So did the screams and the gunshots. That's what he heard in his dreams. Those dreams that awakened him in the middle of the night. He would always wake up in a pool of sweat. It was as if the shooting had happened only yesterday—when those nightmares beckoned him, forcing him to relive that awful day.

After he met Trudy, the dreams that had plagued him for so long had stopped. But now they were back with all the baggage he thought he had thrown out the back door of his subconscious mind. Why put her through that? She didn't need to help him unpack those suitcases he would be lugging into her life.

Trudy was the best thing that had happened to him since that awful day he had decided, on a whim, to carry that gun into that coffee shop. And that very decision had changed his life forever. She needed to hear that he cared. He wanted to marry Trudy. But now he questioned. How could he marry her when she was unaware of the battles that would follow? His battles. He had to tell her, *especially* since the dark endless nights of no sleep were back. He knew he could never escape them.

"Well, if I'm going to lose her, it's going to be because I came clean—not because I threw everything we had away, as if she didn't matter." He couldn't have her thinking that he didn't care. He had always cared, maybe too much.

He decided he would march right up her sidewalk, knock on her door, and say the four words that kept looming over him. Yes, he would say it outright.

"Trudy, I killed a woman."

*****

But he could not turn the car around, not just yet. He had to think. As he continued to drive, he began to think back, way back. Suddenly, his thoughts took him to when he was twelve years old.

He didn't like his freckles. Never had. Girls didn't like them either. He looked in the mirror.

"Ugh," was all he could say.

Twelve-year-old Ted did not want to go to camp. He was a boy who didn't like bugs, and he preferred an overhead light to a campfire. He didn't want sticky fingers from roasting marshmallows, and he especially didn't want to sleep in a cabin full of boys, where all they could talk about was girls. By day they hunted frogs; by night they dreamed of ways to scare the girls with them. Such nonsense.

He took one more look in the mirror. He looked at his open suitcase on the bed. His mom had laid out all his clothes. His job was to put them into the suitcase in some type of order. He could do that. He was what they called a "neat freak."

She had also insisted he have a suitcase with wheels. That's all he needed to go alongside the freckles. All the other boys would have backpacks. He would be teased unmercifully. A suitcase with wheels? Seriously?

His eyes brightened when he remembered the backpack he had secretly purchased and hidden under his bed. His one and only friend, Stan, had said to him, "Just go along with her, pack your things, and then switch them in the car when we pick you up."

"Won't your dad notice and tell my mom?" He always worried about things like that—getting caught doing something his parents wouldn't approve of.

"Oh no, he won't notice."

"Why not?"

"It's an engineer thing."

"An engineer thing?"

"Yeah, my mom said engineers don't notice anything except crooked pictures on the wall and specks of dirt on the rug."

Ted liked Stan. They were alike. They liked "order." And Stan had freckles too.

Yes, those young boys had a lot in common. They could not remember a time when either of them had not been teased. They could go back as far as kindergarten. Back then, they thought it was because both of them wore horn-rimmed glasses. It wasn't until high school they realized it wasn't the glasses at all—it was their minds. They had simply been too smart. Once they figured out why they were teased, they learned how to deal with it.

When they entered high school, they began to tutor the football players. Once those big, burly guys saw that their grades were raising from D's to B+'s, the teasing stopped. And when the most popular wide receiver on the team got an A in algebra, both Ted and Stan were heroes. Nobody messed with them anymore. In fact, they became quite popular, regardless of their freckles and horn-rimmed glasses. Everyone knew that unless "those boys of fall" got good grades, they could not play football, and if they could not play, the best team in the school's history would lose their chance of being crowned champions. Well, Ted and Stan were the cham-

pions that year, and the football team actually cheered them when they gave their valedictorian speeches at graduation. Yes, it had been a "tie."

That all aside, Ted had still settled in his mind that he would be a loner all his life. A lot of techys seemed to follow that pattern. Their career came first. Their computers were their first love. Deep down inside, Ted reasoned that computer love never let him down. Oh, it crashed and burned from time to time, but he could always fix that. Relationships were different. He didn't know how to fix a human who crashed and burned, especially a woman. He was hoping to learn one day. And he thought he could do just that when Trudy walked into his life. She seemed special. She was special. After all, she had told him she was royalty. He surmised she would never crash and burn because of something he had done in his past. God would protect her from him and the awful incident of that tragic day.

He would never perceive himself as royalty—that was for sure. She thought he was wonderful, protective, gentle, and laid-back. But she didn't know the secret that had followed him around like a shadow, refusing to let him go. It was one of those awful secrets that could blow a person apart if they let it. Guilt was hovering around him like a low dark cloud, smothering him. He knew he would have no future with Trudy if he did not rid himself of those two bed companions that had taken root in his heart. Secrets and guilt had overstayed their welcome in his life.

The cemetery seemed the only place for him to go for his answers. He wasn't looking forward to it, but he knew somehow that was where he had to go. And this particular cemetery was not just around the corner from Brooksport Village. It would take him quite a drive to get there. For that was where the secret had become like a spider spinning its web, like tendrils spreading far into his future, unless he brought it into the light. Only then would he be a captive set free…

*****

They were so different. She was outgoing, lighting up every room she entered. She was well-liked, voted homecoming queen, and head cheer-

leader—a beautiful girl. He was exactly at the other end of the spectrum. One always questioned how sister and brother could be so opposite, being raised by the same parents. These siblings were another pair making the exception to the rule a strong reality.

Her name was Tess. He had always called her sis. They became known as Tess and Ted, the two T's. She had teased him unmercifully in those younger years. He smiled now at some of those memories as the miles kept getting him closer and closer to the cemetery he was fleeing to in desperation.

How old had he been when he had thrown a rock through the storm door window, leading to the living room? Five years old. She was fifteen. He was always told that he was their bonus baby. Never a mistake. Sometimes, he wondered about that.

Tess simply loved making faces at him and then running away. She loved seeing him get so mad his face would turn red. He remembered her looking at him the day he threw that rock. She had pointed at the broken glass on the porch, yelling, "Daddy's sure gonna spank you when he gets home!"

Ted remembered sitting in the middle of his front yard and dreading the five o'clock hour, when his dad would be coming home from work, driving his little yellow Comet that looked like a bumblebee. He remembered the drill so well. His dad would get out of the car and look at the broken glass while his sister snickered nearby.

"Who did this?"

"I did. I threw a rock."

His father had never asked why. He had merely sent him to his room and told him to think about what he had done for thirty minutes, and then he was going to get a spanking.

His dad always surmised that thinking about the spanking was ten times worse than actually getting one. He had been right. He did not get spanked. But, oh, the time he thought about it was much worse. And he vowed never to throw any more rocks.

He wished he could bring back those days of his sister's teasing. It was "sibling" teasing, not ruthless. If he had known then what he knew now, things would have been different. He would never have bought a gun.

He kept his eyes on the road, deciding it was time to stretch his legs. He pulled off at the next rest stop and got out of the car.

He saw a group of five-year-old boys, all wearing cowboy boots, running around the picnic tables with their toy guns while shooting at each other. Their parents were trying to rein them in so they could carry on in their journey, wherever they were going. But you can't rein in little cowboys with guns. You had to lasso them.

He used to have a pair of cowboy boots. He remembered trying to be a cowboy way back when; he just didn't quite make it. An outlaw maybe but not a cowboy.

He kept looking at the little boys in their play and thinking about the gun he had purchased so long ago. He knew he wasn't a cowboy; he just wanted a gun. Did he want to prove to himself that he was, indeed, a manly man if not a cowboy? Real, true, manly men carried guns. Or so he thought at the time. Like it or not, that had been his answer. He had since changed his mind about all of that nonsense, especially after what had happened.

Yes, Tess had teased him in those early years, but she had also kept his secrets. She did manage to get him out of heaps of trouble from time to time. Trouble just seemed to always find him wherever he was. That should have been his first clue not to buy a gun when he was of age to do so.

His mom had never liked guns; neither had his dad. Both Ted and Tess knew that. Tess vowed never to say a word about it, especially to their parents. She had helped him actually do everything on the up and up. He had gone to firing lessons and acquired his license to carry. Tess had thought it pretty cool—a techy like him carrying a gun. It had never occurred to him that, one day, he just might have to use it.

"Oh, I feel so protected when I'm with you!" she had whispered to him one day, teasing him, walking arm in arm down the street.

That had made him feel good, especially when she had always been the one protecting him when he was growing up. He remembered those days as he continued to watch the five-year-old boys continue their game of cowboys and outlaws. Of all the things in his life, he always wanted to protect his sister.

He sat at one of the picnic tables and remembered: *Tess had been seventeen when she left for college. He had been seven. He had cried when she left. He missed her terribly. When she graduated and came home, he was twelve years old.*

The major teasing at school had escalated since kindergarten, well into junior high. Tess always flew in like a hawk with a look that would stop a predator in their tracks. By the time he had moved on to high school, she had taught him self-defense tactics. Turned out he didn't need them when he realized he could turn the very thing that was causing all the teasing into something good for the football players. He could never be a popular jock, but he knew how to use his mind to help those other jocks make their grades. And the teasing had stopped. He smiled at that memory.

Yes, he was smart. He had a knack for knowing computers, but his fascination for guns remained. He liked the thought of one day having to protect someone and actually being able to do it. The gun was his confidence, his security. Something that proved his manhood.

*****

Ted returned to his car, got in, and continued to drive as he was drawn back to the present. He looked up at the clouds through the windshield of his car. The wind began to blow. It was a cold wind, much too early for wrapping its arms around a warm October day. The dark clouds continued to gather. But Ted didn't care. He was nearing the town where he needed to be. The cemetery would be coming into view soon. He would park his car and walk up to that grave—even if it poured rain in torrents. He had come this far, and he would continue to go the distance.

He would leave this cemetery with mud on his shoes and drenched to the bone. He was about to experience an abreaction that only God could give him in the pouring rain. Healing rain.

Meanwhile, back in Brooksport Village

Trudy didn't know what to do with herself. She felt helpless. She was supposed to be the *fixer* of everyone's woebegone love affairs. But she was losing her touch. She kept thinking of Gordy and Jasmine; Jasmine was gone. And Gordy sat on his porch alone at dusk, watching inchworms. Even lard didn't seem to help her state of mind.

She kept asking herself, *Where had Ted gone?* But hadn't she told him to go with words that cut to the quick? Maybe he hadn't loved her as she thought he had. Frank hadn't loved her, really loved her, either—as a husband should love a wife. He had wanted no harm to befall her, but he had not ever been *in love* with her. He had been in love with another woman and had given that woman a child. She had finally accepted that. But she made a vow to herself that she would never put herself in that predicament ever again. Loving someone who didn't love you back was a hell within itself. She couldn't even describe it. The wound was too deep.

She remembered Frank and how she had watched his vacant eyes when she tried to have a conversation. She remembered the flinch in his body when she tried to touch him, feeling him crawl to his own side of the bed in the midnight hour and knowing he wanted to be somewhere else. He would always leave the room where she would be standing with not even a shrug or a sigh. She never knew where his mind was. All her attempts at making him happy fell to the floor with a crash only the unloved could hear. That's what she had experienced with Frank, her ex-husband, now deceased. She remembered him asking her forgiveness for all those tearful times when she had waited up for him, eaten dinner alone, and cried herself to sleep. Yes, he had apologized, and she had forgiven him. In her wildest dreams, she never thought she would be put in the same circumstance yet again—this time with Ted.

"I cannot believe he is with another woman," she said to herself over and over. "I just cannot believe that at all."

She would not let her mind trick her into falling into that miry pit. All she could hope for was that he would discover what he was running from and turn around to face whatever it was that had him in such a twit. All she could pray for was that he would come back and tell her whatever it was that kept chasing him from his past and why it was so difficult to put that secret in front of her. She wanted desperately to fight this thing with him. Was it that bad? Somehow, she couldn't wrap her head around anything that could be *that* bad—not with Ted. He was a techy. He followed the rules. He made sure things were always in order. Things that bad did not happen to techys. Didn't he trust her to stand beside him regardless of what he had done or what had been done to him?

She was doing a lot of sighing these days without Ted. Buddy missed him too. She sensed the treats he always carried in his pocket were a big part of the reason.

"Treats! Buddy, I will give you treats tonight, and I will get pizza—and beer!"

Yes, she needed beer with pizza. Maybe that would help. Comfort food and drink. She would give Buddy a treat and take a bite of pizza. Then she would repeat. Over and over. She would sit on her pity pot that night. In the morning, she would get up and be her old self again. She would do it. Yes, she would.

What Trudy didn't realize while sitting on her pity pot, was that her techy had feelings too. And he did have a clue, when others thought he didn't. He hurt. And when he was cut deep, he bled. He was all human, and humans have emotions that can't be denied. He found it hard to share emotions that seemed to clutter his brain and his heart. So he tended to keep it in. He didn't want to bother with it. It kept him from doing productive work that needed to be done. Until—until he found Trudy. Until he wanted to make a future with a woman who needed grease and salt. Until his past collided with his future that he wanted so badly. He believed he had to go away in order to trace back to where he belonged.

He was going to face his giant.

Techys become more human than most when they do exactly that—face their giants. They aren't as closed off as people may think. They become more understanding because they have been trodden upon through the years in ways most don't understand. They have to blend their past hurts into what the future holds and hope that the special woman they meet along life's pathway will understand. That she would be there to help them unpack the baggage they had carried around for so long—a woman who would be there through the nightmares and night sweats. A woman who would cup their face in her hands and tell them she was there and would never leave.

That is what Ted wanted with all his heart. He loved Trudy. His only hope was that she loved him just as much and that she would be that special woman in purple who would hold him when he finally cried.

*****

Ted sat in his car gripping the steering wheel. He looked out at the rain. It had been a different kind of day all those years ago.

Tess had always liked autumn.

"The world is so full of color!" she had exclaimed.

He took a deep breath. The autumn breeze was cold today.

He remembered particularly a warmer autumn day.

"See that pile of leaves over there? Let's go run through them!'

He thought, Why not? Adults could run through leaves too!

Then both brother and sister took off running, spreading the leaves as they ploughed through them.

The park attendant watched in horror.

"Hey!" he yelled. "You two are old enough to know better!'

"We'll fix it!" Tess had yelled back, throwing leaves in the air.

"You bet you will!'

He walked over to them and gave them two rakes and a dozen leaf bags. They had laughed as they raked. When they were done, they had turned in unison to the park attendant and had given him a thumbs-up sign. Tess grabbed her brother's hand and went running toward the seesaw.

"No, no way!" Ted had shouted through his laughter.

"Yes, yes—way! Just make sure that gun you're carrying stays in the holster and you don't shoot your foot!"

"I took classes, remember? I know the safety rules!'

"I know you do, and your secret is still safe with me! In your deepest of hearts, did you ever think about becoming a policeman?"

He had not answered her.

The rain continued to pour as he kept remembering that day.

After leaving the park, they had walked to the local coffee shop and settled into a cozy booth. She would be leaving the next day on a well-deserved vacation.

He had turned to her and said, "I'll never ever look at a leaf in quite the same way ever again."

And she had replied, "Me neither. Don't forget to run in the park from time to time, little brother. Promise me you'll find a seesaw and be a kid again. Promise me you will throw leaves in the air every autumn."

That was the autumn after brother and sister took their last sip of coffee together—when the man walked in. There had been a small child at the counter. As if in slow motion, everything happened so quickly. Tess had seen the man first. She had also seen a small child at the counter, looking at all the pastries. The first gunshot assaulted his ears as Tess jumped and ran to protect the child from the gunman. Ted had turned while reaching for his own gun. He didn't hesitate. He merely shot twice.

The first bullet hit his sister, whom the gunman had grabbed and held in front of him. When she fell, the second bullet hit the masked man.

Ted felt a cold chill run up his back. Both Tess and the gunman lay on the floor. Both dead.

*****

Ted got out of the car. He began to walk toward the grave markers still thinking. Oh, if he could only go back to the days of toasted biscuits, warm syrup, and a side of bacon. If he could only see his mother in that tiny kitchen and his dad rounding the corner driving his bright yellow Comet. If only, if only. If he could have fast-forwarded to that day in the coffee shop. If he could have seen what was about to become a fearful reality.

He would have persuaded her to play in the leaves a bit longer. They would have talked about hummingbirds while sitting on that seesaw. Tess loved hummingbirds. She loved how they could fly successfully backward. She would have talked about how graceful, colorful, and translucent those hummingbirds were. It would have taken up more time. And he would have listened to her every word.

She had been a poet by nature. A rare, beautiful bird herself. They would not have gone into that coffee shop. They would have gone home because it was getting late. Hindsight is the best sight, they say.

He wanted desperately to talk about all of this with Trudy. He wanted to tell her what had happened on that fateful day. He knew she would understand his misery, but would she hold his face in her hands like she used to and convince him everything would be all right? Would she stand beside him and wipe his forehead in the midnight hour? Or would it be easier for her to walk away? All he knew was that he had to face his own personal giants before he could ever ask Trudy to climb the huge mountain that loomed in the distance—that mountain that mocked him with every step he had tried to take forward. It had to come to an end. And this was the place he had been led to end it all.

*****

Rainy days and quiet cemeteries always give you answers. Rain—lots of rain—seemed appropriate to Ted as he stood there, looking at his sister's grave. He was alone. No joggers. No loud music. No alarms. No walking dogs. Only fountains, statues, and grave markers. Some vases filled to the brim with flowers, others empty. He had stopped at the florist and bought the "full to the brim" bouquet. He bent down and put the flowers in the vase.

"You know, someone once said if you are facing a major decision in your life, go to the cemetery. That's why I'm here," he whispered.

He sat down on the ground. He faced the gravesite where his sister had been buried.

"Hello, Tess. You see, I have to make a major decision—how to live the rest of my life. I'm ready for a change."

The wind began to blow the rain in his face. Even though the day was warm, the drops felt like ice against his skin. Sharp ice. Cutting ice.

"The therapist used to tell me I should put away my guilt. So did Mom and Dad. I've tried. But, Tess, the dreams are back. They're relentless. It's both a conscious and subconscious thing. Neither will allow this guilt I carry around to evaporate. It has seeped into every fiber of my being."

The rain turned into a steady drizzle.

"Oh, I tried escaping from the reality of it all—through my computers."

He smiled.

"I help people find lost loves. My job is like an anesthesia that helps me forget what happened to you. I've looked for you everywhere—in stranger's eyes, in blonde hair swaying in the wind, at the ice cream stand where you loved to hang out, *everywhere*, Tess. I looked for substitutes. But I could never find my own sister—because you were here."

He wiped the rain from his face.

"You're the only girl I ever wanted to protect because you always protected me, and you're the one I killed!"

He looked into the distance. He scraped his hands over his face.

"I need to tell you about Trudy."

He began to pull the weeds that were beginning to take root around his sister's marker.

"Am I going to spend the rest of my life constantly thinking of all my regrets? Am I going to still go to bed at night just waiting for the night sweats to begin?"

He stared at his sister's marker and ran his hands over its smooth surface.

"I need you to talk to me!"

He hung his head.

He didn't care if some passerby might think him crazy shouting to a tombstone marker. But he was alone. Nobody was out on a day like this, especially visiting a cemetery.

He looked up at the sky, the clouds still threatening, as the rain continued to fall.

"I killed you, sis. I killed you."

Ted was in need of a resurrection.

*****

He continued to stare at his sister's marker, allowing his memories to settle in the very core of his soul.

There had been no charges pressed. When it came down to the bottom line, the police called it a tragic incident when talking about his sister. The gunman, well, that was a different matter. It was public opinion that Ted had actually been a hero by ridding society of a gunman who had intended fully to "shoot up the place." They had found the letter the gunman had written in his apartment where the police had stormed in shortly after the incident. They were compassionate toward the loss of his sister but wanted to award him with a badge of honor for saving the lives that would have been lost that fateful day. Ted refused. Instead, he had gone to the lake and thrown the gun into the deepest part of the dark water. His sister had been memorialized for saving the young toddler's life. When she pushed the toddler out of the way, the gunman had grabbed her. The rest was history.

His dad and mom went with him to the lake. They tried to console him, but the shadow of death followed him throughout the rest of all the days of his life, right up until the day he had met Trudy. Trudy, the woman who wanted his help in finding a baby, all those years ago, the baby that was all grown up. Trudy, the woman who loved purple. Trudy, who had a cat named Buddy. Trudy, who loved lard. Trudy, the woman who had made everything take another turn in his life. Trudy, the woman who could make him forget until the dreams had returned, along with the night sweats.

*****

The rain began to disperse while Ted sat there, soaked to the bone.

Again, he wiped the marker with his hands.

"I've met a woman, Tess. A woman that I never dreamed would ever come into my life. She's everything to me. I need her. I want her. And yet I keep pushing her away."

Ted continued to pull weeds from around Tess's marker.

"You would like her. She's funny. I think she loves me. I know I love her."

He looked up at the clouds that were now showing a tiny tint of blue.

"Tess, forgive me? Did I react too quickly? I had the gunman in sight. You pushed the toddler away, and he grabbed you just as I pulled the trigger! Oh, Tess, forgive me!"

He stood up and began to circle the gravesite. He couldn't look up, knowing it was not only Tess's forgiveness he needed. Humbled, he found himself on his knees. Finally, he looked up.

A holy sorrow had taken root in his heart.

"Forgive me, Lord. Please forgive me."

The dark clouds were disappearing. The sky became more than a patch of blue. It seemed to be opening wide to new hope for Ted. Still on his knees, he looked down, and a sudden thought crossed his mind. God never forgets his children. God never forgets watching them play in the park, running and jumping in the autumn leaves, no matter how old they are.

It was then he saw it. He couldn't believe his eyes. He had just been pulling weeds there. To the right of his sister's grave marker, tucked inside the engraving of her name, was a tiny heart-shaped leaf. Very tenderly, he plucked it away from the stone and cupped it in his hands, sheltering it from what was left of the rain. Where had it come from? Without asking any more questions, he knew he had been given his answer. He remembered.

"I will never look at leaves in quite the same way ever again."

"Nor will I," she answered.

He put the small leaf in his pocket and made his way to his car. In Tess's own way, she had reached down. He had uncovered his emotions. He had allowed the healing rain to fall upon his face. God had given him his abreaction.

With tears of surrender flowing down his face, he walked to his car, opened the trunk, and took out a cloth that he had placed next to the spare tire. He grabbed it and began to gently rub the cemetery mud from his shoes. There was an urgency in his step as he walked to the driver's side of the car. He started the motor, wiped away his tears, touched his pocket that held the leaf, and began his trip back to Brooksport Village.

A tragic accident. A godly sorrow. And a shadow of remaining guilt disappeared. The light had overtaken it. Once and for all.

*****

One leaf—new birth, pure authentic grace had rained down upon Ted in that cemetery; and a certain restoration began to embed itself into his very soul. Forgiven.

A transition was taking place. Past and present began to blend. A future. Old frames. New pictures. Hope. He had to get back to Trudy. He was going to "come clean" because now he felt clean.

Oh yes, God does work in mysterious ways. Sometimes, he uses a mere tiny leaf to bring you back. The Shepherd always finds his sheep.

*****

Chapter 36

Ted looked at the clock on the dashboard of his car as he rounded the corner to Brooksport Village—2:00 a.m. That was when he saw it. A flicker. Were his eyes playing tricks? He had been driving all night. But then a wall of fire burst out from Trudy's Tresses and Tootsies!

Reaching for his cell phone to call 911, Ted pushed the gas pedal to the floor and sped toward the salon.

As he got closer to the salon, he saw how serious it was. His eyes caught upon something in one of the windows. It shattered, and that was when he saw Buddy jump onto the ground below.

"Buddy!"

Buddy ran straight to Ted. He picked him up. It was at that moment that reality and cold hard truth hit Ted.

"*Buddy goes where I go*," he remembered Trudy saying. "Trudy's in there! That cat is always with her! She is in there!"

As the fire department was arriving, Ted hollered for them to take Buddy, placed him on the ground, and went running toward the burning building.

One of the firemen yelled for him to get back. "You can't go in there!"

"Watch me!" Ted shouted back.

He took off his shirt, wrapped it around his face, knotted it, and dropped to the floor. Crawling around the smoke-filled salon, he heard a weak cough.

"Trudy! I'm coming for you! Get close to the floor! Make another sound, Trudy! Please!"

The smoke was dense. He couldn't see. He felt as if he were floundering, losing his direction.

He screamed, "Trudy! Where are you?"

He heard it again. He was closer than he thought to her. He reached out, and a hand barely touched his. But he knew that hand. That was the hand of the woman he loved.

"Oh, Trudy! Come on! We're going to get us both out of here!"

He dared to stand up, his shirt held firmly over his face. Pure adrenaline pushed him out the door. Then he fell to the ground with Trudy in his arms.

"Get oxygen over here!"

EMS and firefighters were everywhere. The complete team had arrived.

They saw Ted rip the shirt from his face and heard him coughing.

"Get a mask on him! Give him some oxygen now!"

Another EMS team member was working on Trudy.

"Skin color is changing! Her lungs are inflamed! She's going into acute respiratory distress! Let's get going, people!"

With sirens screaming and oxygen masks in place, the hospital was waiting.

Seeing the flames, Seth had run from Crabby's Bar.

"Trudy's place!" he cried to everyone else who was vacating the bar at closing time.

The crowd began to run to the scene, not really knowing what they could do.

Seth was the first to see Buddy. "Come here, little fella. I'll take you to her. Come here."

He held out his hand. Somehow, that cat knew it was safe to run to Seth. Somehow, he knew this young boy, who worked the cracker aisle at Brooksport grocery store, would take him to his Trudy. Seth picked him up, walked back to the bar, and decided he would wait all night if he had to with the owner, giving Buddy water and food. He didn't know what else to do.

"Pray," Leon said, "like you've never prayed before."

*****

"The woods are lovely, dark and deep,
But I have promises to keep,
And miles to go before I sleep,
And miles to go before I sleep."

(Robert Frost)

The hospital staff swung into action.

"Fire victim! Minor burns! Excess smoke inhalation! Must be intubated immediately!"

Ted was rushed into another area, and the curtain was drawn. He knew it only took ten to fifteen seconds for smoke to wreak its damage in a person's lungs. How long had she been in that salon before he had run to her aid? "Intubated"? Did he hear that word?

Trudy was surrounded by the medical team down the hall.

"Where are they taking her?" Ted shouted.

"Let's take care of you. Lie still. She's in the best of hands!"

A doctor pulled the curtain back and walked over to Ted. The nurse looked up, saw the doctor, and said, "So are you. You have the best doctor standing in here beside you."

Ted grabbed her arm. "If he's the best, he needs to be wherever Trudy is. Go to her!"

*****

Trudy couldn't breathe. Everything seemed in slow motion. She heard the distant orders of the doctor, but it was like an echo. Everyone was running around. They were hooking her up to things, putting things down her throat. What was on her face? She didn't like it. It bothered her. She wanted it off, but she had no strength to fight. It seemed she was seeing things—her past, present, and future all colliding in her mind. She saw colors. Oh, what beautiful colors. Colors she had never seen before. She couldn't even imagine all those colors existing. She saw people. She saw purple. Events. Events that meant something from her past. No control.

Where was she? Why was she here? Things were getting hazy, dark. There was a crushing pain, crashing into her chest. Thin slivers of light danced between the darkness enveloping her. She craved her lungs to fill with air—just to take a deep breath. She couldn't move. Another pain hit her hard.

"Doctor!"

Everyone sprang into action.

"She's inhaled too much smoke! We didn't get her intubated in time! She's having a heart attack!"

"Paddles!" the doctor ordered. He kept trying to resuscitate her over and over.

"Too much smoke! Too much smoke! Nothing is going to help!"

Charlie burst into the room. He looked at the monitors just as Trudy coded out. All he saw was the flat line.

The nurses looked with fear at the doctor in charge, asking with their eyes if this was the day Brooksport Village would lose their Trudy. They wanted desperately to bring her back.

The doctor took a deep breath and looked at the clock on the wall before speaking. He raked his hands over his face and gave a heavy sigh.

"Time of death, 3:05 a.m. Cause of death: heart attack due to smoke inhalation."

He turned and left the room.

Charlie couldn't believe it! He wouldn't believe it! Not his beloved Trudy! Not the woman who had never lied to him! Not the woman who had taught him manners when he was growing up! No! No! No! Not his Trudy!

*****

Nothing could keep Ted away from the hallway that led to where Trudy had been taken. "I'm fixed up now! I'm okay! Let me go to Trudy!"

The doctor could not stop him, and Ted was gone in a flash. He nearly ran head on into the doctor that had just left Trudy's room. "Doctor! Please tell me Trudy is okay! You have to tell me she is okay!"

He could not control keeping his hands by his side. He grabbed the doctor's shoulders and stared into his eyes. The look that was returned to Ted made his heart sink and his hands dropped as his knees buckled. The doctor put his arm around Ted to hold him up.

"I'm so sorry. She's gone."

*****

Chapter 37

Kate was restless. She couldn't sleep. It was a little after 3:00 a.m. She propped herself up on her pillow and ran her fingers through her hair. She put both feet on the floor and looked over at Jake.

So handsome, she thought. *So mine.* She smiled. *We made it through, baby. And the redhead was not so bad after all.* She smiled.

Again, she looked at the clock.

"Not good," she said as she walked to the kitchen to get a glass of water.

It always seemed that if something bad was going to happen, it would be in the wee early hours of the morning or the late dark hour of midnight. She didn't like the feelings she was having. She felt something was wrong. Then she heard the sirens.

The phone began to ring only a few seconds later. Kate was midway between the bedroom and kitchen when she began to run.

"Hello?"

"Come to the hospital!" Sarah was screaming.

"What's happened to Charlie! Has something happened to Charlie!" Kate's screams echoed Sarah's.

Jake rounded the corner, hearing the urgency in her voice from the bedroom.

"No! No! It's not Charlie! But he is at the hospital!" Sarah kept screaming. "Oh, Kate, please hurry. It's Trudy!"

At that moment, both Jake and Kate looked out the window and saw the flames. Trudy's Tresses and Tootsies was on fire.

*****

"Please tell me this isn't happening!" Jake shouted, pounding the steering wheel of the car.

Kate sat stunned in the passenger seat. "No! Not Trudy!" Kate was afraid to breathe.

"Kate? Are you with me?" Jake asked.

Kate took a deep breath, her heart pounding.

She suddenly burst into tears. She remembered Trudy telling her she would be spending the night at the salon.

"I've seen too many people die in my lifetime! People who have been so close to me that I felt a part of me died with them! Like someone cut off my arm or my leg or a part of me that I could never replace! Death came and crippled me in so many guises! And then I met Trudy! She can't be dead! Trudy can't be dead!"

Jake pulled the car over and grabbed Kate, enclosing her in his arms. Knowing the heartaches of Kate's past, he held her tightly.

"I'm sorry, baby. Oh, I am so sorry! I love you, Kate. We'll get through this together, I promise."

They needed to calm themselves. Trudy was at the hospital—the best possible place she could be right now. He pulled back from Kate and looked directly into her eyes.

"Ready to go?"

Kate nodded.

"I don't have a handkerchief, but you can use this." He offered her the sleeve of his shirt.

She was grateful but pulled a tissue from her purse. Trudy had always taught her to carry tissues. Kate remembered what Trudy had told her once.

"You never know when you're gonna need one—happy moments, sad moments, a nose always drips!"

Jake pulled out from the side of the road and continued to speed toward the hospital.

"Don't you ever die on me, Jake!" Kate shouted. "Promise me you will never die on me!"

Jake pulled over to the side of the road once again, turned off the motor, and looked at Kate. There were no words. He gathered her in his arms once again, and the two of them sat there, holding on to one another. They were hoping for the best but preparing for the worst. Their tears blended with one another. They didn't notice the rain that had begun to fall. It was a dark, pounding rain. The storm clouds had gathered. Ominous. Bad. It took every bit of strength to hold on.

Jake slowly released Kate and started the motor.

"We have to go. Whatever we find at the hospital, we find it together."

Kate kept wringing her hands.

*****

Jake and Kate found Ted staring at the floor. Sensing their presence, he looked up. "What am I going to do without her?"

Kate went to him, tears flowing down her face. She fell to her knees in front of him. "None of us can do without her."

Jake made a fist and hit the nearest wall. He had to be strong. But it just wasn't fair! Not Trudy! Not a woman who was bigger than life! A woman like her could not, would not, allow a fire to take her out! It didn't make sense. He walked over to Ted and Kate. The three of them cried together for all they had lost in a mere moment of time.

*****

Something was happening in Trudy's room.

"No! No! No! Trudy, I won't let this happen!"

Charlie began barking out orders to the nurses. Quickly they ran from the room to do just what he had told them to do.

"Trudy, you listen to me! You listen good!" Charlie shouted as he continued to do what needed to be done to revive Trudy.

"I want you at my wedding! Do you hear me!"

No response.

"Trudy, I'll have Sarah carry purple flowers in her bouquet, do you hear me!"

No response.

He kept working on her. "Trudy, you need to come back to us! Trudy, I'll even wear a purple tux! Come on, Trudy!"

One of the nurses grabbed Charlie's hand. "It's no use, Charlie. She's gone."

"No! I will not allow her to die! I simply will not allow it!" Charlie kept working on Trudy. The nurses had followed his instructions and brought in everything he had ordered. But no one was holding out much hope. "Trudy, you've always had a strong will! You're a stubborn cuss! Come on, Trudy! Come back to me! You have to come back to me! Do it! Do it! Come on, girl! Do it!"

Suddenly, there was a small bleep on the monitor and then a stronger bleep until finally that flat line had totally disappeared, and those bleeps became more constant.

"Look, Charlie—I mean, Doctor! We have a heartbeat! We have a definite heartbeat!"

Stronger and stronger it became.

"That's it, Trudy," Charlie kept saying over and over as he continued to work his miracle over her body that had fought so hard to come back.

"That's it. Keep on coming back to us, Trudy!"

It was sheer will that brought her back—sheer will and a loving God who knew it was not her time to race to the heavenlies… She had "too many promises to keep and miles to go before she slept." Trudy had just proven that she was, indeed, royalty…

*****

Everyone was running. Back and forth.

Kate shouted, "Why are these people running? What is wrong with them? Don't they know that Trudy is dead? Can't they be quiet!"

Jake held her closely to his side. He didn't know who was holding whom up at this point. He just knew he could not let go of his wife. He would never let go. He would stay steady. He would not run.

Charlie rounded the corner.

"Charlie?" Kate ran to him. "Did you see her before…" Her voice trailed off. Charlie put his arms around Kate. Jake and Ted stood beside her. "She's dead, isn't she?" Kate asked.

Gently, Charlie held her at arm's length. He looked at all three of them. He was tired and shaken, but he spoke firmly. "No, no, she is not dead. She is very much alive. We have some hurdles to jump, but if I know Trudy, she'll do it, and we'll jump them with her."

All three of them nearly fell to the floor. One minute they had been mourning Trudy, and the next minute they were elated.

Charlie pointed to a waiting room. "Come, let's go sit."

A young nurse who had been in the room walked over to them. "Yes, very much alive," she said. "This young doctor would not give up! I think it was his constant screaming at her and her fighting spirit to come back. A miracle, I would say!"

Kate looked at Charlie. With a tearstained face and hair askew, she asked, "When can we see her?"

Charlie smiled. "She would absolutely kill me if I let you in her room to see her now. She doesn't look her best, you know?" Looking at Kate, he added, "Neither do you, Kate."

Through her tears, Kate managed a soft laugh.

"But soon. You can see her soon. Right now, she has to sleep. She has to rest." He turned around to leave but hesitated. "Please go find her cat. Find Buddy. If I know Trudy, she needs to know he survived that fire as soon as she wakes up."

Ted was so relieved that he held on to Jake and cried tears that would not stop. He didn't know where Buddy was, but he did know he had held that cat in his arms and had put him on the ground after yelling for someone, anyone to take care of the cat. He thought it had been one of the firemen. He was bound and determined to find Buddy and personally deliver that four-legged child to her. After all, wasn't he the finder of lost loves? He knew Buddy was alive. He was the very living thing that had led him to Trudy in the first place. Yes, he would find her beloved Buddy.

Ted, Jake, and Kate walked out of that hospital holding on to one another. They had survived yet another storm in their little village town. Brooksport Village had just claimed back one of its own. This time there had been victory.

*****

Ted sat at Trudy's bedside, looking at her. He couldn't lose her now! She had come back to life! He knew it was still touch and go with machines bleeping and nurses coming in and out of her room. He grew to know what nurse was entering the room without looking up just by their gait, just by the scent of their recently shampooed hair. Every sense in his body had intensified. Touch, smell—it seemed that he could even taste the Pine-Sol of the recently mopped hospital corridors. He wanted her to move, even if it were just a finger or a toe. *Blink, Trudy! Just blink!* She didn't move. She didn't blink.

He continued to sit there and stare at Trudy with all the memories of his past colliding inside his head and heart. "You have to live, Trudy! You came back once. You can do it again!"

Charlie had said it would not be an easy road, that everyone had to be patient.

The machines kept bleeping. The nurses kept coming and going. The Pine-Sol was making him nauseous.

Funny how hospital rooms and corridors can make people remember all the other sad times in their lives. Trudy just had to wake up! She had to!

Was she going to die, anyway? he kept asking himself. A woman so full of life. A woman who knew everybody in town, along with their business; but everybody loved her, anyway. She just had a flair all her own and was forgiven so easily. He had brought her a bouquet of purple flowers. He had put them in a vase on the table beside her bed.

"Wake up, Trudy. Please wake up," he pleaded. "I brought you flowers. They're purple." He scrubbed his unshaven face with his hands.

"Trudy, royalty doesn't die like this! Charlie said anything could happen, but I command you to wake up! If nothing else, you need a more dramatic exit than this!" He kept looking at her, pleading with her.

Charlie walked in.

"Ted, I know you'll feel more comfortable at Trudy's place. You need to go back there now. You need to get some rest. And besides, Buddy may show up."

"I can't leave her alone."

"I'll be here."

Ted looked at him, searching his face. "Please tell me she's going to be okay, Charlie."

"She's survived the worst part, Ted. If I know Trudy, she is going to fight her way back to us now, too, and continue being the Trudy we know."

"I don't know if I should leave."

Charlie repeated, "I'll be here. I'll call you if she regains consciousness. I promise."

Reluctantly, Ted got up from his chair and gave Charlie a pat on the shoulder. He bent over and gave Trudy a kiss on her forehead. "I'm sorry, Charlie. You love her. I know you'll be here. I'll go rest now."

Charlie adjusted the tubing that was connected to Trudy.

Ted hesitated at the door and turned back to Charlie. "Is there anything I can do?"

"Yes," Charlie replied, "keep praying."

*****

Trudy opened one eye and turned her head to the chair next to her hospital bed. She wanted to see Ted, but it wasn't Ted. It was Charlie. Charlie, sleeping. Charlie holding her favorite purple scarf. Her eyes misted over. She took an extra moment before speaking.

"So when's the weddin'?"

Charlie jolted awake, nearly falling off the chair. "Trudy! You're awake!"

"It seems so," Trudy could barely whisper.

Quickly, Charlie called for the nurse, shouting out orders. A certain frenzy followed as Charlie and a troop of nurses gathered in that hospital room in ICU. What had to be done was done.

"Call Ted," Charlie said to one of the nurses. He looked at Trudy.

"Ted's not here," Trudy whispered. "He left."

Charlie reached out to touch her hand. "He's back." Charlie looked straight into her eyes. "He's been here day and night. I sent him to your place last night. He needed rest."

Trudy was weak but managed to ask, "He's back?"

"Yes, he's back. Actually, he is the one who got you out of that fire. He risked his own life to save you, Trudy."

"He did?"

"Yes, he did. It appears that timing is everything." Charlie made some notes on her medical chart. He looked solemnly at her. "Really, Trudy, who could stay away from you for very long? Did you really think he would never come back?"

Trudy gave a glimmer of a smile. "It's only fittin' it was you in that chair when I woke up, Charlie. Can I have some water?"

Charlie poured a small glass of water and gently held her head up to help her drink. "Little sips, Trudy," he commanded.

"Yes, Doctor." Trudy swallowed, looked at Charlie, and gave some orders of her own. "Now get me my cat. Where's Buddy?"

Charlie had to find Buddy. Where in the world was that cat? Ted had told him that Buddy had survived. Now it was just a matter of finding him. He prayed Buddy wasn't wandering the streets or worse yet, that he… No, he wouldn't think those thoughts. Buddy was a survivor—just like his mistress. He called Kate.

*****

"Jake! Charlie just called!"

Jake came running into the room.

"Trudy just regained consciousness!"

"Praise God!"

"She's asking for Buddy. We have to find Buddy!"

Kate began scurrying around the room, gathering car keys, her purse, and whatever else she needed to take to the hospital.

"We have to go!"

Jake was at a loss. He had no clue as to where to even start to look for a cat. He had always wanted a dog to fill up the silence in his penthouse. Now both he and Kate had two dogs—a big dog and a little dog. He knew nothing about cats or where they might wander off to. He spoke "dog" now.

"We have to find Buddy! We need to take him to the hospital with us and hand him over to Trudy! She needs her cat! You know how close they are!"

"I know! I know!" Jake exclaimed as he grabbed his own wallet, opened the door for Kate, and quickly ran out onto the porch behind her.

They began their search at the now-boarded-up salon. Nothing. They checked the perimeters. Nothing. Their last stop before going to the hospital was the fire station.

"Did you find her cat?" Jake asked the fire chief.

He shook his head.

Jake raked his hands over his face. "Trudy came to! She wants her cat!"

"That's good news!"

"But no cat? Are you sure?"

"Yes, I'm sure, no cat. But we know the cause of the fire—faulty clothes dryer part."

*****

Across town, Seth heard the news. Trudy was awake! He gathered Buddy, along with a little bed he had bought at the local pet store, and made one stop at Brooksport Village grocery for some Chicken in a Biskit crackers. He thought it might take her a few weeks to eat them, but, at least, they would be waiting for her. He was riding his bike with a few additions. Now he had a little basket with the pet bed tucked inside it, hooked to the handlebars, for Buddy to ride comfortably.

He found Jake and Kate sitting beside Trudy's bed when he walked into her room. They were trying to console her. He didn't know if he should interrupt, but he was having a difficult time controlling Buddy. He wanted to jump down and run to his mistress.

He decided to speak. "Buddy seemed to enjoy riding in the basket I put on the handlebars, Miss Trudy. I think he knew I was bringing him back to you." He walked over to Trudy's bed, looking down at her tearstained face.

"Oh, Seth, you found him!"

"He's fine, Miss Trudy. I saw him outside the salon when all hell was breaking loose…" He looked at Trudy. "Sorry, but it was hellish. Buddy ran over to me when I called him, and I took him home so I could care for him while you got better."

Seth could not contain Buddy any longer as he jumped from Seth into Trudy's arms.

"I guess I should have told someone. I just didn't think. I was too busy prayin'. That's what Leon told me to do."

Trudy cradled Buddy and looked up at Seth. "Oh, Seth, you did good! I owe you all my gratitude. I really do!"

Seth beamed. He had never gotten many accolades in his life. "I brought you these." He handed her the box of crackers. "I thought you might need some lard—when you're up to it, that is."

*****

Buddy stayed with her, and the hospital allowed it. After all, it wasn't every day that someone came back from the dead.

How long had she been here? She didn't know. She didn't care at this point. Hadn't Charlie said that Ted was back? If he was back, where in the world was he? Why hadn't he come to see her?

"What do ya think, Buddy?"

Buddy cuddled up next to her and went to sleep.

"Guess I should do the same." Trudy yawned.

Instantly, she fell asleep to the sound of Buddy's purr.

*****

It was nearing dawn when Trudy opened her eyes and looked around. She couldn't believe that some mornings she remained so disoriented. She focused and looked to the side where there was a man sleeping. This time it wasn't Charlie. It was Ted. Ted, with one leg on the footstool sitting in front of him and the other leg on the floor. His mouth was open. He was sleeping.

"How romantic," Trudy said. "But at least, you're not droolin'."

Ted came instantly awake, nearly falling off the chair.

Trudy reached for her sense of humor. "Seems like that chair likes men fallin' out of it!"

"Trudy, Oh, my God, thank you!" He grabbed her hands.

Trudy looked at him thinking he was the most handsome man she had ever seen. But she wasn't going to tell him that. She was still mad at him.

"You look awful," she said.

"You look beautiful," Ted whispered.

"Liar," she replied.

Trudy tried to sit up but still found that simple gesture difficult to do.

"I have some things to say to ya, Ted, but not right now."

"Get all your strength back first," Ted replied.

"Then you better watch out, 'cause I'm not gonna be nice."

"I don't want you to be nice. I deserve everything you have to say to me, and more. But when you're done, I want you to listen to me."

He continued to hold her hands in his. "Oh, Trudy, it's such a long story."

"I'm willin' to listen."

That was a start for Ted, and that's all he needed to hear.

He kept staring at Trudy. He kept thinking how beautiful she looked.

Trudy exclaimed, "Stop starin' at me, Ted!"

"I can't help it, Trudy. I thought I had lost you."

She grabbed his hand. "You're not gonna lose me, you moron, but you sure have some explainin' to do!"

Buddy had walked from his bed and began nosing around Ted's jacket. Silently, he reached into his pocket and gave Buddy a treat.

"Back to normal, I see," Trudy whispered before drifting off to sleep, still holding tightly to Ted's other hand.

"It takes two to speak the truth—one to speak, and another to hear."

(Henry David Thoreau)

Chapter 38

Ted was determined to make everything right with Trudy. He had gone back to that cemetery to find what he needed, and he had found it. He would tell Trudy everything—from beginning to end and everything in between.

He could never leave Trudy in a thousand lifetimes, and he knew it. He knew he was stuck with the girl who once told him you couldn't stay angry with the world as long as you remembered to put glitter in your hair. And that night, she had done exactly that. They were cleaning glitter for weeks after that fun-filled night. He had never laughed so hard. Trudy was special. Who else thinks like her? Nobody. Just Trudy. And he was glad to be stuck with her.

He shivered to think what could have happened if he had not come back at just the right time. He had gotten her out of that burning building. He had not failed her. He had not let her die.

He had not expected to come back to her and rescue her at the same time from a fire!

He thought he would be coming back to a woman completely bent out of shape. She would be fit to be tied. She was going to chew him up and spit him out. He just knew it. She might still do just that. But he was ready to be chewed up. It would be good for him to be spit out. He was ready for all of that.

He wanted to spend the rest of his life with her. And he was going to tell her. He had faced his giant. He had found all his answers in the cemetery mud.

*****

"Can you live with a man like me, Trudy?"

"You mean a man who keeps his secrets so close to his chest that it breaks his heart over and over again, right along with the woman that stands by his side? Or do you mean a man who can come clean with me, open up, and share whatever it is that is hauntin' him—one that can also celebrate the victories after the roller coaster ride?"

"I deserved that," he replied.

"Yes, you did."

"I want to fix this, Trudy."

"I would like nothing better."

"Then let's fix it—together."

Trudy stared at him, wanting to grab him, pull him into that hospital bed, and comfort him. She wanted to take his face in her hands, put her lips on his, and say, "It's gonna be okay." She wanted to promise him forever right then and there.

But she remained still as a June bug on a summer's night. She had to. She didn't want to get caught with her heart tied to a string ever again.

It was he who needed to speak; it was he who needed to open his own personal alabaster box and let it spill out upon the floor. She had done her share of opening those secret boxes. Now it was his turn. She had dealt with a lot of forgiveness in her life, but there was always room for one more, and she felt there was another one coming. It was he who had to be honest with her and himself. And if it took her to be in this hospital and her salon to almost burn to the ground, then so be it.

"God is good," she whispered to herself and settled under the hospital sheets to listen to what her techy Ted was about to say.

*****

Ted poured himself a cup of water from the hospital pitcher.

"We were in the coffee shop," he began.

Trudy looked confused. "Why don't you start at the beginning, Ted?"

Ted sighed and took a deep breath. "The bottom line is, Trudy, I killed a woman."

Trudy had told herself she was ready to accept anything Ted shared with her. She was just glad he was finally opening up to her. But she had never, in all her wildest imaginings, ever expected something like this.

With all the strength that she had finally regained from the fire, she was able to respond. "Go on, Ted, from the beginning."

"Men can only think. Women have a way of understanding without thinking. Woman was created out of God's own fancy. Man, He had to hammer into shape."

(Rabindranath Tagore)

"I killed her—a young woman, a woman filled with hopes and dreams and so much promise. A woman who had protected me all of my life from the bullies at school who called me Freckle Face. I killed my sister."

Trudy continued to sit very still. She listened. Ted told her the whole story. He left nothing out.

Trudy got out of the hospital bed and slowly walked over to the window. She had her back to him because she wasn't certain what she would say. Could anyone ever feel better after killing the person he loved most in the world? She wasn't sure she could help him in any way. She knew she wanted to, but this was far beyond anything she had ever experienced. She had to think. She had to offer the right words to his outstretched hand.

"I pulled the trigger. If he hadn't grabbed her instead of the toddler that she saved, the first bullet would have been his, not hers."

Trudy turned to face him with great sorrow in her eyes.

Ted took a deep breath.

"I've slept with this. I've had nightmares about this. I've wondered what I could have done differently. And you know what the public said? They said I was a hero. I wasn't. Tess was the heroine. She saved the child. And in one split second, the aim I took killed my sister because the masked man had grabbed her in front of him. The next bullet killed him."

He wiped his eyes as he continued.

"I was holding her when the ambulance arrived. I fought them. I couldn't let her go. They had to drag me away."

Ted joined Trudy at the window. Both of them staring out, looking up at the sky.

Trudy was the first to speak. "What happened next?"

"My parents and I avoided the press. We went to the lake with that gun and took a boat out to the deepest, darkest part, and threw it overboard. I left that lake with a broken heart, tears, and a suitcase full of guilt."

There had always been those rare times in Trudy's life when she had been rendered speechless. This was one of those times. She reached for his hand. He couldn't raise his eyes to look at her.

"What now, Trudy?"

She merely squeezed his hand. Words were not necessary. Human touch was enough.

*****

Within the week, Trudy was released from the hospital. She was moving in slow motion, but she was alive. She had had plenty of time to think about what Ted had told her. Did she love him enough to wake in the middle of the night with a cold, wet washcloth in her hand for his forehead when the nightmares came? Yes. It had been a tragedy. But she had lived through tragedies before, and she was stronger because of them. She loved the man, and it was time to show him.

He would be arriving at her house tonight. She would tell him then. She would walk through fire for this man, and he had proven he would do the same for her, literally.

Buddy had taken up his old space on the couch, as he had always done right before Ted's arrival in their lives.

"We're gonna help Ted through this, eh, Buddy?"

Buddy stood up, stretched, and lay back down. Trudy saw Ted approaching her house. She smoothed down her hair and walked to the door.

*****

They were sitting on the couch when Trudy reached for his hand. Ted was the first to speak. "Can you see yourself understanding me through my mood swings and night sweats—through the nightmares that still haunt me?"

Trudy wanted to calm his unwarranted fears. Yes, she would see him through anything, gladly. The man who had sat so faithfully through her worst hours, well, yes, she could see him through his own private hell.

He ran his hands over his unshaven face. He got up from the couch and walked across the room. He turned and looked at Trudy. He dared to ask the question. He needed to know her answer.

"Can you help me unload all the guilt I've felt through the years? Can you do that, Trudy? Can you help me unpack my dark side? You have to know you're not getting a prize package here, don't you?"

Ted stopped talking and began walking around the room, every nerve in his body tense.

"Ted, come sit back down," Trudy whispered.

He looked at her with questioning eyes, dreading what her answer might be.

"But, first, see Buddy over there? Go pick him up, put him on your lap, and be quiet. Cats relax you. And they like it best if you don't move around so much."

Ted only shook his head and obeyed this woman he had come to love more than his next breath. Once he had settled himself with Buddy cozied on his lap, Trudy began. "I want you to know something," Trudy said as she opened the drawer of the end table next to the couch. She took a purple square piece of cloth from its resting place. "You probably never knew that I crochet."

Ted smiled, but his look told her he was somewhat bewildered.

Trudy couldn't help smiling. "I know, I know. It seems crazy. I, who throw glitter in my hair, can sit still at times. I find peace in crocheting. I crocheted a shawl for Kate once—a prayer shawl. I prayed over every stitch I created in that shawl for that sweet woman. She had become such a big part of my life through the years of her arrival in Brooksport Village. Tears fell on that shawl along with some spilled coffee and a few wine drops. She and I have quite a history together. One day, I will tell you."

Trudy sat a little straighter in the chair opposite Ted. "When you went away, I got my crochet hooks out of my drawer, along with the same yarn that came from Kate's shawl, and I began to form this little square, once again praying over every stitch. I wanted to give it to you one day. I wanted you to be able to always carry it with you wherever you went as a reminder that God is always near. I didn't know when the time would be right, or at the time, I didn't even know if you would ever come back. But I trusted God to bring you back, and then God, being the God that he is, would show me the exact time to give it to you."

Trudy handed him the remnant. "Today's the day."

Ted took it from her.

Trudy continued. "As you know, the town's right when people say you can't hide anything from me. Eventually, I find out everything that the crevices in a person's forehead are signaling. And Ted, my dear, you had signals clear across that handsome brow of yours. I knew you had a big secret the first time I met you. I seem to have that 'talent' with people. You people with secrets give off a certain vibe, if you know what I mean. You liked, a little too much, being 'holed up' in your computer world. At first, I tried to convince myself that you were just a loner, and I could convince you to run free one day alongside me. You know—throw some glitter around."

Ted dared to smile.

"But then you became distant. That secret was getting in the way. And then you just plain and simple decided to ghost me."

"Ghost you?"

"Yes, ghost me."

"What do you mean?"

"You just plain disappeared with no word of goodbye, no closure, no nothing."

Ted looked down at Buddy. "I ran."

"Yes, but you ran to find answers. There's a difference. You came back." Trudy took his hands in hers. "When someone asks questions, they are usually ready to hear the answers. You asked questions, and I am so glad you went back to that cemetery to find your answers." She squeezed his hands. "And then the fire happened," she whispered.

"Yes."

"You've been told I died for a moment, haven't you?"

"Yes."

"But I came back."

"Yes."

"God wasn't ready to have me come home yet."

"So he sent you back?"

"Yes."

They both looked at each other.

"What I'm trying to tell you is that if I can survive a fire, I can see you through all your mood swings and night sweats. I can comfort you through your nightmares. And, yes, I can help you unload your guilt and help you unpack your dark side. Neither one of us are 'prize packages,' as you say. But we're trying to make the most of what we are and be the best of who we are."

Ted felt his eyes tearing up. So were hers.

"I want you to take that little purple remnant you're holdin'. I want you to carry it with you and remember the prayers that were prayed over it—the prayers that covered you. Prayers that you would find your answers. Prayers that you could leave the ghosts that haunted you behind. Prayers that you would find your true purpose and prayers that, the Lord willing, would return you to me."

"Your prayers were answered, Trudy, right there in that cemetery with my sister. And here I am."

Trudy smiled through her tears. "I just didn't think it would be a fire and a rain-soaked cemetery that would bring you back. But that's our God, isn't it? Always up to something good, even in the middle of our unsettling circumstances."

Trudy stood. Buddy jumped from Ted's lap, stretched, and went back to his secret place for yet another nap. "Now I'm gonna get my afternoon exercise by walkin' you to the door. I want you to go home, take a shower, *shave*, get cleaned up, and come back here. I've been cravin' a Stumble In burger since I got home from the hospital. Charlie said I could have one or two if I wanted!"

He cupped her face in his hands. "I don't want to live without you, Trudy."

"You don't have to. Hurry back here, ya hear?"

When he left, he was holding the purple square remnant from the same yarn as Kate's prayer shawl right next to his heart.

God's healing rain, God's healing balm. "Pharmacon."

Yes, he knew what that was now, and God's secret elixir was beginning to work its will. Healing from past hurts, past tragedies, and past secrets. Oh! The sweet victory attained from God's glorious grace!

*****

Before Trudy could begin to freshen up her makeup, there was a knock at the door. She slowly walked across the room, looked out the side window, and saw Charlie.

She flung open the door.

"Charlie! A man who saved my life doesn't have to knock on my door! Come on in!"

"You taught me manners, Trudy, remember?"

Trudy smiled and motioned for him to sit down. "Just move Buddy and sit."

"Nope, that cat can sit wherever he wants, whenever he wants. He's been through as much as you have." Charlie reached in his pocket and pulled out a prescription bottle. "You forgot these when you were discharged."

Trudy rolled her eyes. "No, I didn't. I left them on purpose. I don't want to take them. Those pills make me goofy!"

Charlie handed her the bottle. "You're already goofy. Take them, anyway."

Trudy took the bottle and began to laugh.

"What's so funny?"

"You."

"Me?"

"Yes, you. There was a time when you wouldn't even think for one second to sass me. But look at you now! All smart-ass!"

"Watch your language and take those pills, as prescribed."

Trudy sighed.

Charlie took her by the arm, led her to the kitchen, filled a glass with water, and stood there while she opened the bottle and popped one of the pills in her mouth.

"Swallow," Charlie commanded. Before leaving, Charlie said, "Stick out your tongue."

She obliged him.

"Good girl. Now do I have to come by here every eight hours to make sure you take those pills?"

"No, I'll do it, but I don't want to. They make me goofy."

That being said, Charlie left the house, shaking his head, hollering over his shoulder, "Like I said, you're already goofy!"

*****

PART 7

POLLY APPEARS

Chapter 39

Trudy had fully recovered and was back to her old self, finding comfort in the loving arms of Ted and craving lard. A different face came into town after the fire at Trudy's Tresses and Tootsies. Polly arrived with no fanfare, but, clearly, she appeared as a woman on a mission. She knew the town. It had been described to her in great detail by Jasmine. She knew the layout. She knew the people. She knew where they "hung out." And she knew Trudy the minute she saw her walk out of Brooksport Grocery. She knew she was heading to Belle's. The day was sunny. Polly only hoped it would be as sunny when she said what she had come to say.

She took a deep breath and headed straight to Belle's. She was going to go against her best friend's granddaughter's wishes, *but* it was for Jasmine's own good. And she had not promised she would not try to fix what was going on between Jasmine and Gordy. It was true that she had approached Jasmine with the thought that Polly herself should visit Brooksport and talk to Gordy, but Jasmine had flipped her lid at the suggestion.

"*Tell me you won't do that, Polly! Tell me you will not go to Brooksport!*" *Jasmine had exclaimed.*

"*Okay, I'll not think about it,*" *Polly had answered.*

Well, she did not have to think about it. She had already made up her mind! Sometimes you just had to do what you thought was right, especially when the granddaughter of your best friend was in serious trouble of losing what she most wanted. She just didn't know it yet. And it took people like Polly to get things straightened out once and for all.

She walked into Belle's Bakery, ordered coffee, and sat down to wait. Gordy was bound to come in sooner or later.

Belle kept watching her.

"You here for a vacation?" Belle asked.

"Well, it sure is a sweet little town," Polly answered, "but I'm just here for a short spell. Got some business to handle."

Belle was cleaning the counters when Trudy walked in. "Hey, Trudy!"

Polly looked up. She imagined that Trudy was a character. But she was also Jasmine's friend, and Polly decided she liked her and all her purple before even being introduced.

"I'll have my usual, Belle!" Trudy exclaimed while looking at Polly, who was sitting in the corner at what had now become known as the confession table.

Trudy looked at Belle with a silent question. "A newcomer or tourist?"

Belle mouthed, "Newcomer."

That was when Gordy walked through the door.

Polly said to herself, "S——t fire, that's him!" I know that is him! What do I do now?"

He greeted Belle and Trudy and ordered coffee. He looked over at Polly. That was when Polly saw his eyes. Blue. That was him. She summoned up all her courage and walked over to him.

Looking Gordy straight in the eye, she asked, "You the only fellow in this town with blue eyes?"

"Excuse me?" Gordy questioned.

"You heard me. Are you?"

A smile forming on her lips, Trudy looked up. Who was this woman? "I believe he is the only man in this town with eyes as blue as his," Trudy answered.

Polly took a deep breath. "You and I have some serious talking to do if your name's Gordy," Polly said.

Trudy kept looking at Polly with a smile of intrigue upon her face. "That's Gordy," Trudy said.

"Good," Polly exclaimed. "Can we go somewhere for something stronger than coffee? I have a lot to say to you."

"Who are you, and what are you talking about?" Gordy questioned.

"My name's Polly, and I'm here to talk to you about Jasmine."

Trudy blurted out, "Crabby's Bar! Just down the street! That's where you can go! Much stronger stuff than coffee!" Trudy looked at Polly and turned to Belle. "I don't think she's from the city."

"Me neither."

Trudy stirred her coffee. "But she's a woman with something on her mind!"

"Seems so."

Both Trudy and Belle continued to stare at the two of them as they left Belle's.

"Well, well, what do ya know, Belle! Sure says somethin' about Gordy following that woman over to Crabby's, don't ya think?"

"Seems like Gordy might still have a 'thing' for Jasmine, eh, Trudy?" Belle asked.

"Yep, sure seems that way. Indeed, it does."

Trudy got up to leave.

"Trudy, where are you going?"

"Where do ya think?"

"Crabby's?"

"You bet!"

Belle chuckled. "Gonna be some more excitement here, I'm guessing," Belle whispered as she went to wait on a new customer who had just entered the bakery.

"Excitement, did you say?" the new arrival questioned.

"Oh yes," Belle answered. "What are you having today? Got some fresh deep-fried doughnuts!"

*****

Gordy and Polly found a quiet table in the corner of Crabby's.

"Look, I know I am a surprise to show up here. Frankly, Jasmine would absolutely kill me if she knew I was here!"

Gordy kept looking at her with his questioning blue eyes.

Polly ordered her drink and looked at Gordy. "S——t fire! Your eyes are really blue."

Gordy couldn't keep himself from smiling. "Yes, I get them from my grandfather. It's in our lineage."

The server brought Polly her drink and Gordy's ginger ale.

Polly raised her glass to Gordy. "Some fine lineage, I would say." Polly took a sip of her drink and slapped her hand on the table. "All right, down to business!" Polly ordered another drink to maintain her courage. "Look, I don't want to feel like I am betraying my best friend's granddaughter, but I have to talk to you about Jasmine—things you need to know."

Gordy looked at her, truly, wanting to hear what she had to say.

"I don't want her making the same mistake that Ellie made."

"Ellie?" Gordy asked.

Polly took another sip of her drink. "Yes, Ellie. Oh, I need to start at the beginning, don't I? Ellie, Jasmine's grandma."

*****

Halfway to Crabby's, Trudy changed her mind. This was not her business. Not yet anyway. She would visit Gordy later. Maybe she would take him something to eat—like a casserole. He would tell her everything. Of course, he would! She would pester him until he did. He knew that.

She would find out who this Polly was! She would find out how she knew Jasmine. And she would find out what she told Gordy about Jasmine. Oh yes, she would!

One thing Trudy felt in her bones was that this Polly woman, whoever she was, was here to help Gordy see that he needed to get on with it! He needed to make a move! At least, that was what she hoped. This woman would not have come to Brooksport Village to risk talking to a blue-eyed man named Gordy if she did not love the sweet flower that was named Jasmine. Would she? No, of course not! What purpose would she have, except for that?

Gordy and Jasmine had both suffered long enough. So much time had passed. She was absolutely sure they had both worked through what needed to be worked through. It was time. Then she remembered. She looked up at the sky.

"Sorry, God, I'm not trying to get ahead of you this time! I'm really not! But won't you please say it is time now! It is time for these two! Why else would you have sent Polly?"

Oh, how exciting! She could hardly wait to tell Ted! Trudy's matchmaking had just come back to life—with the help of Polly, of course! And God. Not necessarily in that order.

*****

Polly didn't look at Gordy for a long time. She kept looking around the bar, thinking someone she might know would walk in. It made her nervous. What did she think she was doing? Should she walk out?

"S——t fire, no!" she exclaimed only in her own mind. She had never met Gordy. So why did he look familiar?

"Everybody has a twin," she said to herself and probably because Jasmine had talked about him so much.

She took another sip of her drink.

"Look, I've known Jasmine all her life. Her grandma was my best friend."

"So you've said." Gordy joined the conversation. "Ellie?"

"Yes, Ellie. And it's Ellie that would want me to do this. She would want me to come to Brooksport Village and set things straight. She would not want Jasmine to make the same mistake she made years ago!"

"What mistake was that?"

Polly sighed. "Not allowing love to come in."

*****

Gordy encouraged Polly to talk. "I'm listening," he said.

Polly told Gordy every last detail about Jasmine and Andrew. "I watched her grieve—" Polly interrupted her own thought pattern. "Anybody ever watch you grieve, Gordy?"

Gordy thought of Trudy. He thought of the casseroles, the Bible verses she shared, the advice she had to give, the green shirt with the twinkle lights. And he thought of the flashlight those sweet kids had given him to help him find his way out of the dark. Come to think about it, a lot of people had watched him grieve.

Polly took the napkin and wiped her eyes.

"Sorry, just watching that girl through that period of her life and remembering it now makes me so sad. I didn't think that girl would ever get over Andrew."

Gordy looked at Polly. She could see his eyes softening. Perhaps it was her tears. Most men could not bear to see a woman cry. Gordy must be one of them. She had met a few of those men way back when—one in particular.

Gordy took a sip of his ginger ale before speaking. "You don't 'get over' it ever. You learn to live with it. Grief continues to come calling, usually in the most unexpected ways. My therapist calls them grief bursts."

Polly stared at her drink. "I know about your Jessie and little Sam," she began. "Jasmine told me. I'm so sorry that happened to you." Polly took a sip of her drink. "I think that is what attracted you two in the beginning. You shared parallel griefs."

Gordy stared at her. Was she right? Maybe in the beginning, but, no, they had much more than that. Their downfall was that they didn't really *talk* to each other about how life just struck out at you when you didn't expect it. They should have talked, instead of pushing all the sadness away, thinking happiness had snuck through the back door of their hearts.

Polly looked at Gordy.

"Let's talk about those 'grief bursts,' Gordy. Have you learned that you don't have to let them take up root in your heart? You can pay attention to them for a while and then send them on their way? Have you learned that, Gordy?"

He looked at her. "Has Jasmine learned that?"

"Yes, she has. I've watched her go through them. She's learned not to linger with them too long, and she's learned that it's perfectly okay to have them."

Gordy nodded in agreement. "I've learned that too."

Understanding, Polly smiled. "Look, I've never lost someone like the two of you have. But I have lost good friends, especially one." Polly suddenly retreated inside herself, staring at the door. Who exactly did she think was going to walk through that door? She turned her gaze back to Gordy. "It is taking me a long time to get over losing my best friend."

"Ellie?" Gordy questioned. "Jasmine's grandmother?"

"Yes, Ellie. I still cry sometimes, mostly when I'm tending her garden. I promised her I would take care of her flowers. I also told her I would watch over Jasmine. That's why I'm here." Polly looked at Gordy before continuing. "Ellie raised Jasmine when her mother died after giving birth to her."

Jasmine had never talked about her grandmother. He would have remembered that awful fact—that her mother had died after giving birth! They had never talked about their pasts that much. They should have. He realized that everyone became a product of their past in one way or another. Yes, they should have talked about their past instead of hiding it somewhere in the dark. That was their first mistake.

Finally, Gordy spoke. "I didn't know that about Jasmine."

"You don't know a lot about Jasmine. And something tells me she doesn't know a whole lot about you either. Other things got in your way."

Suddenly, Polly laughed. "You two became an item quickly, much too quickly. You both were in love with love, don't you think? You only had time for the 'present.' And that's okay. I understand that. But there comes a point you have to settle your hormones down and forget the chemistry for a while. You have to talk about cold hard truths because the fantasy of love disappears like a vapor. I think that you two weren't ready to know a lot about each other. Both of you still had tears blocking your vision of what could be."

Polly sighed and took a deep breath. "What I want to tell you is that Andrew was her life. That girl mourned. She wept. She muddled through for a long time, toting that load." Polly ordered another drink, knowing full well she shouldn't. "She took photos of their final months together with this little camera she bought. Those photos were sad—all black-and-white. No color. They shouted *lonely*. They dripped tears. They spoke to the lonely heart. She was in a dark place. I know grief can put you there. I was so worried about her." Polly took a sip of her freshened drink and looked at Gordy. "Then came you."

*****

Polly continued to talk. "She and I talked every day after she met you. She was a little embarrassed at first—I mean the way you first met."

Gordy remembered that night very vividly. He chuckled. "She did have a little too much to drink."

"When she asked you to dance."

"I think it was the green twinkle lights in my shirt that lured her over to my table."

"I felt she was really making progress, getting on with her life. She was starting over, and I was thrilled. And then—"

Gordy shifted in his seat. He raked his hands over his face. He finished Polly's sentence. "Then she saddled up Star Bright."

"Yes."

*****

"I'm not here to tell you what to do, Gordy—no! Of course, I am! And this is what I'm going to say! I've come this far! I may as well go all the way! It's time to come clean, Gordy. Time to share what's bottled up inside your mind! Time to tell Jasmine a thing or two about yourself. Time to tell her about all the hurt you suffered. And it's high time she did the same!"

Gordy remained silent, thinking about those times of total darkness in his life. Polly was right, of course. He needed to tell Jasmine about it all. He knew she would listen, and he would listen to her in turn. But how? It had been a long time since she had left Brooksport Village.

"When Jasmine left, she didn't tell me where she was going. I figured she wanted to be left alone. She did say goodbye after apologizing to me. I wouldn't even know where to go look for her."

Polly threw her hands in the air! "What is it with men, anyway! Didn't you think she would have gone home to her roots? She came back to her grandma's house! She came back to me! But that's not where she belongs—in the past! She belongs here, with you! Now do something about it!"

*****

Polly had given Gordy a lot to think about. It was true he had never stopped wondering where Jasmine had gone. It was true that he wondered about what her reaction would be if he went in search of her and found her. He had thought about having Ted find her but never followed up on it.

Polly was right. He was a dunce. Why wouldn't he think about her going back to her own hometown? But then they never really talked about her hometown, among other things they should have spoken out loud to each other.

He knew Jasmine was a treasure. Could he do it? Could he weave the memories of his past with the reality of Jasmine in his present? Could he accept it? Could he commit to it?

A treasure is something you hold on to—it's precious. You hold it closely because you want to. He was learning that he had to share his memories with someone who had memories of their own in order to form a future. He was learning that memories didn't haunt him anymore. They had just, one day, become a part of him. A sweet, valuable part of him that had made him exactly who he was today, a harmless heart.

Could he do it? Could Jasmine? Was there still a chance for them? Polly thought so.

*****

Polly stayed at Open Door that night, before leaving Brooksport Village the next day. She had grown to love the town in a matter of hours, and she left with the promise that she would return to visit. She had a new understanding of Gordy and had half fallen in love with him herself. And he had insisted she stay at Open Door because of all the drinks she had consumed—building up her courage.

The next morning, Gordy helped her pack her things in the car after she promised to come to a special birthday party that was going to be held in his own grandfather's honor during the Labor Day celebration in Brooksport.

"How old will your grandpa be?" Polly asked.

"Ninety."

"S——t fire! I'll be there!" She looked out at the lake. "Have I given you some insight by coming here? Have I given you something to come in search of and grab ahold of?"

Gordy put his thumbs in the pockets of his jeans and followed her gaze to the lake. "It's taken me a lot of years and tears to come to this point. I was still fighting it. And then there you were—at Belle's."

"And?"

"I have a lot to think about."

"That's a start and good enough—for now."

Polly got into her car. Looking up at Gordy with a smile, she said, "I hope that you'll know what you want soon. I don't know how much longer I can put up with my sweet, sad sack Jasmine. I think you're the man who can help her recapture that smile again. Aww, s——t fire! I know you are!"

She began to drive off, stopped the car, and hollered out the window, "Gordy, it's time to admit it! Love's done gone and snuck up on you!"

Thinking of Trudy, he watched the car disappear, whispering to himself, "Another one who leans toward a dramatic exit."

*****

Halfway back to her home, Polly wondered what she would tell Jasmine. She would have to tell her something. Well, she would make up something. Jasmine and Gordy had to get back together before she could confess the truth of where she had really been. Everything would have to be smoothed out, wrinkle-free.

"I will tell her I had a rendezvous with a man." She eased her conscience. "Well, I did, in a way."

She found it quite fun making up ridiculous stories when it came to love…

*****

"You did not!"

"I did!"

Jasmine went to the cabinet and secured two glasses for the wine that was sitting in the middle of the kitchen table, begging to be uncorked. "Do tell all!" Jasmine exclaimed.

Polly made up the biggest story she could think of that had Jasmine giggling through the night. Was it so out of the question? Polly wondered. What was so funny about her meeting up with a man on a rendezvous? Maybe she would do exactly that when those two got back together. She would show them all!

Polly came to the conclusion that whatever the outcome, she knew in her heart that she had done the right thing. It wouldn't take Gordy long before he came to their little town that Jasmine called home.

That night, Polly prayed for forgiveness for telling a little white lie to Jasmine, and she promised God she would continue to stay where she was and tend Ellie's garden. She would not go trapesing off on any kind of rendezvous. It was then that she closed her eyes and slept soundly for the first time in months.

*****

Chapter 40

Polly was looking at the calendar. Jasmine walked into the kitchen. "Are you counting the days until your next rendezvous, Polly?"

"Child, you nearly scared me to death coming into the kitchen so quietly!"

"Sorry. Hey, don't let me stand in your way when you want to go! Hey, why don't you invite him here? I can meet him and give you my thumbs-up or thumbs-down sign! What do you say?"

"I say calm down! I'm not wanting anything serious!"

"Then why are you looking at the calendar and counting the days?"

"Oh, I don't know!" Polly was clearly frustrated. "I'm going to the garden."

"Okay, I think I'm going into town for a while. They asked me to work part-time at the gift boutique. I think I'll do it."

Polly stopped walking and turned to face Jasmine. "I personally think you have some thinking to do—not work in the boutique!"

"Polly, don't start! What I had—or what I thought I had—with Gordy is over. It didn't work. I have to start thinking about a job—"

Polly interrupted her. "You don't need a job! You have so much money you can't fold it fast enough! You know that. Andrew, God rest his soul, saw to that! You need to think about your memories and start weaving them into your future, girl!"

Jasmine was stunned into a quietness she didn't quite understand.

Polly mumbled as she left the house for the flower garden, "Why can't people see love when it's staring them right in the face?

First Ellie and Carson. Now it's Jasmine and Gordy. What in tarnation am I supposed to do with these people and all their unrequited love issues?"

*****

Jasmine was talking with the owner of the boutique when she looked up and saw what she thought was a familiar face. A very familiar face.

"Pardon me, but I have to go!"

She ran out of the store, but he had disappeared. She must have imagined it. He wouldn't be here, anyway. He didn't know that she had come back here. Her mind was playing tricks on her. Probably because of Polly talking so much about him lately. Polly was putting ideas in her head, and thoughts of Gordy had manifested in her subconscious mind. Of course, that was what it was. He wasn't thinking of her. There were times she wished that he was. There were times that she hoped she haunted his dreams. There were times she was just plain angry. Then she was sad. Then she didn't care. Then she cared too much. But she simply refused to contact him. She would not. Didn't someone once say, "*A lady always knows when it's time to leave*"? Well, she was a lady, and it was time for her to, once and for all, get him out of her head. She would take this job she didn't need. She would buy a little house near Polly. She would drink wine and celebrate Polly going on her carefully planned rendezvous. And she would force herself to be happy.

She shook her head to clear all the feelings that were bombarding her mind. It was her imagination playing tricks on her. Gordy wasn't here. She sat down on a nearby bench.

"What just happened?" She was thinking of Gordy and only Gordy. Not Andrew.

*****

Dinner was quieter than usual with Polly. Polly was thinking, and they were not good thoughts about Gordy. What was wrong with him? Where was he? He should have at least called. Why hadn't he come riding in on his white horse and rescued Jasmine, who was in distress and didn't even know it?

It was Jasmine who broke the silence. "I thought I saw him today."

"Who?"

"Gordy."

Polly dropped her fork. "Where?"

"In front of the boutique. I ran outside, but he was gone. Decided it was my mind playing tricks on me."

Polly remained silent and held out hope that perhaps Gordy *was* doing the right thing. But why would he not go into the boutique if he had seen Jasmine standing there? Polly replied nonchalantly, "You love him."

"Not possible."

"Why else did you run out of the store to see if it was him?"

"Friendship."

Polly took a deep breath and sighed heavily. "Think long and hard about the question I am about to ask you, child. Do you still love him? I think you do, but you have to answer that question yourself. And if the answer is yes, you should hightail it back to Brooksport Village. Men don't wait forever."

*****

Did she love Gordy? Alone in her room that night she did exactly as Polly had advised. She thought long and hard. Why was she missing him so much after all this time that had passed? Why was she thinking about him in the middle of the night? Why was she actually thinking of swallowing her pride and going back to Brooksport Village for a visit? Should she?

Yes, she decided. She needed closure. And if it took her to a dreaded place of rejection, well, at least, she would have her closure. She would tell Polly tomorrow of her plans.

"Do you still love him?"

Still? Does that mean I loved him, once upon a time? With wild abandon, did I love him? I must have. Why else would I feel this way? Those were the questions hammering on her heart as sleep evaded her, thinking only of Brooksport Village. She got out of bed and began to pack.

*****

Jasmine found Polly in the flower garden the next morning mumbling to herself and digging up weeds with a furor.

"What are you saying to yourself, Polly?"

"Nothing that would interest you."

Jasmine put on the extra kneepads and knelt to help Polly with the weeds. "I have something to say that might interest you."

Polly kept digging.

"I'm going back to Brooksport Village."

Polly jumped up with delight, dragging Jasmine up with her. A big bear hug followed. Polly took a deep breath and stared at Jasmine.

"I've rendered you speechless?"

"Lordy, child, you have, indeed! Come on back to the house! I'll help you pack!"

"Already have. Did it when I couldn't sleep last night, thinking about your question." Both women removed their kneepads. "And you know what else, Polly? After I thought I had seen Gordy outside the boutique, after I had run outside to see if, indeed, it was him, I was so let down because he wasn't there anymore. I went over to that little bench outside the store, and I had what one calls an epiphany. It just happened. I realized I was only thinking of Gordy—not Andrew."

Polly gave her another bear hug. "The time is right, child. Now the time is right. Go get your Gordy."

*****

Polly watched as Jasmine's car disappeared. It was nearing dusk. She walked up to her front porch and took a deep, cleansing breath.

Those precious petals were beginning to unfold—the jasmine plant. She decided to sit outside for a moment longer.

She looked up at the sky. "Oh, Ellie, I must tell you," she whispered, "you would be so proud of your granddaughter." She cupped her hands together. "I'm watching her reclaim all the pieces that had once been her life. It feels damned good." She looked once again at the horizon. "Looks like she's getting ready to take flight and reclaim the rest."

*****

Perhaps it was the honesty. The pureness of Brooksport Village. People would arrive at Brooksport's garden gate filled with questions. Some had to leave to find their answers, only to return with balloons in their hands or pockets with holes, spilling out their secrets all over the floor. Some had to travel to the city and all of its racket to find their answers. But the heart, along with the "pilgrim," always returned to Brooksport Village. Always.

A calmness of spirit could forever be found there. All who had left and all who had come back found a peace they had not known before. People seemed to find themselves on their journey to and from Brooksport. It taught them that sometimes they had to go back in time to look at their lives in earnest. They had to look at certain chapters in their life—the chapters that had turned their world upside down—once upon a time. Only then would they be able to run toward their future. They needed a blending of their past into their present—a blending that would, most certainly, lead to hope for the future. They needed a transition. They needed to breathe deeply and walk through another door. One had to realize that their self-made penance was over. Finished.

Yes, a new light dawns when you first set foot in Brooksport Village. You find yourself eventually putting new pictures in old frames.

PART 8

"SETH"

Meanwhile, back in Brooksport Village…

Chapter 41

Seth decided it was time to visit Trudy now that she was home from the hospital and had some time to get fully settled into her recovery. He had come a long way since he had first set foot in Brooksport Village, since he had been sent to his new foster home in a rural area, a few miles north of Brooksport. Zeke, the owner of the grocery store, had given him a job at Brooksport Grocery; and that was where he had met Trudy for the first time.

She had scared him to death demanding her Chicken in a Biskit crackers. The woman wanted lard, salt, and grease. Zeke had told him to always have those crackers on the shelf where she could see them.

He learned even more about her from the "regulars" and some of the tourists who had met her. After the fire and his taking care of Buddy while she got better, he had decided he liked her. She didn't scare him anymore.

He further decided to visit her often at her house while she was continuing to recover from all the side issues of smoke inhalation. He decided he would deliver her groceries until she could walk those aisles herself.

He had ridden his bike to Trudy's house with a bouquet of purple flowers in the basket that had once carried Buddy to her hospital room, and he had stopped by Belle's to get her some extracrispy doughnuts. He found her sitting on her porch with Buddy on her lap. He parked his bike, retrieved the flowers and doughnuts, and began walking toward her.

"I see you're takin' it easy like Doc Charlie told you to do! Miss Trudy, you scared me to death!"

"When? A few years ago at the grocery store or after the fire?"

"Both! I brought you these flowers and these doughnuts."

"Why, thank you, Seth. You're a good boy!"

Seth smiled and walked up the steps to the porch where Trudy was sitting. "I appreciate you telling me that, Miss Trudy. I don't get compliments too often." He shuffled his feet. "Can't remember when I ever did, matter of fact."

Trudy took a deep breath. "Is something troubling you, Seth? Come here and sit with me. Tell me about it. It matters not what it is. Just tell me. Is it about girls?"

"No, not really. It seems like I'm lookin' for somethin', and I'm not sure what it is."

Trudy remained silent.

"It's not your Chicken in a Biskit crackers with lard! I do know that!"

Trudy could not help but laugh, hugging him in the process. "Oh, Seth! You are such a delight to be around! And you are so very kind and compassionate. I do so love all of that about you!"

"Oh, wow, another compliment. It's really nice gettin' compliments, Miss Trudy." Seth looked at Trudy with such a sadness. Trudy held him tighter, rocking him back and forth. There, in the shelter of her arms, he said, "I just feel like I don't really belong anywhere, Miss Trudy. I feel so alone sometimes."

Trudy understood. She felt she had always been looking for something, too, hiding behind her humor—after Frank—until Ted. "Oh, my darling boy, you just need someone to love and someone to love you back."

He pulled away from her slowly. "Miss Trudy, I don't want a girlfriend! I've heard all about your matchmakin', and I'm too mixed up for a girlfriend!"

Trudy couldn't resist. She grabbed him again and chuckled. "Oh, you are such a smart lad, too, Seth! Don't worry! We'll figure out where you're goin'! We'll figure it all out!"

Seth began to squirm inside her arms. "This huggin' has gone on long enough, Miss Trudy!"

"I want to thank you, Seth."

Seth looked at Trudy.

"I'm not talkin' about thankin' you for just these." She pointed to the flowers and doughnuts.

"Somethin' tells me you're gonna hug me again."

"I will if you want me to."

"I'm good, Miss Trudy."

She took a doughnut from the bag and offered him one. As they took bites from those extracrispy delights, Trudy pointed to Buddy. "I'm also talkin' about my cat, over there sleepin' like a baby. Just so you know, he likes the pet bed you bought him too."

Seth looked at Buddy.

"Thank you for savin' him."

"It was my honor, Miss Trudy."

She smiled. "I've been meanin' to ask you, what were you doin' in Crabby's Bar after 2:00 a.m., anyway? You're too young to be in there."

Seth looked up from where he was sitting. "My second job. I clean up after hours."

"When do you sleep?"

"When I can."

"Where are your parents, Seth?"

"I don't have parents, Miss Trudy."

"What?"

"I belong to a foster home just about five miles from here, on a farm. My parents died when I was a baby, in a car crash."

"Oh, Seth, I'm so sorry."

Suddenly, the doughnut didn't taste so good, and all the pieces to the puzzle were coming together. No wonder he felt like he didn't belong. She looked at Seth, remembering the first time she had seen him in the grocery store aisle at Brooksport Grocery.

"I'm sorry I was so hard on you that day in the grocery store, ya know, when I needed my special crackers?"

"With salt and lard. I remember. I'll repeat: you scared the livin' daylights out of me that day! But that's okay, Miss Trudy. I get stronger when people are tough on me. At least, that's what I've been told."

Trudy thought for a moment before speaking. "You know somethin', Seth?"

"What's that, Miss Trudy?"

"I never could have children of my own, but if I could have had a son, I would want him to be just like you."

"Well, if I were your son, Miss Trudy, I'd make sure you always had those crackers you like. I know you get ornery without your lard."

Trudy smiled. "You wouldn't want me gettin' ornery, eh?"

"No, ma'am!" It was at that moment Buddy decided to wake up from his nap and stroll over to Seth. Seth picked him up, patting his head ever so gently. "We both love her, don't we, Buddy?"

Trudy's heart melted then and there. Seth was so much more than a grocery store—aisle stocker for the summer and a "cleaner upper" after hours at Crabby's Bar. So much more. She wondered how much of his hard-earned money at both his jobs did it cost to buy Buddy that bed, all those cat toys, and treats—not to mention the flowers that he had just handed her. How much, indeed?

"Be strong and courageous. Do not be terrified; do not be discouraged, for the Lord your God will be with you wherever you go."

(Joshua 1:9)

Chapter 42

Seth was having a meltdown.

"Clean up in aisle ten! Pallet tipped! Ice cream, everywhere!"

Zeke appeared in aisle ten and witnessed it all. He walked over to Seth.

"To my office, son."

"Sir?"

"To my office. I'll handle this."

Seth dropped his head and slowly walked back to Zeke's office. This was serious, he thought to himself.

Zeke called for his assistant manager, and the two of them positioned everything back to order and organized the ice cream in the proper freezers. Zeke walked into his office where a dejected Seth sat and walked around his desk. He sat down and looked at Seth. Seth did not lift his head.

"How old are you, son? Really, tell me really how old are you?"

"I lied."

"Last year?"

"And this year."

"Why?"

"Because I need this job."

Zeke remembered Seth had insisted on cash as payment for his work. He remembered Seth's actions after Trudy had scared him nearly to death. Young, he had thought then—but time had gotten away from him, and he had forgotten all about his suspicions. Seth's reaction over the overturned pallet brought the question front and center once again.

"People have told me I look a lot older than my age."

"I agree with that, Seth. You may look it, but you don't act it."

Seth continued to hang his head. "Are you going to fire me, sir?"

Zeke cleared his throat. "No, son, I'm not going to fire you."

Seth jerked his head up. "Really?"

"Yes, really." Zeke placed his elbows on his desk and leaned toward Seth. Seth looked at Zeke, tears forming in his eyes. *Young*, Zeke thought again. "Seth, how old are you?"

Seth hesitated only for a moment. "I'm thirteen, sir."

Zeke leaned back in his chair, never taking his gaze away from Seth. Seth thought this was it. Instead, Zeke shoved his fingers through his hair and thought about his reply. He took a deep breath and sighed. "Where do you live?"

"With foster parents, sir, out in what they call the rural area—on a farm."

"And you ride your bike to work every day—here?"

"Yes, sir." Seth began shuffling his feet. He was looking at the floor once again.

Young, Zeke thought over and over again. "Are they good to you, your foster parents?"

Again, Seth's head sprung up. "Oh yes, sir! They are real good to me! We have food, and when it rains, I hear the pounding on the roof at night, and I know I'm safe and warm. I feel good about that."

Zeke felt a knot way back in his throat. "You're not fired, Seth." Zeke stood up, walked to the window, turned to Seth, and said, "Look at me, Seth." Seth forced himself to look straight at Zeke. "In fact, I'm giving you a raise, and you will continue to be paid in cash."

"What do you want in return, sir? More responsibilities?"

"Honesty," Zeke replied, "honesty."

*****

Trudy had to know more. She found herself walking to the grocery store to talk to Zeke. Zeke saw her come through the door and ran up to her.

"I thought Seth was delivering your groceries, Trudy! Come in my office! I want you to sit down! You look peeked!"

"Oh, stop it, Zeke! I am fine! I had to get out of my house for a spell. But I will come into your office. I want to talk to you about something."

Once settled in a chair, Zeke brought her a bottle of water. Then he sat at his desk, across from her.

"Talk to me about Seth."

"What do you want to know?"

"Everything."

Zeke folded his hands in front of him. "I'm thinking Seth has had a rough life, Trudy."

"Go on."

"Exactly what do you know about him already?"

"I know his parents were killed in a car crash when he was a baby, and I know he lives with foster parents on a farm a few miles from here." Zeke sucked in his breath and felt a rush of sadness. "He told me about his foster parents, but he did not tell me how his parents died."

"I'm thinkin' he was underage when you hired him."

Zeke sighed. "Yes, I just found that out this morning, actually. He looks so much older."

Trudy sipped her water. "You know he has bills down at the pet store?"

"What?"

"He has bills down at the pet store—and the florist."

"What are you talking about, Trudy? I've lost you."

"That young boy brought me flowers nearly every day while I was in the hospital. He bought a bed for Buddy—and toys, plus all the cat food. He took real good care of Buddy when I couldn't. He brings me doughnuts from Belle's, but they're free—Belle told me—on the house."

"He's too young to have bills."

"I stopped at the pet store and the florist before I came here. He has bills."

Zeke cupped his forehead in his palm, shaking his head. "That's why he wanted more hours here," Zeke murmured.

"You know he works at Crabby's after hours, cleaning up?"

"A second job?"

"He had just started when the fire happened. He was wantin' to save some money, but he ended up spendin' a lot of it on Buddy and me." Trudy finished drinking her water.

"I guess what I'm tryin' to say Zeke, is if you can, give him a few more hours. He's a proud boy. He's a hard worker. Plus, he's in school. Seems like he wants to make his own way, but he likes takin' care of people too. Don't fire him because he's underage. Give him cash."

"I already do."

Trudy looked at him and smiled. "I'll bet you even gave him a raise too."

"I did."

"Thanks, Zeke. I always knew you were a good fella." Trudy rose to leave.

"What are you thinking, Trudy? Are you going to help that boy in some way?"

"What do you think I'm gonna do? I have a whole lot more to learn about him, but I'm gonna help in some way. I'm gonna start by payin' off his bills." She winked at Zeke and walked out the door.

Trudy did have a plan. She had to talk to Ted, and both she and that handsome techy man of hers had some Sunday-go-to-meetin' days ahead of them.

*****

Chapter 43

Gordy decided to do a turnaround for a change. He took Trudy a casserole.

Trudy opened the door to a smiling Gordy, who was handing her dinner for the night.

Trudy laughed.

"I cooked it myself," Gordy said.

"Sure, you did."

She took the casserole from him, opened the door wider, and invited him in. "Let me put this in the kitchen. I'm glad you just showed up. I want to talk to you about somethin'."

Gordy sat and waited for Trudy to come out of the kitchen. "I hope you are not going to try to get my love life in order, Trudy."

"Nope, I've given up on you."

"Good."

"It's about Seth."

*****

"Would you hire me part-time, Mr. Gordy?"

Gordy looked at Seth. "Seth, you are working at the grocery store, and now I hear you are working at Crabby's, after hours. Why do you need another job?"

"I have bills."

"What kind of bills?"

"At the pet store and the florist."

Gordy walked over to Star Bright and stroked her mane. "And how did you get those bills?"

Seth stood firmly. Gordy seemed to see a little man standing there. Trudy had already told him all about Seth. She had even told him to expect Seth to come to him for another job. Now, it seemed, she had become a prophetess. He felt it important that Seth tell him on his own about his "financial" situation.

"I bought a bed for Buddy when the fire happened. Well, I charged it, kind of. And I took Miss Trudy flowers while she was in the hospital, and I just kept bringing her flowers when she came home to recuperate. I thought those flowers would cheer her up. So I just kept charging."

Gordy's heart took a gentle leap. "I see."

"So I need another job to pay those bills off."

Gordy petted Star Bright and gave him a carrot, looking at Seth. "I see," he repeated. Gordy walked over to Seth. "Let's go talk." "I'll tell you what," Gordy began. "I think those bills can disappear."

Gordy already knew that Trudy had paid them off. She had told him so. But she didn't want Seth to know. He remembered what she had said, *"He's a proud boy. He needs to know he worked to pay off his bills."* Trudy had thought that Seth talking with a man about his bills would help him stand a little taller.

"How can those bills disappear, sir?"

"Out of the goodness of a person's heart, son. I'll tell you what. How about you working here for two weeks in the stable with Wes, and we'll call it even, and those bills will be paid?"

"So the money I would make would go straight to paying my bills?"

"Yes, that's the bottom line, Seth."

"You would do that for me, sir?"

"Yes, I would."

"But is two weeks enough time for everything I owe?"

"It's enough time."

Gordy couldn't help thinking of his own son, little Sam. Looking at Seth, he was glad he could help him out, and he was grateful for Trudy confiding in him. Her parting words were, *"Make sure he stands tall. Let him work for what he owes."*

Seth broke into Gordy's thoughts. "Oh, that would be wonderful! I will make you proud! Thank you, Mr. Gordy!" Gordy smiled and held out his hand for a handshake. "You won't regret this, Mr. Gordy!"

"Wes will show you what to do, Seth. Report to work this weekend."

And so Seth's bills were paid. All was right with the world. Or so Gordy thought.

*****

"Wake up, Ted! It's time!" Trudy was standing over him with a big purple hat on her head.

"What time is it?" he managed to question.

"Time all old dogs are dead. Aren't you glad you're a pup?"

"It's still dark outside."

"Get up! We have to talk! Or, rather, I have to talk to you!"

He knew better than to fight whatever this battle was with Trudy at 6:00 a.m. He got out of bed and began to walk into his living room—Trudy close on his heels. He pulled her down alongside of him on the couch.

"Okay, I give, what exactly is it time for? And why did I ever give you a key to wake me up this early?"

"It's time to tell you my secret. Only one other person knows in this town. But soon, there will be three of us. I need to come clean with you, and what better way to do it than ridin' to Carsonville?"

"I thought I knew everything about you."

"You don't. But you will—on the way to Carsonville. We'll stop for breakfast. You may need a mimosa by the time I've told you half of my story—maybe somethin' stronger." Trudy walked to the mirror and adjusted her hat. "Get dressed, city boy. And hurry! I'm takin' ya to church!"

*****

The ride was too short for him to absorb everything she was telling him. And she was right; he had needed something stronger than a mimosa, so they went to the infamous country bar serving Bloody Marys that had a live band and dancing every Thursday night. It was there, sitting at the end of the bar, with that big purple hat on her head that he learned all about Frank.

"I was the reason my baby died. At least, I thought that for a long time. The doctor said the miscarriage was caused by stress. I blamed Frank for making me feel stressed. I blamed his affair that had caused me to lose our baby. I blamed everybody I could think of. I blamed the other woman. I blamed the cashiers in the department store for selling me baby blankets and onesies far too soon."

Ted was holding her hand tightly.

"So you see, I understand what you felt with all your guilt about your sister. I want to help you to unpack all of that guilt, and I want you to help me continue to unpack mine. I want to bring in the 'new' Ted. I want to trust again. I want to love again. I want to feel alive again, with you."

"Oh, Trudy, I want the same." He tried to kiss her, but the purple hat got in the way. When they left the bar, they were laughing with fingers intertwined.

"Who goes to a bar before church?" Trudy questioned.

Ted smiled and replied, "You, Trudy, only you."

They walked into that little country church in Carsonville and took a seat.

Sitting next to him, she pointed toward the altar and whispered, "I found myself at that very altar in this very church many years ago, Ted. I want to find myself again, with you by my side."

He felt so at peace. She was glowing, and by the time the service was over, so was he. It had taken a cemetery conversation and a fire to get them to this point, and now both of them knew just how much fire does, indeed, refine and how pouring rain can, indeed, heal.

Ted and Trudy remained true to that Sunday morning gathering from that moment on. Every Sunday, they left Brooksport Village at 7:00 a.m., had a nice breakfast, and sat in that little town church holding hands—her in her purple hat and Ted with his purple chapeau placed on his lap.

*****

They grew closer as they unpacked their past heartaches and all their guilt. Honesty made them shine. Iron sharpening iron. They became solid as a rock.

"Even though I could have no more children," she told Ted one of those Sunday afternoons, "I became the 'mother of many.'"

He understood what she was saying. He had watched her when she was around children. She loved them; they loved her. She was widely known as "the fun Miss Trudy," as well as the "don't mess with Miss Trudy."

"You ever see that tower of polished stones around the corner of my house?"

He nodded.

"That's my personal Ebenezer stone."

He looked perplexed.

"I remember the day I built it."

She took his hand and looked straight through him.

"It was a beautiful spring day. Over the years, when I felt so alone and forsaken. I collected polished stones along the lakes edge. I had put them in a jar—didn't know what I was gonna do with 'em *until*—" Tears were beginning to form in her eyes.

"Until what?"

"Until God told me he had been with me through all my twists and turns in life and he was not going to ever stop loving me. That's when I built my tower."

"What does it mean, Trudy?"

"It means, *God has brought me this far*. It means he will never forsake me. When times get rough, I go to the corner of my house. I look at that tower, and I remember. I affirm over and over that faith in what I can't see will get me where I'm goin.'"

"Where's your path going now, Trudy?"

"It's goin' somewhere that I need a real strong shoulder alongside me, Ted." She came close to his ear and whispered, "I want you to consider…"

His answer was in his smile and the squeeze of his hand. As the two of them left the church, a few forgotten leaves rustled around their ankles. They knew the meaning of those leaves sent down to them at just the right moment. They looked at each other and smiled. A major decision had been made with a whisper in Ted's ear, and the mere nod of his head. And now, the final affirmation from the leaves, floating around them upon a soft breeze.

*****

Chapter 44

This day would be a day of nostalgia for Wes as he arrived at the stable. He touched the small plaque with only one word engraved upon it: *Love*. He knew instinctively that he was standing in front of Star Bright's stall. He held out his hand, and the horse nuzzled it.

Wes whispered, "Oh, how she loved you." He reached in his pocket retrieving a small sugar cube. "You still miss her, I know."

He stroked the horse's soft nose. "We all do, buddy. We all do."

Wes sat down on the bench close to Star Bright. "It's hard to forget someone you've grown up with. Not that you want to."

The white horse neighed.

"Oh yes, I remember that day as if it were yesterday—9/11, the day two sweet sparks left our small village town—Jessie and Sam." Wes stood and walked to the feeding bins. He began to fill the buckets for the horse's morning meal.

"Well, a lot of years have passed since then. Wounds have turned to scars. Life has moved on. Charlie is now a doctor. Sarah is returning in a few more months…" He broke off and began walking back to Star Bright.

"Hey, buddy! She is going to be your vet! My daughter! How about that!"

Again, the horse neighed.

Wes smiled. "Sure is nice carrying on a conversation with you, fella!" He began to fill the feeding trough. "We're going to have some more help around here for a couple of weeks. That young Seth fella is coming over. I think I'll make you his responsibility for that time. Is that okay with you, buddy?"

Star Bright began to eat. Wes continued to talk to the horse. "Gordy was devastated when he lost Jessie. Then he met Jasmine. I wondered if he met her too soon, but Reva reminded me it had been nearly four years after 9/11 when they had met. She told me not to worry about it, that Gordy knew what he was doing."

Wes patted the horse and sighed. "And then she decided to take a ride with you, and the rest is history."

Star Bright neighed. It seemed he understood every word Wes was saying.

"I know you liked her. But grief is a monster of the shadowy kind. You never know when it is going to jump out at you. It lurks behind chairs where Jessie once sat. It hides behind computers where she once wrote, and it struck a sad chord when she saddled you up to meet Gordy that fateful day."

Star Bright finished eating as Wes continued to talk. "Maybe she'll come back. Maybe Gordy will be ready to have her come back one day." Wes prepared to go tend to the other horses. "Whatever happens, we'll always be there for Gordy, right, you big, majestic fella?"

He rubbed Star Bright's nose once again, gave him another square of sugar, and whispered, "*No man left behind*."

As Wes walked away from Star Bright, that special horse looked out over the pasture where he would soon run. His gaze also took him to the path where he had watched Jasmine walk away. And just like the night when Gordy had repeated the bedtime story that Jessie had always read to Sam, that horse blinked. Seemed like he had understood everything that Wes had said to him that morning. He kept looking at the path. Perhaps she would come back one day as quickly as she had left.

*****

Wes's nostalgic day would soon take on quite another turn. The thought of working with young Seth and training him with the horses, even for a few short weeks, had given Wes a sense of delight. He was looking forward to Seth's arrival.

Seth arrived with an eagerness that pleased Wes as well. He introduced Seth to all the horses but especially took more time with Star Bright.

"This magnificent one will be your responsibility the next two weeks," Wes said.

Seth was thrilled. He knew how special that horse was. "How about giving our buddy his bath today?" Wes sensed Seth's uneasiness. "I'll give you the instructions, and this fella won't give you any trouble. He loves his baths."

Wes told Seth where all the supplies for the bath were, patted him on the shoulder, and told him he would do just fine. With that, Wes left the stable for his regular storytelling hour with all the tourist kids. He loved doing that, and they loved every single one of his made-up stories, even if they had heard them more than once.

*****

Seth took the ladder over to the hayloft, climbed up, and walked to where all the supplies were stored. He gathered the sponge, cloth, shampoo, scraper, and hose—just as Wes had instructed. Attaching the hose to the water heater, he then plugged it into the socket and began his climb down from the loft. He walked toward Star Bright.

"Hey, big fella, we're gonna start with your legs, get you used to the water, just like Wes said." He continued to talk to Star Bright as he worked. "Don't worry. I won't spray the water anywhere near your face or ears." He reached for the small sponge and gently washed the horse's face and eyes. "You likin' this, big fella?" All went very well as Seth completed his first responsibility at the stable. He took a deep breath and decided he liked this job more than all the others.

It was nearing late afternoon when Seth took all the supplies back up to the loft to store them away, paying particular attention to the hose. He had to leave soon for his other job at Brooksport Grocery. It had been a good day. He was pleased with himself, and he hoped both Gordy and Wes would be pleased too. He looked around and decided everything was in place. He patted Star Bright on the nose, got on his bike, and began his ride to his second job.

Everything was not in its place. Seth had forgotten one major detail. And that one thing would turn his world upside down.

*****

Wes was running late with his story hour with the kids and was walking back to the stable, hoping Seth would still be there. He walked up to Star Bright's stall.

"How are you doing, fella? Did you enjoy your bath? I'm going to take you out to the pasture soon." He patted the horse on his mane. "Seth, are you still here?"

No one answered.

"Guess not. Let's get you out for some fresh air!"

With that, Wes prepared Star Bright and led him outside. He walked back to the stable. He decided to climb up to the loft and drop down a bale of hay for the horse's morning meals. He carefully pushed the ladder into place and climbed up. This was familiar territory for him, and he had become quite the master of doing all the daily chores. Blindness did not hinder him. And Gordy had installed all the necessary equipment and braille signs that served as his road map.

He began to whistle as he walked toward the corner where the bales of hay were always located. He was thinking of spending a nice evening with Reva when his foot caught on the cord to the water heater. He did not have time to react. He tripped forward and began his decent down to the ground below. His head hit the hard ground, and everything turned black.

*****

When Gordy returned home, he noticed Star Bright was still in the pasture. That was odd. He was sure Wes was home by now. He would never have left the horse this long. He should have been settling in for the night.

Gordy walked over to his horse.

"Hey, buddy, you waiting for the stars to come out? Let's get you inside."

As Gordy approached the stable, he saw something on the ground below the loft. He soon realized that it wasn't a something; it was a someone, and that someone was Wes! He ran to his friend's side, speaking his name and reaching for his phone at the same time.

The ambulance arrived and took Wes, with sirens blaring, to the hospital. It was only when Gordy had called Reva and settled Star Bright into his stall that he went up to the loft to see what might have caused Wes to fall.

It didn't take long for him to discover the cord still plugged into the socket for the water heater. His heart sank. He should have given Seth more guidance. He should have gone over safety rules with him. He just didn't think. You cannot measure a teen with an adult yardstick. He should have watched out for his blind friend. What was wrong with him? He had to get to the hospital to console Reva and tell her exactly what had happened.

*****

Chapter 45

Where was he? The hospital? What had happened? Wes shook his head trying to remember. A sound from the hallway, something falling from a shelf somewhere, brought it all back.

He had been in the stable, his fingers searching the braille sign. L-O-V-E—he had been talking to Star Bright, giving him sugar cubes, rubbing his nose, talking about Jessie.

What had happened next? He continued to hear low murmurs in the hallway. Were they whispering about him? He tried moving his legs. Check. His arms. Check. His fingers and toes. Check. His head? Although painful, it moved. Check.

"Thank you, Lord."

He could feel the breeze from the open window. What was that smell? A fragrance. It was sweet. Calming. And in some strange way hopeful. Then, as if something had clicked in his mind, he remembered the fall.

He had stepped up the ladder to retrieve a few hay bales for the next morning. Then he had stumbled, tripped. A cord of some kind in his path—not supposed to be there. He had gone tumbling to the hard ground below.

"Anybody here?" he questioned.

No answer. He was alone. He ventured to believe it was late night or early morning. He knew Reva would be there as soon as first light broke on the horizon.

He tried to sleep, to no avail.

"I guess this is our alone time, eh, God? You want my full attention?" he whispered.

Wes didn't know how right he was with that question. Something life changing was about to happen, and the only two who needed to know were the only two in the room. Alone time. With God.

*****

Why is it that nighttime always seems and feels darker than it usually is? The pain in his head had eased. He was grateful for that. The doctor had said he could return home in a few days. He was restless. He wanted to get out of bed and walk over to the window. He wanted to walk toward the breeze where that sweet smell of hope kept lingering from what seemed hours before. He knew it was still dark outside; there was less activity in the hallway.

He dared not move. He didn't know his way around this strange room with the sweet fragrance, hovering around him. He had promised Reva he would "stay put."

"I know how stubborn you are," she had said, jabbing her finger in his chest. *"Promise me you will stay in that bed!"*

He had promised. That seemed to placate her. She had always trusted his promises.

Nevertheless, he flung his legs over the side of the bed. She would never know—unless he fell again. But he had promised. Slowly, he put his legs back on top of the bed and turned on his side. It was almost too quiet, he thought. And in that quietness, a certain peace came upon him. A calming of his spirit. A sigh of release found his lips.

"It's jasmine," he whispered. "It's the sweet fragrance of jasmine that I smell."

How could that be? It wasn't dusk. It was way too dark. Was there a jasmine plant outside his window? He felt confused, disoriented, and yet calm.

That was when it happened. The calm after the storm of the afternoon of his fall. He couldn't believe it.

Sometimes that is exactly what happens when one is alone with God. Mysterious fragrances. Insights. Miracles. One does not question a gift. One does not try to explain it either. One accepts it with palms open. And one always remembers the sweet fragrance that was only shared by two.

The sweet fragrance of jasmine—gift from God. Yes, God's fingerprints were all over that hospital room. And the gift he had given this time was labeled *priceless*.

*****

Across town, Seth kept watching the clock on his nightstand. Would morning ever come? The night seemed to crawl, just like it did when Trudy was in the hospital—the night of the fire. He would have to go. He remembered his bike had a flat tire. He would hitchhike if he had to. He had to go first thing in the morning to see Wes. He kept kicking himself for not unplugging the socket to the water heater. He wasn't thinking. Where had his mind been?

He was thinking about how to make enough money to buy Christmas presents this year, even though Christmas was months away. He had to plan early. He had to save early. It made him sad he couldn't buy for the people who had taken care of him these past few years, his foster parents.

He had stayed in numerous homes in his lifetime, but this old farmhouse with the rain pounding on the roof this endless night had been his home now for several years. He worried about them. They were getting older. What if something happened to them? Where would he go? What would he do? Would he have to leave this place where he felt so safe and secure? Could he make it on his own in Brooksport Village if he had to? Yes, that was what he was thinking when he became so negligent. He needed to concentrate on the things at hand, not worry so much about the future.

It was all his fault. Wes didn't deserve that fall. It seemed he had lost days of his life before Seth got the call from Trudy, telling him that Wes had regained consciousness. Trudy kept telling him not to be so hard on himself, but he was. She was only trying to make him feel better about himself. Seemed funny now that the woman clad in purple who had once scared the living daylights out of him was trying desperately to make him not feel so guilty. Yes, now they were buddies. Maybe it was because he understood her now. It wasn't just her need for lard that he recognized; it was her compassionate heart. He appreciated her trying to convince him that accidents happen and not to blame himself so much. All he knew was that he had to see Wes. Come hell or high water, he had to see him. He had to pay his penance. He had to give his apologizes. He had to ask for forgiveness.

It was 5:30 when Seth decided he may as well get up and start his day. He couldn't sleep. He walked to his closet and took the jar of pennies, quarters, and dimes to his bed. He dumped the contents on his pillow and began to count—the money he had saved since the beginning of the new year, preparing for this year, this winter, this Christmas. He would have to start over. Because he was taking his savings to buy Wes something—in way of apology. He had to do something. He just had to. He hoped that Wes would understand and forgive him for being so unreliable. He got dressed, slid the change into his pocket, and left. It would be a long walk. But he decided that was probably good. He needed to clear his head. He would be soaked to the skin when he arrived at the hospital, but that was okay too. So many things had gone wrong in his childhood; this was just one more thing. He would visit Wes at the hospital and then go to work at the grocery store—and start saving all over again.

*****

Seth stood outside Wes's hospital room with flowers in one hand and a box of candy in the other. He had done it. He had to charge it. He was in debt again. Gordy had been so kind to let him work to pay off his other charges, and he had failed him for all his good will by causing Wes's accident. He felt awful. He looked awful. Because he was, indeed, soaked to the bone.

He began to question himself. What in the world was he thinking? You didn't give flowers and candy to a man, but he couldn't quite come to grips with giving him a teddy bear either. Maybe he should just give all he carried to the nurses for taking care of Wes. That seemed the most logical thing to do. But he wanted to give Wes something, so he dared to knock on the door and enter with his tokens, trying to make things better.

"Come in," Wes answered to what seemed like a feeble attempt of someone who was questioning if they should enter the hospital room at all.

"It's me, sir, Seth."

"Hello, Seth."

"I brought you some flowers and candy."

"Well, thank you—"

"I didn't know what else to bring, but it sure seems funny bringing a man these things. I've only had experience with Trudy when it comes to hospital visits."

"Come, sit down, Seth." Wes motioned for him to sit.

He couldn't sit. He wouldn't sit. He had to walk over to Wes. "Sir, I'm so sorry, not unplugging that heater! I wasn't thinking, and now you're here! You fell, and it was all my fault. You hit your head—"

"Seth, it's okay." Wes interrupted. "We all make mistakes."

"But this one, oh, sir, I thought you were going to die!"

"But as you can see, I didn't."

"Thank goodness! I find it hard enough not to feel guilty about that big knot on your head, much less if you had died! Oh, I cannot even imagine!"

Wes smiled. "Don't feel guilty, son." Wes reached up and patted Seth on the shoulder.

"I do."

"Don't." Wes pushed the electric button to raise his body up for a more comfortable position. "Do you believe in God, Seth?"

"I do now."

"Why?"

"Because I begged God to let you live."

"And I did live."

"God answered my prayers, didn't he?"

"He sure did." Wes threw his legs over the side of the bed and looked in Seth's direction. "Do you believe that sometimes God gives us even more than what we ask for?"

"I guess he could since he's the boss."

Wes smiled. "Yes, I guess we could describe him that way."

Seth continued to stare at Wes. "You're not angry with me, are you, sir?"

"No, I'm not angry with you." Wes stood up, continuing to look at Seth. He was breaking his promise to Reva. But that was okay now. He walked steadily over to the table where Seth had left the flowers and candy. Seth watched. Wes opened the box of candy, took a piece, and brought the box over to Seth. "I hear that chocolate-covered cherries are quite tasty," Wes said.

Seth took the box of candy, continuing to look at Wes. "Sir, I don't get it. I would be mad at me!"

Again, Wes smiled. He pulled a chair over for Seth to sit down. He pulled another chair over, and he sat down directly in front of Seth. "You have blue eyes," Wes said.

"I do, but how—"

Wes took Seth's hands in his and held them with a firmness that shouted appreciation that Seth had come to visit him. He thought to himself that, yes, God was always on time. Never late. Never early. Always on time. It was only fitting that Seth should be here now with the flowers and candy, unbefitting as it seemed to Seth. Sometimes things are not as they seem.

"I'm not mad at you. I want to thank you for leaving that heater plugged into that socket so I could fall over it."

Seth didn't say a word; he just looked confused as Wes continued.

"Yes, Seth, God answered your prayers for me to live, and he went one step further."

"What are you saying?" Seth questioned. "What else did he do?"

Wes looked directly into Seth's bluest of blue eyes. "Thank you, Seth. You are going to be the first to know. I can see."

*****

Seth couldn't move. He just kept staring at Wes. "You look just as I pictured you in my mind, Seth."

Seth could not speak. He just kept sitting there with his mouth open.

Wes smiled. "Nobody else knows yet, not even the doctors. I started seeing shadows early this morning," Wes began. "I heard the birds outside the window and turned to the sound. Suddenly, the shadow cleared, and there was this little bird sitting on that ledge just outside."

He grasped Seth's hands a little tighter. "I want to thank you for leaving that cord I tripped over in my path. If not for that, this may not have happened." Suddenly, Seth came to life and could not help himself. He embraced Wes with a hug that would not let go. "It's okay, son. It's okay. No more guilt, you hear me?"

Seth stood up from his chair before they both threatened to topple over while sitting knee to knee. He looked at Wes with fresh eyes. "No, sir. No more guilt!"

He left the room, running for the front door entrance of the hospital. He could not tell anyone, not yet. Wes would tell everyone in due time. It was Wes's miracle to share.

While leaving the hospital, he nearly collided with Reva.

"Sorry, ma'am." Seth apologized.

Reva noticed the tears in his eyes as she stood silent a moment, watching Seth run.

"Poor boy," she whispered. "I do hope Wes made him feel better about himself."

Suddenly, Seth turned around and ran back to the doorway where Reva stood and gave her a hug. Without saying a word, he turned and began running down the street.

She knew with Seth's hug that Wes had done just that—made that guilt-laden boy feel better. That was just Wes.

*****

Wes was sitting up in bed when Reva arrived in his room.

"Did you keep to your promise last night, Mr. Stubborn?"

"I did. I did not get up and walk around last night." Well, that was true. He had only walked this morning. In fact, just a few minutes ago.

"Good."

She began gathering things, putting them in the suitcase she had brought along with her.

"I just saw Seth leaving the hospital."

"Yes, he was here. He brought me flowers and candy."

Reva smiled. "I hope you eased his mind. He looked like a drenched mouse when I saw him coming out the door. I felt so sorry for him. But he was smiling. He even gave me a hug. I figured you had made him feel better about himself."

"I eased his mind."

"Good."

"Reva, could you go to the window and tell me if there is a jasmine plant out there?"

Reva turned and faced him. "You must have hit that head of yours really hard! Sweetheart, you are six floors above the ground! There's no jasmine plant outside your window!"

"I thought not."

"Should I call the doctor? Are you sure they are going to release you today?"

"No, you do not need to call the doctor, and, yes, they are going to release me today. I need you to come sit down beside me for a minute. I want to talk."

"We can talk at home! Don't you want to get out of here?"

"Yes, I do. But I need to talk to you first."

Reva sighed. "Everything is ready for your arrival at home. Trudy has brought her pizza casserole. Sarah has made sweet tea, and Charlie will be checking you out every hour of the night. He is going to stay at our house."

"There's no need for that! Reva, please come here and sit down!"

She pretended not to hear him and continued to race around the room, packing his clothes for his return trip home. "Charlie said he would hunker down on the couch. He said all he needed was a blanket. He would bring his own pillow. He wants to keep an eye on you. I think that is wise." She kept talking incessantly.

"Reva, Reva, come sit down next to me, please."

She walked over to Wes and sat down, taking his hands in hers. "I'm just anxious to get you home!"

"I know you are." Wes squeezed her hands. "The last time I saw you this hyper was when we discovered Kate was Sarah's natural mom."

Reva thought for a moment. "You're right. I tend to get this way when the tide suddenly shifts around the ones I love and throws us all into chaos."

"I know you do."

Reva captured Wes's gaze.

"And I love you for it. You love with all your heart—every smidgeon of it."

Reva sensed the importance of the moment. Wes was holding her hands almost too tightly. She took a deep, cleansing breath. "We are going home today, aren't we?" she timidly asked. Wes loosened his grip. "Aren't we?" she whispered. She took her hands from his, running them over her face. "Aren't we?" she kept asking as a lone tear ran down her cheek. "Has something else happened that you're not telling me? Something from all the tests they have run?"

Wes took his fingertip and traced that tear on her cheek, wiping it away.

"What aren't you telling me, Wes?" She kept looking at Wes with her questioning eyes. "You seem different. You look different," she stammered. "Do I even want to know?" She stood up. "Have the doctors found something else that is going to take you away from me?"

Wes could understand her overactive imagination. She had been taught, through the years, to prepare for the worst and hope for the best. He took a deep breath, stood up, and held her face in his hands. "It's what they call something similar to spontaneous remission."

"Oh, my God, Wes! I knew there was something! What is spontaneous remission? Is it treatable? Are you going to die? What's happening!"

Wes began to laugh. She looked at him as if he were crazy.

"Why are you laughing? This sounds really serious, Wes! What are we to do next?"

"Oh, Reva, my dear, dear, sweet Reva! It's not a disease I'm talking about! You need to put your overactive imagination to rest! You need to stop thinking that everything that happens to me is bad!" He walked to a nearby chair and sat down, patting his lap for her to come sit with him.

"You want me to sit on your lap while you tell me about something that is scaring me to death? And you're laughing about it?"

"Come, sit!"

She walked over to him. He reached out and pulled her onto his lap. It seemed the "lap posture" was something they had carried throughout their marriage when something very important was about to be discussed. She braced herself and waited for his laughter to stop.

Wes pressed her head down to his shoulder. She was beginning to cry. He began to rock her back and forth before turning her to face him once again.

She dared to ask, "Do you have cancer?"

"Oh no, no, my sweetheart. What has happened to me the doctor said is similar to spontaneous remission that sometimes happens in cancer patients. When I fell, I hit my head—really hard—and something wonderful happened because of it."

She looked confused. He held her tighter.

"Reva, this thing that happened to me that is similar to spontaneous remission is something good. Very good. Look at me, darling."

She looked at him with her tearstained face.

Looking straight into her eyes, he said, "Reva, I can see. And it's all because of God and something similar to spontaneous remission. The doctors can't explain it. They didn't even try. God just wanted to give me back my sight, and he went about it by allowing me to take that big fall. Mysterious, eh, our Miracle Worker?"

*****

It didn't take long for the word to get around Brooksport Village. There would soon be a celebration. Jake was already on the phone ordering the balloons. The whole town was talking of the miracle that had taken place and how God had turned something that had been so bad all those years ago into something so good that they would be talking about it for decades to come.

Oh yes, this celebration would be extrasweet, and those launched balloons would also bring back home one of its own…

PART 9

KATE AND SARAH

Chapter 46

Through the years, since Sarah had discovered that Kate was her natural mother, the two of them had come to a point of complete restoration and understanding. Kate had prayed for that day to happen. She did not push. She did not pry. She merely let life flow. She was always there for Sarah, and Reva played a huge part in everything going smoothly, as the family blended together, welcoming into their midst the heart that was Kate.

Kate wanted Sarah to feel that she could come to her to talk about anything. She wanted Sarah to feel comfortable and free with honesty, and she prayed that she, too, could be just as transparent.

That day did come. There was no fanfare. Just sweet, simple honesty and trust. The day had arrived with a whisper of a breeze as both Kate and Sarah sat in the flower garden, enjoying their sweet tea. It was also a day of reckoning—not exactly how either had planned. But then one does not plan for such days—they just happen.

"You know, Charlie never did like this stuff," Sarah began.

Kate laughed. "I know. I remember, well, the day he told me he preferred lemonade!" Sarah sighed. Kate could sense something in the air. "What's on your mind, Sarah?" Kate questioned.

"Just thinking about life in general. Wondering why it is that men seem to keep running away from the women they love."

Kate took a sip of tea. "Well, some do come back—like Jake *and* Ted."

"True, but I don't understand why they run away in the first place."

Kate looked at her daughter. "I guess some people just have to run to think things out in their own minds when they are so full of questions."

"Well, I'm glad Jake and Ted came to their senses!"

"Me, too, sweet girl, me too." Kate looked out at the lake. "Are you afraid Charlie is going to run away?"

"Oh no! Charlie and I talk about everything. We know each other pretty well. My goodness, we've talked about everything since we were teenagers, and even younger."

"That's the bottom line really, Sarah. You have to communicate. You have to dig in and accept certain things in a person. And you have to make sure your expectations of a person are reasonable—that you don't expect something that they cannot give or possibly be." Kate looked at Sarah. "Charlie would never run away, Sarah."

"I do know that, but I was wondering…" Sarah stopped herself and put her tea on the garden table. "I don't know if I should ask you this."

Kate looked perplexed. "You can ask me anything. I'll always be honest with you."

Sarah shifted her body in her chair. She was going to ask Kate. She had to. She just needed to know.

Pensively, she looked at Kate.

"Where is your mind taking you, Sarah?"

"Did my natural dad run away? Who was he, Kate?"

*****

Kate shifted in her chair. Could she be as honest and transparent as she had prayed to be? "We still have some of life's lessons to talk to each other about, don't we, Sarah?"

"Yes, I think we do."

Kate placed her glass of tea on the table beside Sarah's. "I want to do that, Sarah. I really do." She cupped Sarah's chin in her hands, looking at her. "I want you to trust me enough to tell you exactly what you want to know. But, first, I need to talk to someone else about this. Then the two of us will sit down with you, and we will talk. Can you do that?"

Sarah nodded and got up to leave. No other words were necessary. Kate watched her go.

"Oh my," Kate whispered to herself, "what now?"

Sarah's natural father?

"Oh my," she said yet again while looking out at all the bleeding heart flowers that were surrounding her. Delicate yet, oh, so strong, enduring through the storms and the brittle winters. She touched the tiny tear at the tip of one of those fragile flowers. Survivors, never forgetting the pain that had seen them through to a new season, a new spring.

She had to think. She had to talk to Trudy. The two of them would determine how to share the answers they would give to this inquiring girl who needed to know the truth about the other man who had run away.

*****

Kate stood and walked into her bedroom. She opened the dresser drawer and pulled out the shawl that Trudy had crocheted for her. She remembered the day Trudy had given it to her.

"I prayed over every stitch of this, Kate," she had said. "Sometimes we have to be reminded we're royalty, sugar."

Kate wrapped herself in the shawl and walked to the window. Maybe Frank should have had one of those purple shawls. Maybe that would have kept him from running away from Trudy in the first place. Maybe it would have kept him from running away from her too. Maybe he had needed to be reminded that he, too, was royalty. Maybe. Maybe. Maybe. Seemed like the world was full of maybes.

Kate stood at the window for a long time. She looked up at the sky and began to pray. Trudy saw her from the distance. She was coming to Kate with a bag of extracrispy doughnuts—just for a little R & R away from the salon for a while. She stopped walking and stared at the image in the window.

"Somethin's goin' on," she whispered to herself. She saw the shawl wrapped around Kate's shoulders. "Oh my," she whispered.

She began to walk slowly toward Open Door. She was preparing herself for the fact that this visit was going to be more than just a little R & R.

*****

Trudy sat on the front porch step, waiting for Kate to emerge. One just did not interrupt another while they were standing at a window, looking up at the sky, wrapped in a prayer shawl.

She was munching on one of the doughnuts when Kate stepped out of the front door. Trudy looked up at her. "I couldn't think of anythin' else to do but eat while I was waitin' on ya."

Kate sat down beside Trudy and took a doughnut for herself. "I agree."

Trudy sighed. "What's goin' on, sugar?"

"I don't know how or where to begin," Kate answered.

"The beginnin' always works for me," Trudy replied.

"It's Sarah."

Trudy took another bite of her doughnut. "What's wrong with Sarah?"

"Nothing is wrong, but she's searching for a name and a face."

Trudy looked out at the pathway that led to Open Door. "You gotta make sense, sugar. A name and a face of who?"

"Her natural father."

Trudy dropped the bag of doughnuts. "Oh, dear."

Kate sighed. "She wants to know who her natural father is. She wants to know if he ran away from me and from her."

"Oh, dear."

"How are we going to tell her, Trudy?"

"Oh, dear."

"Please stop saying, 'Oh, dear.'" Trudy looked at Kate, not knowing what to say next, since she couldn't say, *Oh, dear.* "What are we going to say to her? How are we going to tell her?" Kate questioned again.

Trudy looked up. "We're not."

"I can't believe you said that! I've prayed for the day that Sarah and I could talk honestly with each other about anything! And we have been able to do that—until this very minute!"

Trudy stood and began to walk down the path.

"You're running, Trudy!" Kate blurted out.

Trudy turned. She knew Kate was right. Sooner or later, people just had to learn to stand still and reason things out. She supposed this was her time. She walked back to face Kate.

"Trudy, I've prayed about this."

"I know. I saw ya at the window."

"Secrets eventually come out. We have to tell her, and we have to tell her, together."

"No, we don't."

"Yes, we do."

Trudy sighed. Wringing her hands, she looked at Kate. "Oh, sugar, I know you're right. Secrets are powerful over us when they're hidden in the dark. I've learned that… For Pete's sake, what is wrong with me! Of course, you are right! No more secrets!" Trudy flung her arms in the air. "Still couldn't we make up something?"

"No!"

"You're right. You're right! But how?"

"I don't know. But it has to be done. She is not going to let this go."

Trudy raked her hand through her hair. "Okay. Let's go to the lake and talk."

*****

The two of them walked to the lake, still munching those doughnuts.

"Why do people eat when they have issues?" Kate questioned.

"For comfort, I guess, sugar." They found two beach chairs and sat down.

"Trudy, we have to do this, together."

"I know."

"Good. Then let's map out a plan."

*****

Sarah arrived at Open Door early that next morning. Kate was ready.

"Let's take a walk," Kate said.

"Where?"

"Trudy's."

"Why? Does she know something about my natural dad?"

"You'll know soon enough."

Trudy saw them coming. She still wasn't quite sure how this would work out, but Kate was right. Sarah needed to know.

Sarah was perplexed sitting in Trudy's living room across from both of the women.

Trudy began, "Sugar, I know you are puzzled about being here." Trudy fiddled with the purple scarf in her hair. Sarah had learned from the past, as well as Kate, that when Trudy wore a purple scarf in her hair, there was "business" to be dealt with, serious business.

Trudy jumped up. "Want some tea?"

"Nobody wants tea, Miss Trudy," Sarah quipped. "I just want some answers, and I don't understand why I am here for my answers!"

"Well, I don't want you drinkin' alcohol, so I'm makin' tea—sweet tea," Trudy simply answered.

Sarah looked at Kate with questioning eyes. "Is it that bad? My natural dad? Was he mean?" Sarah stood up. "And why do we have to discuss this in front of Miss Trudy?"

"I heard that!" Trudy exclaimed. "You'll have your answers!" Trudy continued her walk to the kitchen for tea. She thought maybe she'd throw in a couple of cookies in the mix, too—for good measure. They were all going to need some comfort.

Kate began to fiddle with her hair.

"That bad, huh?" Sarah questioned.

"No, it's not bad. It's really not bad. You were born. And that is good. You are a blessing, Sarah. Both Trudy and I believe that with all our hearts."

Trudy sat the tea on the coffee table, along with the cookies, but no one reached for them.

"Your dad was a kind man," Kate began. "He was quite handsome too."

Trudy cleared her throat. Sarah looked at Trudy, still wondering why Kate and she were there in the first place.

Again, she questioned, "Why are we here, at Trudy's? What does Trudy have to do with all of this?"

Trudy jumped up. "Okay, enough! Let's stop dancing around all this and give this child the truth!" Trudy walked over to Sarah and looked her straight in the eye. "Sugar, you and Kate are here in my house together—with me—because your father was my husband."

"What?" Sarah could not believe her ears. "I don't understand." Sarah looked at Kate and then at Trudy.

"We're going to explain," Kate whispered.

Sarah looked down at her feet, refusing to allow them to run out the door. She needed answers now, more than ever. She would not run. Women didn't do that, right? Only men.

*****

It was Trudy that began. "Kate is right. Your dad was a kind man. A gentle man. He was younger than I when we met. But at that time, I didn't see that age would matter." Trudy shrugged before continuing. "It did—in the long run."

Sarah continued to stare at them both. "Go on."

"We were married. I wanted a baby so badly. In fact, I wanted a houseful of children." Trudy's eyes began to brim with tears, remembering her past with Frank and the baby she had lost. Some things she would not share. Some things other people did not need to know. This was one of them. "Your dad was good at everything he did. He traveled a lot. He was a darn good salesman."

Sarah began to fidget.

"Our paths began to take different directions."

"I see." Sarah suddenly spoke. "That's when he found Kate."

Kate straightened her back. "Yes, that's when he found me."

"Did you know he was married?"

"No."

Trudy intervened. "Your dad betrayed both of us. He didn't tell Kate he was married. Kate thought she had met the love of her life. And the rest became history."

Sarah could barely get the question out of her mouth. "You slept with Trudy's husband?"

"I didn't know at the time. I was so young. I was so in love. I couldn't see anything but Frank," Kate confessed.

"That is his name?" Sarah questioned.

"Yes," both women said in unison.

"Where is he now? I want to meet him. I want to look him in the eye and tell him he did you both wrong. I want to slap his face!"

"You can't do that, sugar," Trudy said.

"One of you tell me where he is!" Sarah exclaimed.

Trudy looked at Kate. Without a word, Trudy rose from her seat on the couch and went up the stairs.

*****

Silently, Trudy went to her closet. How long had it been? She searched the shelf for the little black box that held so much of her past. She had not opened it since that dreadful night she had learned the truth about Kate and Frank. She vowed to never open it again. Why hadn't she just destroyed it all those years ago after she and Kate had made their amends? Why, indeed?

Because it would lead to this day. That's why. Another day of reckoning.

She spilled the contents of that ancient box upon her bed once again. She took a deep breath rummaged through the contents and found the picture of Frank. His daughter needed to see his face. But she would not be able to slap it. She put the photo in her pocket and headed back downstairs.

Both Kate and Sarah waited in silence. Trudy walked over to Sarah and handed her the photo.

"This is your dad. Unfortunately, you cannot slap his face. But you can look at his picture."

"I want to see his real face!" Sarah cried out.

"You can't," Kate replied.

"Why not? Is he nearby? Where is he?"

Trudy put her arm around Sarah's shoulders.

"Sugar, your dad is dead."

*****

Sarah became very quiet. She began taking deep breaths.

"In through your nose, child. Out through your mouth," Trudy began saying over and over.

Sarah minded her. She didn't know what else to do. And she was *not* going to run. Running would not become her pattern, as it had so many others in her life, or so she had learned.

Sarah sat down. She merely looked at both women and said, "I think I'll have that tea now."

*****

From beginning to end, Kate and Trudy revealed the complete story to Sarah. They just kept talking until they saw a certain light come into Sarah's eyes, helping them to know that she finally was, at least, coming to grips with all the emotions that had run rampant between Trudy, Kate, and Frank. They understood it was a lot for Sarah to take in. They knew it would take perhaps a longer time for her to understand it all. Then, and only then, did they sit silently, anticipating Sarah's reaction.

Sarah swallowed and took yet another deep breath. She folded her hands in her lap. "It's okay," she finally said. "I'm okay. I know how hard it was for both of you to face this truth with me. I'm glad you did. Because, you know, I would have discovered the truth sooner or later. I'm glad it was sooner. And I'm glad it was the both of you who told me." She looked intently at both women. "Both of you are so special to me. You already know that. You've been honest with me. I only have one question left."

"What is that?" Trudy questioned.

Sarah looked directly at Kate. "Did he know about me?"

*****

Before Kate could speak, Trudy intervened. "No, Sarah, he never knew about you."

Sarah stood and walked to the door. She turned to both women. "I'm glad to know that. At least, I know he didn't run from me." Sarah picked up the photo of Frank. "May I have this?"

"Of course," Trudy replied.

She tucked the only thing she would ever have of her fathers into her pocket, kissed both Kate and Trudy on the cheek, and walked out the door.

"Trudy, you lied."

"I know, and I'm *not* sorry!"

"We were trying to be honest here!"

"And we were—to a point."

Trudy retrieved the tray of empty glasses and uneaten cookies and began to walk to the kitchen. Kate followed her.

"Sugar, this is one of those 'ponderous' moments. Some things you just have to ponder in your heart. Some things people just don't need to know, especially if they're your daughter. Some things are too much to handle. They're better off not knowing. This is one of those moments."

Kate had to agree. Sarah had enough to think about. It would all be okay. Trudy and Kate made a pact never to mention any of this again. It was best for Sarah to remember Frank as the good man both women had believed that he was. He had been confused. He had loved two women at the same time. Trudy believed that a man could barely handle one woman, much less two. Yes, he had made mistakes, but who hadn't made blunders in a lifetime? Kate had to agree.

Sarah had his photograph. She had a name and a face, and that was what she had wanted. She would love him just because he was her natural father. She found comfort in the fact that he had not known about her. He hadn't known what to do with his life that had become so confusing, loving both Trudy and Kate. The main thing to Sarah was he hadn't really run away. He had just disappeared, reappeared, and sought forgiveness. Sarah would hold on to that.

That night, Trudy and Ted took a boat ride. She took the black box, along with the remainder of all its contents, and destroyed it. She would make sure she never opened it again. Nor would anyone else. Both she and Ted watched it sink to the bottom of the lake. Over and done. Time for new pictures in old frames.

PART 10

SIFTED, STIRRED, AND BLENDED

"Piece by piece, I reenter the world. A new phase. A new body, a new voice. Birds console me by flying, trees by growing, dogs by the warm patch they leave on the sofa. Unknown people merely by performing their motions. It's like a slow recovery from a sickness, this recovery of one's self."

(Toby Talbot)

As Jasmine was driving back to Brooksport Village, she remembered the evening Polly had found her standing in front of the jasmine plant outside, what used to be, her bedroom window. She had been staring at that plant for a long time when Polly came up from behind.

"What are you thinking about, child?"

"Him."

"Gordy?"

"No, not him. I'm thinking about the man who planted this flower bush. The man who did great funerals. The hummingbird safely buried next to this plant. The day he sang 'Taps' as we lay that sweet bird to rest."

"Ah, I see," Polly said.

"I was very young, but some things are coming back to me about him." Polly looked up at the sky. Jasmine followed her gaze. "I want to know more about him, Polly. Can you tell me more?"

"Only if me telling you about him will make you have second thoughts about what you need and truly want in your life. Only if you will not make the same mistake your grandma did! Only if my telling you about him will make you think about going back to Brooksport Village to get your Gordy!'

"Polly, he's not my Gordy."

"Ah, I see."

"Is that all you can say?"

"Yep. Other than, it sure is true—the acorn does not fall far from the tree!'

"What are you talking about?"

"Your grandma thought the same way. He was not 'her' Carson, either."

"So you're saying that my grandma let Carson slip through her fingers?"

"Yep, that's exactly what I'm saying."

"They loved each other?"

"Yep."

"But he didn't come back for her either."

"Oh, but he did, child—too late. You know that! Don't let the same thing happen to you. You need to go get that Gordy of yours!' Polly held up

her hand before Jasmine could reply. "Don't you dare say it! He is yours. You just don't see it yet." Polly turned and walked away mumbling to herself, "I'm so sick of all this 'star-crossed lovers' mumbo jumbo! People who think they can't be together! Rubbish!"

Jasmine didn't know if it had been the plant that brought all the memories crashing back into her mind or Polly and her mumbling. All she knew was that she had made up her mind to do exactly what Polly wanted. She was going back. If there was a second chance waiting for her around the corner, she had to risk it. She was going to take back something that she never thought was hers in the first place. Exactly how? She didn't know.

Those were her thoughts that kept bombarding Jasmine's mind as she drove the highway going back to the little town she had tearfully left a few short years ago… What she would find remained to be seen… One thing was for certain—Polly had been very pleased with her decision to go…

"Weeping forward" can be a mind-boggling experience for someone on an unexplainable journey, not knowing the outcome. They're not even sure they should be on the road, much less expecting the beautiful scenery that would surely unfold.

Just around the corner that Jasmine would turn would be quite a surprise that was already in the making. Who would have ever thought? But isn't that just one of the things our God does best? Oh, how he loves to surprise his children!

"You can't cross the sea merely by standing and staring at the water."

(Rabindranath Tagore)

Chapter 47

Jasmine needed a friendly face before driving the final fifteen miles to Brooksport Village. She determined to stop in Carsonville. She parked her car, got out, and began her walk to the antique store on the corner. She hoped he was still there. She hoped he was still putting bowls of water on the sidewalk for his four-legged friends and for the cat that refused to go out in the heat. She hoped he and his wife were still happily together. Well, she would soon find out. She would see that friendly face, and then she would go have one of her "pink" drinks at that little country bar where she met Gordy for the first time.

She was glad that her heart had not toughened during the time she had been away trying desperately to find pieces of herself that had drifted away on the clouds of grief. She had softened. She had become better, not bitter. She remembered that, at first, her journey had seemed like she was prowling around in a mind that was not her own. She had dug through all of that. Her therapist had handed her the shovel.

"It's going to be a lot of hard work, Jasmine," the therapist had said. But she had done it. She had faced her giants of grief and she had "replanted." She had "wept forward" instead of continuing the process of "weeping backward." She prayed Gordy had found some answers of his own. Oh, how she prayed for that.

Jasmine had finally reached a decision with a clarity of mind that she could not deny. She could move forward without forgetting her cherished Andrew. Although she had ranted and raved at

Polly, it was her own emotions that she had been fighting. Coming to know that she, indeed, wanted Gordy in her life had become a gentle release from the chains that had bound her for so long. Her only hope was that he would want the same.

Both Gordy and Jasmine's wounds had left scars, but the painful process of healing can become a victory. Her memories had become smile makers. Classic movies had been lovingly placed on shelves that could be retrieved if the moment allowed. And at long last, she could now make macaroni salad without shedding tears, using onions as an excuse for her eyes leaking.

Her detour in Carsonville was exactly what she needed right now. She needed to take a few deep breaths on that park bench that faced the antique store. The gentle breeze was telling her summer was on its way. It was the wind chimes that brought her back to the present. She took yet another deep breath and looked up.

He came out of the store with a bowl full of water.

"For your four-legged friends?" Jasmine questioned.

"Hey, girlie! You back?" There he was once again, the owner of the store venturing out to join her on the bench.

"I was hoping you would be here," she replied.

"I've wondered what happened to you. It's been a while since I've seen you."

"A good long while," she replied.

He looked up at the sky. "Did you find your answers?"

"How did you know I had questions?"

"Everybody has questions."

"Well, I do believe I have found my answers."

"Good. It's always good when you learn that it's time to take the gloves off. It's good to know when the fight is over, and the spoils await." He took a deep breath, still looking at the sky. "Well, lookey there, would you?" He pointed up to the sky. The balloons were lazily floating higher and higher.

"Must be another celebration of some kind over there in Brooksport Village."

She looked up and thought to herself, *I hope it's not too late. I hope it's not a wedding celebration of some kind. Not Gordy.*

He interrupted her thoughts. "You going up there to see what those balloons are all about this time?"

"I do believe I will."

"Good. You report back to me, will you?" He seemed so all-knowing. She smiled at him and gave him a kiss on the cheek. He stood and walked toward the entrance of the store. Turning, he said, "Go find him, girlie."

*****

She stood up from the bench and walked toward the country bar at the end of the street, hoping that one more friendly face she needed to see was still there.

It was Thursday. She saw the familiar sign, "Live music on Thursday Night." She walked in.

"Well, well, look who just walked through the door!"

"You remember me?"

"Hard to forget you, missy! You stomped on our dance floor really good and hard that first night I saw you. Want one of those pink drinks you like so well?"

"It's early, but, yes, I do believe I want one of those pink drinks!"

He prepared her drink and set it down in front of her. "You'll see I didn't forget how to make that foo-foo drink!"

She took a sip, pretending to swoon.

"Where have you been? I haven't seen you and that fella here in quite a while."

"I've been healing."

He nodded, looking at her intently. "You going back up to Brooksport Village? You have unfinished business up there?"

"You might say that."

"Anything to do with that fella I haven't seen in a while either?"

She only smiled and took another sip of her drink.

He leaned over the bar, touched her nose, smiled, and said, "Thought so."

*****

She had needed a friendly face before driving the last fifteen miles to Brooksport Village. She had found not only one but two in front of that antique store and in the country bar where there was live music every Thursday night, just where providence had led her a long, long, time ago…and she sure needed that pink foo-foo drink…

*****

The ride to Brooksport Village was truly just "a little piece up the road." She was nervous, and she still questioned if she was doing the right thing. What was the worst that could happen? Gordy turning away? What was the best? Gordy confessing, *"I've been thinking about you"?* Regardless of his reaction, Jasmine knew she had reached a turning point that would spring her forward. This was the start of a new beginning—with or without Gordy.

She parked her car and wondered if she should see Trudy first. Maybe she should find out why all the balloons were now disappearing behind the white clouds. Yes, that's what she had to do. She walked toward the salon.

Trudy's Tresses and Tootsies had been restored to its original purple status since the fire, and Trudy was busily going through her mail. She had promised both Ted and herself that she would do that task *daily*. She wanted no more surprises like the fire—ever again. She would watch those warranties like a hawk, especially if it got her on a list to advise her about faulty parts. The fire inspector had told her that the fire had been caused by a clothes dryer faulty part, and she had almost died because of it.

The bell above the salon door rang as Jasmine walked in.

"Be with ya in a minute!" Then she looked up. "Well, 'pon my honor! Jasmine, girl!" She jumped from her chair and ran to her. "Aren't you a sight for sore eyes!" She grabbed Jasmine, hugging her as if she would never let go.

Jasmine returned the hug and felt the warmth of her special friendship being rekindled. She secretly thought, *If only Gordy would react the same way.*

Trudy drew back to look at her. "When did ya get into town, sugar?"

"Just a few minutes ago. I wanted to see you before anyone else."

"Come, sit down. Tell me what you've been up to. Let me look at your face."

"My face?"

"Yes." Trudy took Jasmine's face in her hands and peered deeply into her eyes. "Well, merciful heavens, thank you, Lord! She is not forlorn! In fact, she looks at peace!"

Jasmine smiled. "I am at peace, Trudy."

"You've come back for the dude?"

"That depends."

"On what?"

"All the balloons that were flying in the sky that I saw from Carsonville."

Trudy gave her a side glance. "I see."

"What do those balloons mean this time, Trudy?"

"Well, life has gone on here in Brooksport Village, sugar, since you've been gone."

Suddenly, Jasmine felt a twinge of regret. "Usually those balloons are launched because of some kind of celebration," Jasmine forced the words out.

Trudy nodded.

"Tell me, Trudy, has Gordy found someone else?"

"Would it stop you from going to see him?"

Jasmine pondered that question before answering, "No, we still have unfinished business."

"That's what I was hopin' you'd say, sugar!"

*****

Suddenly, Jasmine found herself at Crabby's, sitting beside a very smug looking Trudy.

"Looks to me like you've learned a very important lesson. Seems to me that you have learned that in order to receive something in life, you have to release something else," Trudy quipped.

Jasmine could not help but smile. Trudy was always right.

They ordered their wine. Trudy kept waiting for Jasmine to say something.

"You lost your voice?"

"Kind of."

Trudy sighed. "Okay, let me put your mind at ease. I am so glad you are back! I am sick and tired of preparin' casseroles for Gordy, walkin' up his path, and lookin' at his poor, pitiful face. That's what I'm tired of, missy!"

A glimmer of hope appeared in Jasmine's eyes.

Trudy took a sip of her drink. "It seems to me that the both of you are finally gettin' tired of bein' lonely." She sat back in her chair, waiting for Jasmine to admit that simple fact.

Jasmine just fiddled with her hair.

"Stop it! Don't fiddle, girlie! It's time for a showdown at the cowboy's Dude Ranch! It's time for you to get galloping! You need to lasso that cowboy once and for all!"

"Trudy, you're getting carried away!"

"Nope! I'm not! You can't hide under your sheets anymore, girlie! You have to get out from under and start shaking your tail feathers! You need to march right up to Gordy's door and knock on it!"

"I can't just do that!"

"Why not?"

"I don't know. I just know that I can't!"

"Yes, you can." Trudy ordered more wine. "Sit back and relax, sugar. I'm gonna tell ya a story… Right after you left our little town, Gordy came to me and asked me if Ted knew how to mix up some kind of elixir to make him find a part of his mind he had lost." Trudy scooted her chair a little closer to Jasmine. "I told him I didn't think so. I told him Ted helped to find people. He didn't help people trying to find their minds. I told him a therapist did that."

Trudy took another sip of wine. "He said to me, 'But it's a part of me I've lost, Trudy. If he finds people who are lost, maybe he could find me.'" Trudy sighed. "Honestly, that cowboy can sure be profound sometimes." She began fiddling with her hair before continuing. "And sometimes, even stupid. Don't tell him I said that." Trudy sighed.

"I told him that I knew what he needed, and it wasn't Ted's brilliant mind to concoct some magic potion to guide him down the path to finding himself. He asked me what that was. I told him that not too long ago I knew a man who was searching for his own answers—a man runnin' away from everything he knew and loved. I told him that man needed pharmacon."

"Somewhere, you've lost me, Trudy."

"Never you mind, sugar. I told him Ted couldn't boil water much less mix up an elixir. Then I looked at him straight in the eye and told him he needed divine alchemy."

"What did he do?"

"He went and found himself a Christian therapist."

*****

Jasmine finally spoke. "I'm tired of being lonely. Gordy and I just had bad timing and not communicating about our past—things we should have talked about."

"True. Gordy's tired of being lonely too. I know."

"And you do know everything, right?"

"Right."

Jasmine finished her wine and kept thinking of Trudy's earlier comment about casseroles. "Are you saying that Gordy was grieving my departure? I mean, was that because you kept taking him casseroles?"

"That's exactly what I'm sayin'! But it's a different kind of grief. He's grievin' what might have been and thinkin' that you're the one that got away. He's wishin' he had stopped you, *but* he wasn't really ready to do that in his own mind. But it seems also that you took part of his mind with you because he couldn't find it." Trudy finished her drink. "He was a walkin', talkin' lovesick fool until he found somebody to help him with that mind of his, and…"

"And what?"

"His grandfather decided to move here. He's been livin' with him for some time now. They're both alone up there on that ranch takin' each day as it comes. That's why you saw those balloons in Carsonville. Those balloons just got out of Gordy's hands before he could secure them. That happens sometimes around here! Gordy's havin' a big party for his grandfather—turnin' ninety years old. Lots of people are comin' in for that party." Trudy stood up. "I'm hungry. Let's go eat."

*****

Stumble In was their next stop. While seated, waiting on their burgers, Jasmine leaned in to Trudy and began talking.

"I do care for Gordy, Trudy, a lot."

"It's called *love*, sugar."

"Okay, I do love him."

"Then you tell him! Goodness' sakes, I would have thought the two of you would have learned to talk about things by now, after all you've both been through!"

The burgers came, and both women looked at one another.

Halfway through the meal, Jasmine spoke. "I can't be compared to Jessie, and he can't be compared to Andrew."

"He knows that now." Finishing their meal, Jasmine folded her napkin and put it on the table. Trudy did the same. Trudy motioned for the check. "Let's go to the lake. You have questions? It's when you look out on a clear lake, at a clean slate, that you discover answers."

Trudy took Jasmine's hand in hers. "You can't see the forest for the trees inside a closed room with dirty windows. I've discovered when you look out into the distance, ya get clarity."

*****

The two women were walking along the lake's edge when Jasmine looked out into the distance and asked, "What if he turns away?"

"I don't know. Maybe he will tell you to get lost. Maybe he won't. But one of you has got to make the first move. I'm here, standin' in front of ya, tellin' ya it has to be you. That's just the way Gordy is."

"Did he wait for Jessie? When she went away to New York before they were married?"

Trudy thought long and hard before answering her question. "Yes, he did. He did not go chasin' after her like a crazy man. I think he thought he just might do that at times, but he didn't. I think he just didn't wanna trespass on her space and try to force her to come back. In a way, I think that's good. Gordy's a smart man. He thinks that once a woman has made up her mind about somethin', she's more determined than ever to get what she wants, and she's more determined than ever to make it work—through thick and thin. That's just Gordy. He leaves it up to the woman to make the first move."

"Do you think that's what he's doing with me?"

"I know it is."

"How are you so sure?"

"He told me so."

*****

It was nearing dark when the two left the lake.

"You wanna stay at my place tonight and get some more advice?"

"Let me think about that."

Trudy grabbed her by the arm, and before Jasmine knew it, she was sitting on Trudy's couch with Buddy on her lap.

"Cats calm ya, ya know?"

Jasmine had to agree as she began to pet Buddy. "Do you think that Gordy loves me as much as he loved Jessie?"

"Oh, sugar, stop it! Don't start comparin' yourself to Jessie! That is the worst possible thing ya could do! That's when ya get into deep water! I can tell ya that he loved the very air Jessie breathed. More than life itself. He grieved hard when she and their son died in that horrific plane that crashed into those buildings on 9/11. But I can also tell ya that Gordy has a big heart. He has plenty of room for you in there too."

Trudy was preparing to go to bed. She turned at the stairs.

"I'm gonna be honest with ya. Gordy will never forget Jessie or little Sam. None of us will. They were a part of our lives that brought us much joy and wonderful memories. Neither will ya forget Andrew and the love the two of you shared. Both you and Gordy have to come to grips with the realization that the relationships you had with Andrew and Jessie will never be replicated with each other. But you can definitely be a golden thread that weaves its way into one another's life. A thread that forms a new pattern, a new chapter, and a new outlook in a life yet to be lived."

She continued to walk up the stairs to her bedroom. "Make yourself comfortable, sugar. I've a feelin' it's gonna be a long night of thinkin' for ya. Have some hot tea, turn on some music, take a hot bath. You'll know what to do when the sun comes up."

*****

Jasmine had a fitful night of practically no sleep. But Trudy had been right. The sun was coming up, and she knew exactly what she was going to do. Trudy was right, always right. She couldn't hide under her sheets anymore. She needed to open the blinds. She needed to set things straight. She wanted Gordy in her life.

She put both feet on the floor, got dressed, and walked downstairs to greet Trudy.

Trudy was in the kitchen, sipping on coffee, still in her robe. She looked up.

"I see you are dressed. Ready to hit the road and gallop on up to that Dude Ranch and claim your own?"

"You make it sound so simple."

"It is. Sit down. Fresh coffee is what you need. Plus something else I have to tell ya."

"Oh, Trudy, dare I ask?"

Trudy placed a fresh cup of coffee before Jasmine. "Drink."

"Yes, ma'am."

Trudy sat down across from Jasmine. "Look, I told Gordy pert near the same thing I told you yesterday! Oh yes, I did. When both of ya get your heads on straight, ya may just run into each other on Highway 84! Ya just happened to get on the road quicker than him. And just for your information, he listened to me, just like ya listened and are still listenin'. No doubt in my mind that he loves you, sugar, none at all."

Trudy got up and walked over to the sink. She rinsed out her cup. "Get your ducks in a row. I told him the same thing. I've thrown the ball on the field for both of you. No coin tosses here. No one team against the other. It's up to you two if you fumble the ball or go for the touchdown. And besides that, I'm tired of playin' cupid. I'm givin' it up. I got bigger fish to fry of my own! I have plans to make, and I'm makin' 'em with Ted!"

She walked over to Jasmine, took her by the hands, and pulled her up from the chair. "Now go on! Go on, and get outta here! The next time I see ya, I want to see a smile on your face with that blue-eyed, sad sack turned happy, grinnin' fool right beside ya!"

"The Master exults in newness. He delights in stretching the old."

(Max Lucado)

Meanwhile, back in Jasmine's hometown…

Chapter 48

Polly wiped her brow. She was sitting on her front porch, waiting for the mail. She was mumbling to herself, "Why doesn't that child let me know what is going on in Brooksport Village?"

She saw the mail truck coming down the road. She got up and walked to the end of the street to meet the mailman.

"You must be expecting something, eh, Polly?"

"I would like to hear something from that Jasmine girl."

"Well, today may be your day. Something in there from Brooksport Village."

Polly took the mail and ran back to her porch. "Well, what's this?"

She quickly opened the envelope. Inside was an invitation. She smiled as she remembered that Gordy had verbally invited her to his grandfather's ninetieth birthday party. Now she had the formal invitation. She quickly went inside, signed the RSVP that she would be attending, and walked to her car. She had decided to deliver it to the post office personally. The sooner her reply got to Gordy, the better.

Another trip to Brooksport Village would answer all her questions since Jasmine was being so quiet about everything. She would just go there and find out for herself. And what better excuse than a party?

Chapter 49

Jasmine was sitting by the lake. The time had come. She looked up at the seabirds as they flew above the water. Taking a deep breath, she could almost hear Mona, Andrew's mother, speaking to her.

"Someday, down the road a bit, you'll meet another man. People say that sometimes history repeats itself. If you are blessed to meet a man similar to my Andrew, you go for it, girl! He may even have emotional limitations like our Andrew had at times. But you seem to have a knack about you that opens closed hearts. Don't give up on him, whoever it may be. Try like the dickens to make it all work. You need to fall in love again."

Oh, sweet, wonderful Mona. Jasmine vowed to see her again soon.

She got up from her chair and walked along the water's edge. She was tired. She had traveled so many miles in her mind as to what she was going to say when she stood face to face with Gordy. She knew what her heart was telling her. She hoped the words would not betray her. She would soon find out. She dared to take the first step toward Gordy's ranch.

*****

Gordy was standing in his kitchen, looking out the window when he saw her. He shook his head, as if to clear the vision walking toward him. Was he seeing things? Or was that really Jasmine walking up his path?

Another man was watching her approach as well. He was doing the same thing—shaking his head. He was turning ninety years old. He determined that his eyes were deceiving him because when he looked again, she had disappeared. But she had arrived on Gordy's front porch.

Jasmine took a deep breath, walked up to Gordy's front door, and knocked. Gordy jumped. He had not imagined it. She was here. He walked to the door and opened it. They stared at each other. Neither one saying a word. He motioned for her to come inside.

The man upstairs also had heard the knock on the door. It wasn't his imagination either. He liked the way she had walked, like a woman with a purpose.

He took a sip of his Gatorade that Gordy and Charlie had demanded him drink periodically during the day. Something about dehydration at his age.

Bunch of malarkey, he thought to himself.

But he drank it always making sure Gordy saw him. He was tired of everybody giving him advice. The only way he could get them to quit fussing over him was to do exactly as they said. Life was so much easier that way.

*****

His attention turned back to the downstairs, where he could hear Gordy and the woman talking. He opened the door just a smidgeon to hear them more clearly. A woman in Gordy's life? Gordy had not told him anything about a woman. Well, he was for sure going to eavesdrop on his grandson! He, a soon-to-be ninety-year-old, could do whatever he pleased. He could do whatever he wanted to do, especially when it came to Gordy. He listened intently to the voices below.

"So how are you doing?"

"Okay, how are you?"

The man upstairs took a swig of his Gatorade, thinking to himself, *A pretty woman, as far as I can tell, and that's how Gordy greets her? I'm thinking my grandson has lost his touch with the ladies. Been alone too long.*

He leaned in closer to the open door.

"I didn't know if I should come, Gordy, and I don't know what will happen, but Polly persuaded me that it was the thing to do."

Just then they heard a thump at the top of the stairs. Gordy's grandfather dropped his Gatorade bottle on the floor. While watching the liquid spill out on the floor, Gordy heard him say, "Oops!"

"You okay up there, Granddad?"

Caught in the act! Now what? He had to go downstairs and see this pretty girl for himself. Plus, he had to clean up his mess. He walked to the stairs and slowly began to step down. Midway down, Jasmine's eyes locked onto his.

Gordy noticed a certain connection between the two. Both Jasmine and the birthday boy were transfixed with each other. Gordy raked his hands over his face and broke the silence. "You two look as if you may know each other."

Jasmine was very quiet.

"Granddad," Gordy began, "are you okay?"

"I made a mess up there. I have to clean it up."

Jasmine found herself walking toward the stairway. She walked up the remaining steps and took the man's hand in hers, whispering a question, "Do you ever sing *Taps*?"

"Only when I help little girls bury hummingbirds."

*****

"Hello, Carson."

Those two words had him reaching out to her and pulling her into his arms. "Jasmine, my sweet, sweet Jasmine."

Gordy, still standing at the bottom of the stairway, dared to speak. "Would someone please tell me what is happening here?"

Carson gently pushed Jasmine from him and looked at Gordy. "It's a long story," he said. "But we have all day. Let's all go take a walk by the lake."

*****

They walked in silence for a short distance before Carson spoke. He looked at Jasmine. "I only knew one person named Polly in my entire lifetime. When I heard you speak her name, I dropped my Gatorade."

Gordy guided the two of them to the beach chairs. "Forget the Gatorade! Please tell me what is going on here."

The three of them sat. Carson looked out at the water. Jasmine followed his gaze. Seagulls sang their songs above them.

Carson looked at Gordy. "I'll begin with Ellie."

*****

It was on that summer day that Gordy learned about the part Jasmine had played in his granddad's life. And, yes, it was a long story.

Gordy remembered the times Carson had come back to help his daughter, Gordy's mom, when Gordy had been a baby. Carson's ex-wife had moved out of the country without a second thought or a side glance to either one of the men in her life or her own daughter. He remembered when Carson had come back to help him through the death of Jessie and Sam after 9/11. He remembered it all. The puzzle pieces were coming together. And he remembered the mystery trip he had taken—when he had come back home with a look that personified sadness. Gordy dared to speak.

"When you came back here so saddened from the trip you took a few years ago, *was* that when you had gone to get your Ellie?"

"Yes."

Jasmine remained silent.

"But I was too late. Ellie had died."

Jasmine whispered, "I saw you there at the memorial. I was so young when you left, but something about you was so familiar. When I tried to find you afterward, you were gone."

Gordy looked up to the sky, sheltering his eyes from the sun with his hand. "I don't know what to say, Granddad."

"Then say nothing," Carson replied.

Jasmine rose from the chair. "I'm going to give you two some *alone* time."

Carson looked up. "Come to my party tonight, would you? You remind me so much of my Ellie. I used to love to watch her dance in the kitchen, always throwing me an easy laugh over her shoulder. I loved the way she looked at me. I would like to see her again through you. Please come to the party."

Jasmine looked at Gordy with a question in her eyes. Should she?

Gordy looked at Jasmine and then his granddad. "You should come. Someone else you know is coming. I've invited Polly." Both Jasmine and Carson looked at Gordy. He had to give them answers. "You see, Polly came here a few months ago."

"To talk to you?" Jasmine questioned.

Gordy nodded.

Jasmine sat back down. "She was playing cupid, no doubt?"

Carson smiled. "That's Polly! Well, well, seems like all my past is coming back like a boomerang! It'll be good to see the gal again!" He slapped his legs with his hands and got up to leave. "You two need the alone time, girlie. You stay." He pointed a finger at Gordy. "And you stay too. We'll talk later, Gordy. Tonight, we celebrate!"

*****

"Hic et nac—here and now. Do what is necessary—here and now."

(Cokie Roberts)

Chapter 50

Polly arrived in Brooksport Village with a flair and an urge to celebrate. She didn't know what she would say to Jasmine. She wondered if Gordy had told her of her previous visit. Didn't matter. She was here now and ready to party.

Trudy was the first to see her.

"Polly, girl, ya here for the birthday party?"

She grabbed her, giving her a big hug. "Why, of course! Haven't met Gordy's granddad yet, but if he is anything like Gordy, I'm assuming he's a good man!"

"That he is!" Trudy agreed. Trudy linked her arm with Polly and began walking her toward the salon. "Let's go do somethin' with your hair, sugar!"

*****

Carson took a deep breath. He knew what he had to do. Gordy had told him that Polly had stayed at Open Door on her last visit. That's where he was going now. "Yep, getting older," he whispered as he approached the bed-and-breakfast.

It was a slow walk, but he had to see Polly before the party, and he was determined to do it without anyone else knowing. Surprises startled some people. And he felt his appearance would surely startle Polly. But most importantly, he wanted his reentry into her life to be private.

Thoughts of talking to her about old times made him smile, and he wanted to talk to her about Ellie. He didn't want scads of people around. The moments he, Ellie, and Polly had shared were too precious to be interrupted with well-wishers, presents, and birthday cakes.

Yes, he was huffing and puffing when he walked around back to Kate's flower garden. He knew that was where he would find her. Oh, how Ellie had loved her flowers. Polly had worked alongside her in that garden of hers many mornings before the heat of the day would take them inside for their sweet tea.

He saw her, sitting on a bench in the midst of those bleeding heart flowers that Kate loved so well. Her back was to him.

"You never did like to pull weeds, Polly, girl, but, oh, how you loved to sit and admire all those flowers with their different colors."

Polly gasped. A familiar voice. Could it be? She slowly turned toward Carson. She jumped up from the bench, still staring at him. "S——t fire! Carson, is that really you!"

He merely smiled for lack of anything to say at the moment. She ran from the bench, came face-to-face with him, and pinched him.

"Owww! Why'd you do that?"

"You are real!"

"I'll have a bruise on this thin skin of mine in a matter of seconds, Polly, girl!" He rubbed the spot where she had pinched. "I'd have preferred a hug!" Polly grabbed him into a huge embrace, grabbed his hand, and guided him to the bench.

"Where did you come from? Did you just drop out of heaven into this garden?"

Carson laughed. "I wish I had just dropped from there, Polly, girl. I could have been visiting with my Ellie."

Polly smiled, squeezing his hand. "I miss her, too, so much."

Carson nodded. "Did you know I came back to get her?"

Polly nodded. "I know. I couldn't understand why you didn't stay." Her voice trembled before continuing. "I mean—just to talk with Jasmine and me, just to console one another. Why didn't you?"

Tears began to form in Carson's eyes. "I couldn't. I was overwhelmed. I was prepared to hand her a bouquet and throw her over my shoulder to bring her back with me. I had determined that this time I was not leaving without her." He shuffled his feet and wiped a tear from his eyes. "I was anticipating her wrapping her arms around me and saying that, yes, it was time. I was ready for anything, but *that...*"

Polly's eyes were brimming with her own tears as Carson continued. "I couldn't speak. I could barely feel my heart beating. I was shattered. My heart was broken. You and Jasmine needed a strong shoulder. Mine was bent."

Polly understood.

Carson continued. "I went to the cemetery and talked to Ellie—just spilled out my heart to her. I left the bouquet there in the middle of all those other flowers. I apologized to her for coming back too late and walked away for the last time without her."

Polly faced him. "She loved you. I know you know that."

"I do." Carson looked out at the lake. He raked his hand over his face. "I loved her too. I always wanted to see her dance again—with me."

Polly was crying openly now.

Carson handed her his handkerchief. "Old habits die hard," he said as he handed it to her. "I still carry a hanky in my pocket for occasions like this. You never know when tears are going to pop up out of nowhere."

She took the hanky and dabbed at her eyes. Looking up at him with tearstained cheeks, she spoke. "You know, you still haven't answered my question."

Carson looked at her. "Where did I come from?"

"Yes, why are you here, of all places? Why now?"

"Oh, Polly, girl, I'm the birthday boy. Gordy is my grandson."

Polly's reaction was just like long ago. "Well, s——t fire! You don't mean it!"

"I do mean it. And I also mean that I need some help walking back to Gordy's." He stood up and pulled Polly up beside him. "What do you say we walk back there together and plot on how we get that Jasmine girl and my grandson together, right where they're supposed to be. We have to make sure those two don't make the same mistakes Ellie and I did."

*****

Little did Polly and Carson know that Gordy and Jasmine were doing some talking of their own privately with no mediators and no matchmakers. Nothing but the wide-open sky while they sat on a blanket in the middle of a green pasture where the horses grazed.

That is where all the words spilled out. They shared, truly shared, for the first time honestly. They cried. They laughed. They swore. They hugged. They looked back. They looked forward. They looked outward in the same direction. Salty tears mingled and unspoken smiles urged them forward. With fingers linked together, they walked back to the house.

Trudy saw it all. (Of course, she did.) With a smile as big as Texas on her face, she pretended to be busy in the kitchen, still preparing for the party, when they entered.

"Where in tarnation have you two been?"

She hurried around the kitchen, knowing that she was only walking in circles, talking with every step she took.

"Polly was supposed to be here! She's probably still at Open Door. Carson has disappeared, and you two are standin' around like nothin' is happenin' in a few hours! We have a party to get ready for!"

She pointed to Jasmine. "Get to makin' that sweet tea, girl!" She pointed to Gordy. "And you, go help Ted get those chairs set up outside! He's sweatin' bullets! Make sure some of those chairs are in the shade! And take him some water! He's gonna pass out from heat exhaustion, and I sure don't need that to happen!"

The two of them saluted her and went to work.

Trudy turned back to the kitchen sink, still trying to act busy, with a grin that traveled from one side of her face to the other.

*****

Everyone was there. The birthday song was sung. The candles were blown out, and the wishes were made. The balloons were launched, and Carson turned ninety years old when the clock struck 11:00 p.m.

"I'm turning in," he announced, and everyone began to talk about finding their way back to their homes.

"Thank you, everyone," Carson shouted before walking toward the house. "It has surely been an eventful day!"

"I want, by understanding myself, to understand others. I want to be all that I am capable of becoming... This all sounds very strenuous and serious. But now that I have wrestled with it, it's no longer so. I feel happy—deep down. All is well."

(Katherine Mansfield)

Chapter 51

Carson woke early the next morning. He was determined to talk to Gordy again. He brewed coffee and poured two cups. Ellie had told him once that some of the best conversations, and most of the biggest decisions were made over a good cup of coffee. He hoped that would be the case this morning with Gordy.

He found Gordy on the front porch.

"You're up early, Granddad."

Carson handed him a full cup of steaming coffee. "That's why I have to nap before lunch."

Gordy laughed.

"I want to talk to you, Gordy."

Gordy rolled his eyes. "Please, not about your last will and testament again."

Carson took a sip of his coffee. "No, not about that. I want to talk to you about women—two in particular."

*****

Carson took a deep breath, looked at Gordy, and began to speak. "I was hopelessly lost and didn't know where I was until I met Ellie. When I say I was lost, I mean literally lost in a town where I had taken a wrong turn, gone down too many one-way streets, and found myself way out in the country with no one to give me directions. And I've never liked maps. They give me a headache."

"No GPS back then, huh?" Gordy questioned.

Carson chuckled. "No." Carson settled back, propping his feet up on a nearby stool, looking up at the sky. "Then I saw this house with a beautiful flower garden in the front. So I drove over to it. It was a beacon to me back then. As I drove closer, I saw her—in that flower garden with this big, floppy hat on her head, shielding her from the sun. She looked up, and I said, 'I'm lost.'"

He smiled at the memory. "'No, you're not,' she said to me. 'You are merely temporarily misplaced.' She must have trusted me from first sight, because she invited me in for a cup of coffee." He smiled before repeating, "Good things can happen over a cup of coffee."

Carson set his cup down on the porch and looked intently at his grandson. "What I'm trying to tell you is don't get lost, Gordy. With everything that has happened to you, I understand it could be easy to have the earth just swallow you up. But if you can, try to look at it as if you have been temporarily misplaced for some time. You've grieved long and hard, but don't get stuck there. Jessie will always be a part of you—engraved upon your heart that no erosion will ever take away no matter how old you get. Her memory will never leave you—nor do you want it to."

He leaned in closer to Gordy. "You're not pushing Jessie out. You have to realize that fact once and for all. You are not betraying her. She will always be a part of you, *just* as Andrew will always be a part of Jasmine." Carson settled back into his own chair. "You're not selling the house. You are merely rearranging the furniture. You need to make it a happy and safe place for the years you have yet to walk this earth."

He raked his hands over his face. "Jasmine comes from great stock. I know of which I speak. Don't make the same mistake I made with Ellie. Time eventually runs out. I know of which I speak. You love that girl. I know you do. She loves you too. I can spot true love a mile away. And I'm telling you that you need to go get that girl and make her your own. It's time."

Both Carson and Gordy looked out at the pasture where Star Bright was grazing.

Carson took a big gulp of his coffee before standing up. "Don't lose tomorrow, Gordy, by looking back at yesterday. Don't let the past dictate your present. You still have a lot of life left to live. Go get that beauty you met on the dance floor, and waltz into the present with her. Good memories of days gone by are not meant for you to become a captive to them. Yes, those memories are to be cherished, but they are not meant to make you a prisoner."

Carson turned and began to walk back into the house.

"Where are you going, Granddad?"

"Back to bed. You have some decisions to make on your own. I've said what I had to say. You don't need me hovering over you."

Gordy watched him go back into the house. He took the final sips of his coffee and looked down on the porch floor. There it was. That little inchworm.

"Hello, little buddy. You inching your way back to oblivion, or are you going forward?"

Gordy could have sworn that little worm stopped and looked at him at that exact moment before beginning his journey forward again. He reached down and let the little creature wind its way up his finger. He took that little guy to the nearest tree and watched as it made its way onto the nearest leaf.

"Keep pushing, little fellow. Keep pushing."

He turned and walked into his house straight to his bedroom and closed the door. He sat on his bed, dropping his head into his hands. Finally, he opened the drawer to his nightstand and took out two photos. He placed them side by side on the bed.

His granddad was right. It was time to "un-stick" himself. He and Jasmine had talked. He smiled, remembering that day—the day of the party. Had it only been two days ago? The big blue sky, the blanket, the green grass, the horses. Star Bright in the distance. Star Bright—where the breakup had all started. The gloom that followed. The many sessions in therapy. Trudy bringing him numerous casseroles. It had started with Star Bright, Jessie's horse.

He picked up one of the photos, looked at it, and smiled. He traced the face on that photo with his fingertip.

"What do you think, Jessie?"

He knew deep down in his heart she would want him to move forward to love again. And after torrents of tears and pounding walls, he felt he was finally ready to do just that.

He placed the photo back in the drawer and picked up the second picture.

Jasmine.

His heart swelled to overflowing, looking at her face.

Was the old saying true? *"Life is for the living."*

Was it time for him to come out of being temporarily misplaced? It had not escaped him when his granddad emphasized *temporarily*. Had he stayed too long, gazing over his shoulder instead of looking forward. Had he been stuck?

Again, he looked at the photo of Jasmine.

He got up from the bed, still holding the photo, and walked out of the room.

*****

Polly was having a chat with Jasmine, woman to woman, just a few miles down the road at Open Door.

She left Jasmine looking out at the lake, hoping she would find her answers soon. It was time. It was past time.

When she reached her room, she opened the window and hollered down to Jasmine.

"I don't want to see you coming back to my house unless you have that Gordy fellow on your arm! Do you hear me, girlie!"

Jasmine looked up at her and smiled. She needed to take a walk. A long walk.

She heard Polly hollering something else that sounded like, "And if you show up without him, I'll charge you rent! Yes, I will! Think on that!"

Jasmine heard the window slam. Yes, she knew Polly meant business. Bless her heart.

*****

It was one o'clock in the afternoon before Jasmine decided to go to Gordy's ranch. Yes, they had talked. Yes, they had mended fences, and, yes, they had crossed over bridges that thankfully had not been burned that afternoon before the party. But could they, would they, really be able to have a future together? Questions remained. She had decided there was only one way to find out.

As she approached the ranch, she saw Cason sitting on the front porch. Carson saw her coming. He knew a secret, and he was keeping it to himself—for now. She would soon know, anyway.

"Good morning, girlie! Glorious day, isn't it?"

She took a deep breath, continuing to walk toward Carson. She sat down beside him, saying nothing.

Carson broke the silence. "I think you should take a walk."

"I've already been on a walk."

"And did you think about things on that walk?"

"Yes."

"Is that why you're here?"

"Yes. Where's Gordy?"

Carson pointed toward the stables.

"Do you think I should walk over there?"

"Depends."

"On what?"

"If it's *yes* or *no*."

"But what if—"

"Stop it! Stop it right now! No more whys, buts, or ifs! Just get yourself up there now!"

Jasmine continued to sit still.

"You need a forklift, girlie?"

"I thought I might help with the cleanup from the party first."

"Girl, the party was two days ago. Everything is cleaned up. Trudy and Polly did it yesterday. You are a day late and a dollar short! The only cleanup that needs to be done around here is you and Gordy!" Carson smiled before continuing. "Besides that, he told me to tell you to come to the stable. For some uncanny reason, he thought you just might show up today. He's waiting for you."

Those were the words that made her stand up.

"Go to him, girlie." Carson watched as she began her walk to the stable. *So much like Ellie. Ah, my sweet Ellie*, he thought.

He went inside and walked over to the fireplace mantle. Time to revisit the *secret* he had known since this very morning.

He had seen Gordy just a few short hours before come out of his room. He had watched him walk over to the fireplace mantle, where Gordy had thoughtfully run his fingers over the deep carvings of the wood. It was there, he watched his grandson breathe deeply into the joy that was to be his future. He watched as he put Jasmine's picture in an old frame, and he watched as Gordy placed it gently on the fireplace mantle. Carson saw it all and smiled.

*****

Jasmine found Gordy there, talking to Star Bright. He looked up. He walked over to her and took her hands in his, leading her to Star Bright.

"Ever ridden bareback?"

Her hands were trembling from his mere touch. She wasn't afraid of riding bareback. She was afraid she was going to start crying because she knew what riding Star Bright really meant.

"No, can't say that I have," she whispered.

"It's time." Gordy mounted Star Bright with no saddle in sight.

She looked up at him. "Gordy, are you sure? I mean—it's Star Bright."

"I'm sure. We'll ride him together." He reached down. She clasped his hand, and he pulled her up to sit in front of him. They both took a deep breath. "Ready?" he questioned.

She felt his arms around her, strong and steady. "Ready."

*****

It all came down to one word, *ready*. Love had come to stay. The road they had traveled had been full of ruts, turns, and detours. Nevertheless, they had gone full circle to wind up back here where they both belonged.

This was the horse that had been the trigger, leading them on an incredible journey of healing. The same horse that was now leading them into an amazing adventure of forever.

Once Gordy had made up his mind, once he had gone to his fireplace mantle and placed the photo of Jasmine there, he knew. And it was then that his love for her became as an avalanche, removing the mountains both he and she had tried so hard to climb on their own.

But what it took, we all really know, when you come right down to it, don't we?

It took a *Way Maker, Miracle Worker, Promise Keeper, Light in the Darkness*. Yes, that's what it took.

Star Bright took off in a gallop. It was, indeed, time. Old frames, new pictures…

Epilogue

Trudy Speaks

"Well, here we go again, folks. Another Memorial Day weekend is coming to Brooksport Village. Jake has ordered the balloons—just like that first Memorial Day way back when he met Charlie for the first time. All red, white, and blue for our patriotic and righteous town. A big launch is planned. We always have *big* launches. Memorial Day—a day of rememberin'. Brooksport Village has a lot to look back on, from honoring war heroes to the ups and downs of life that leave behind both smiles and tears.

"The town just keeps on keepin' on, managin' to avoid callouses on our hearts. We'll never be bitter. But, oh, how we do remember how the scars got there. They remain forever evident. But I believe what everyone else believes in this town, of which we have been through so much—someone once said, *Scars don't define who you are. They only tell you where you've been.* I believe that's true. Just look at all of us! And I always say, 'Brooksport Village doesn't want to know where you've been. We only wanna know where you're goin'.' Jake found that out. I told him that the first time I set eyes on his handsome face. Just like I told everyone else who graced our streets with their wanderings, worries, and woes—always in search of somethin', *especially* those people who fled from the city with their forlorn looks. Just ask Jasmine and Kate.

"Yes, we've learned about those pits we all fall into, sometimes because of bad decisions we have made or sometimes because someone else made decisions for us. But we also know all about the mighty arm that reaches down from the heavens, rescues us, and pulls us up and out. And believe me, a smart person knows not to walk down that same road again. If they haven't learned, we'll teach 'em.

"Through the secrets—and you know our town has had 'em—through the tragedies, the storms, the mysteries, the miracles, and the love stories, we have survived and will continue to do so. Oh, how we have learned that relationships take work, and lots of it. I learned a lot when smoke literally got in my eyes.

"Kate and I learned a lot about love. Slow and steady. That's what it should be. A fire that stays warm after the shine is gone. Have to say Jake and Ted learned that, too, and Kate and I have been the balancin' act in those boys' lives. Yes, siree, all four of us have ridden that roller coaster and screamed in fear. We've pounded walls and slammed doors. But in the end, we had to take that knot out of our throat and say what we had to say. Sometimes, we could barely speak, but we discovered that a whisper sometimes works easier than a shout. When our sky fell, we needed someone to hold our umbrella. Truth, trust, and transparency—that's what it's all about. You gotta protect each other and what you have. You gotta meet somewhere between the streetlights of Trudy's Tresses and Tootsies and Gordy's Dude Ranch. And we sure took a lot of walks to "Open Door." We were drawn like a magnet to those bleeding hearts. We learned how fragile they were and how strong they could become. Just like us.

"Be grateful for the scars that tell where you've been, and be aware of the promises that take you where you're supposed to go. It's all about blendin' the two. When Thanksgiving arrives with its many blessings and when Christmas comes with its biggest star in the east, be grateful. Don't hurry here and there. Take your time. It is so much more than turkey and bright tinsel. Get away from the racket of New Year's Eve. Find yourself a cozy little church like Jake did. You may be in for a surprise—just like Jake. New promises just may unveil themselves long after the stroke of midnight. Resurrection power at Easter is what I'm talkin' about, and those fireworks in July are so much more than beauty and noise. It's about freedom.

"There's gonna be another weddin' sometime soon. Charlie and Sarah. I can hardly wait to see Charlie in that purple tuxedo—the one he talked me into 'comin' back' for. I consider him royalty, too, you know. God gave him a healin' hand. Look what he did for me! Reva will cry. Kate will cry. Happy tears. Charlie understands those kinds of tears now.

"Open Door continues to flourish. Joshua visits Jake and Kate during his school breaks. Lydia encourages it. Jake reveres it, his past sins forgiven. Joshua works alongside Kate in her garden where Charlie and she used to kneel, pulling those weeds around those bleeding hearts. Kate has made room for Joshua in her heart. She has many rooms in that great big core of her being, that Joshua is now a part.

"Gordy and Jasmine have come out to the other side of their own personal griefs. Someone once said that one day *mourning* does turn into *morning*. It's happened with those two. They understand. They are together. All is well. I guess I won't be taking Gordy any more casseroles.

"I know you're itchin' to know about Ted and me. So sit down. I'm gonna tell ya.

"Ted and I are married and expecting our first child. Now before you go countin' on your fingers as to how old I am, let me tell you the rest of the story. (I ask you to remember that day I whispered in Ted's ear and he nodded his head while sittin' in that little church in Carsonville.) An adoption was being planned.

"This child will arrive at our front door next week. Both Ted and I will be standing at the window, watching and waiting. We will open the door of welcome to our home before the doorbell rings. This precious one will not arrive buckled in a car seat but will arrive with flowers in his hands. He has a habit of bringing me flowers.

"This child will be standing on our front porch, with a suitcase. Seth is his name."

From the Author

Dear reader,

It has been a joy to walk this journey with you. And it seems I cannot give Trudy up just yet. Like a boomerang, it all comes back to Trudy, just like the sweetest echo you never want to forget. The very heart and soul of Brooksport Village. Defying the odds, rising from the ashes, literally, she will continue to walk the walk, talk the talk, and fix every cowboy who comes to town.

You know she always insists on having the last word and will always bid us goodbye with a dramatic exit. I just can't let her go, just yet. Can you? And this is what I imagine her to be saying to me, especially, and to you…

"My friends, take in the fragrance of the jasmine at dusk. Be tender with bleeding hearts. They are so fragile. Remember that some of your biggest decisions are made in cemeteries. And over a good cup of coffee.

"Keep those young ones in your life busy with their hands. That is when they tell you what's on their minds. Make salads together and have ice cream with caramel and nuts on top and, once in a while, a dollop of cool whip.

"Go to the city with your questions if you have to, but come home with answers. Cook lots of casseroles. Walk that extra mile to give them to someone.

"Tackle grief. Walk through it, not around it. Stay steady and strong. Know your Anchor.

"Take shelter during storms. Sometimes closets bring out the best in us. Ask Phil. Keep your grocery clerks in line. Make sure they have crackers made with salt and lard on the shelf. Otherwise, you may get ornery.

"Go to church, *especially* on New Year's Eve. Make snow angels. White as snow. Ask Jake. Eat extracrispy doughnuts, sometimes with chocolate frosting. Go ahead—splurge.

"Go to coffeehouses and listen to songs about hometown girls. You just may change your mind about leaving and come back for your happy ending. Ask Jake and Kate. Ask Gordy and Jasmine.

"Pet lots of cats. They may save your life. Ask me. Love those dogs that lick your hands after tragedies. Put little red bows on Yorkies who walk down wedding aisles.

"Send in your warranties. Pay attention to recalls. Walk hospital corridors. Pray.

"Scratch your itches, no matter how much it hurts. Come clean. You love somebody? Tell them so. Ride horses. Wear purple.

"Sadly, it's time to say goodbye, my sweet friends. Look to the sky. My hope is that every time you see a balloon rising lazily through the clouds to the heavens, think of us. Think of new beginnings and second chances. Think of putting new pictures in old frames. The fingerprint of God is all around them. Just as he holds Brooksport Village in his hand, he holds you."

About the Author

Old Frames, New Pictures is Judy Baldwin Lord's second novel, a sequel to *Open Door*. Having grown up in a small town, Kingsport, Tennessee, she remembers the close relationships with the people, as well as their dedication and loyalty to one another. Small-town living becomes a natural setting for her novels.

She currently lives in Michigan with her husband, Ron, and her little yorkie, Ryder. She has one daughter, Mandi, who is married to Steve; and two grandchildren, Madison and Cole. Her favorite hobby is loving on those grandchildren and spoiling them as much as their parents will allow.

CPSIA information can be obtained
at www.ICGtesting.com
Printed in the USA
FSHW012229251021
85694FS

9 781639 616749